CAUGHT
IN THE
CROSSFIRE

WATCH VIDEOS OF MATINA'S WARTIME EXPERIENCES WHILE YOU READ

Caught in the Crossfire trailer
http://www.youtube.com/matinajewell
Download the free reader at **get.beetagg.com**

QR Codes like the one above are placed throughout this book to bring videos taken during Matina's posting in the Middle East directly to your phone.

To watch these videos, simply download the free QR Code scanner at http://get.beetagg.com/en/qr-reader/download

Then hold your phone's camera a few inches away from the QR Code images and you'll immediately be taken into the action.

Tag the QR Code above to watch the book trailer.

Or you can visit Matina Jewell's YouTube channel at
http://www.youtube.com/matinajewell

CAUGHT
IN THE
CROSSFIRE

An Australian peacekeeper
beyond the front-line

MATINA JEWELL

ALLEN&UNWIN

Published by Allen & Unwin in 2011

Allen & Unwin
Sydney, Melbourne, Auckland, London

83 Alexander Street
Crows Nest NSW 2065
Australia
Phone: (61 2) 8425 0100
Fax: (61 2) 9906 2218
Email: info@allenandunwin.com
Web: www.allenandunwin.com

Cataloguing-in-Publication details are available
from the National Library of Australia
www.trove.nla.gov.au

ISBN 978 1 74237 567 0

Map by Guy Holt
Set in 12/16 pt Bembo by Bookhouse, Sydney
Printed and bound in Australia by Griffin Press

10 9 8 7 6 5 4 3 2 1

Contents

For my team-mates, my brothers: Wolf, Big Mack,
Du and Hans-Peter

Part of the proceeds from this book will be donated to the Khiam
Memorial fund, which has been established by the Podmore
Foundation to help educate young Indigenous Australians.
The Podmore Foundation is committed to returning opportunity
to young people who may need mentors and role models as well as
financial support. It provides a vehicle to give back to the community.
For more information on the Podmore Foundation or to make a
donation visit: www.podmorefoundation.org.au

Prologue

Unarmed Sitting Ducks

Knowing what's coming, I put on my sky-blue UN armoured vest and helmet. My team-mates laugh and joke about how cute I look in my little blue armoured suit. But after the first 1000-pound aerial bomb hits a nearby town seconds later, smashing buildings apart, the mockers scramble for their own flak jackets and helmets.

It's my turn to joke now, as they frantically put on their body armour behind the parapet of the observation platform, which, though made of reinforced concrete, would be no match for a direct hit. Our excitement and fear grow. Adrenaline is pumping through our bodies, making our voices high-pitched and speech rapid.

The Israeli artillery batteries open up from the Golan Heights. *Crump-crump-crump!* They are after the Hezbollah headquarters and other bases in and around the town of El Khiam. We are in their line of fire. Freight-train sounds crack overhead and then—*Kaboom-kaboom-kaboom!*—the town is ripped up. I cringe at the thought of hot metal flying into buildings, cars and people.

The artillery barrage continues for twenty minutes and then it stops. Silence. Time freezes. The artillery lifts to allow an Israeli fighter jet to fly in on its bombing run. Lethal load inbound. Then in slow motion—at eye level from me, just a cricket pitch distance away—comes a massive 1000-pound laser-guided aerial bomb. With its fins out, it glides smoothly and relentlessly to its target only 75 metres behind our observation post.

We dive for cover. Instinctively tucking our bodies up into self-preservation positions on the deck behind the ramparts, my team-mates and I await our fate. There is an ear-splitting explosion as the bomb hits the Hezbollah bunker, right on target.

A compression blast rocks our observation deck like an earthquake and an enormous fireball ignites above our heads. Large pieces of steel shrapnel, chunks of concrete and metal reinforcement crash into our compound and bounce back into the sky as I bury my head between my knees. I pray that a big piece of debris doesn't fall on me.

The chunks of metal and concrete and clods of dirt continue to fall around us. *Clunk! Thud!* They rain down—big bits and small bits. The air is stained with dust and smoke. I wait for a cry of agony, as something heavy smashes an exposed arm or leg—or worse. I hope that it will not be my own cry for help.

Suddenly the noise stops and my ears are ringing. Wolf's voice breaks through: 'Bunker! Bunker! Go! Go! Go!' The five of us run towards the spiral stairs that lead down to our underground bunker.

And so, on 12 July 2006, began another ordeal in a military career that had already had its trials and adventures. When I graduated from the Royal Military College Duntroon in 1997, I could never have imagined the operations I would become involved in, both in the Solomon Islands and the North Arabian Gulf. Or that, nine years later, I would be running for my life in southern Lebanon as a member of a team of bright-blue peacekeepers—unarmed sitting ducks in the middle of a war.

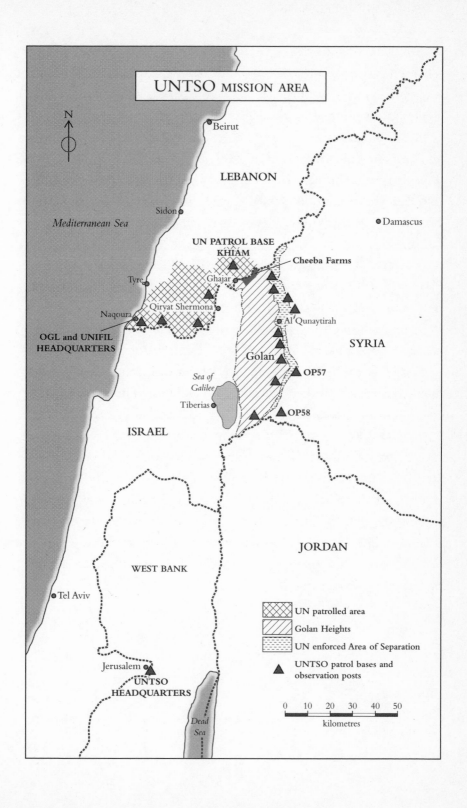

1 Educating Marwa

In August 2004 I received a phone call from Major Ian Ford, my army careers advisor, telling me that the Australian Army had selected me for a prestigious role with the United Nations. This was an amazing and unexpected opportunity for me to serve as a peacekeeper—or a United Nations Military Observer (UNMO), as the role is more formally described—in the Middle East for twelve months.

In my seven years since graduating from Duntroon, I had, first as a lieutenant and then as a captain, been posted to Perth, Sydney, the Solomons and the Middle East. I had worked with the Australian Army, Navy, Air Force and Federal Police, as well as with the military forces of our allies. I was now 28 years old; it was expected that I would complete two more years as a captain before being promoted to the rank of major. I could not think of a better final posting as a captain than working for the UN as a peacekeeper in the troubled Middle East.

In the preceding three years I had been deployed on four overseas military operations, virtually back to back. It had been an unusually hectic and gruelling schedule, during which I had accrued almost an entire year of annual leave—unfortunately, due to operational requirements, I'd not been able to schedule much time off to visit family or friends. Leave is precious and if I didn't use my leave credits, I would lose them. It was not common, but certainly possible, for military personnel to be granted approval to work for other organisations during extended periods of leave. So I had originally planned to have a twelve-month working holiday in London, where I could pursue an opportunity Volkswagen UK had offered me in Birmingham. The prospect of a new challenge, in a totally non-military environment, had been extremely enticing and also seemed like a sound investment for my future, should I ever decide to leave the military. Not to mention that this opportunity had the added bonus that would see me living only a couple of hours away from my brother, Mark, who had been working in London for three years.

However, Major Ford guaranteed that I could take my year's leave in the UK after I served with the UN in the Middle East and that my leave credits would be held over during my deployment with the UN. It seemed I was being offered the best of both worlds. After discussing the offer with my family and military mentors, and with their blessing and encouragement, I delayed my trip to London and decided to seek adventure with the army one more time.

I took the opportunity to enrol in an Arabic language course. I hoped that learning this language would enhance my communication skills as a UN peacekeeper, and would show my respect for the culture I was about to immerse myself in.

The language course was held over a gruelling and extremely intense three months, conducted at the Australian Defence Force (ADF) Language School at the RAAF Base Laverton, just south of Melbourne. The school's facilities were second to none, and my class had the luxury of an extraordinary staff-to-student ratio of eight teachers to only three students. This meant that we had terrific interaction and individual attention from the teachers. However, the flip side was that there was absolutely nowhere to hide in a classroom of only three students. Even a minor lapse in concentration was very noticeable.

My two classmates were Ash Collingburn and Naomi Kinsella. Ash was a fellow army captain, who had also been selected to be an UNMO on the same UN mission that I was preparing for.

Ash would head to the Middle East a month or so before me; it was reassuring to know that he would be, of sorts, my very own reconnaissance party. Ash would send me vital first-impression information prior to my own arrival at the UN headquarters in Jerusalem—at the very least, this would aid me greatly in my decision about what to pack in my removal and what was simply not required.

Naomi was a civilian working within Defence. She had a great sense of humour, never took herself too seriously and was a huge asset to our class, adding a completely different dynamic to the group. Thankfully, the three of us were at much the same level, which made life easier for our teachers; we encouraged and spurred each other on, particularly during those inevitable days when we all felt like throwing in the towel.

During the first lesson we were each given an Arabic name starting with the same letter as our English Christian names. We would be referred to by our new Arabic name for the remainder of the course. No longer was I called Matina, or my nickname Matti, but instead I was now Marwa, meaning 'fragrant plant' in Arabic. Ash was Ahmed, which means 'highly praised', and Naomi was Nadiyya, which translates to 'delicate'. Surprisingly, it didn't take long for us to become comfortable with our new names and Ash enjoyed teasing me by dragging out the pronunciation of Marwa in an Aussie-style drunken drawl, saying 'Hey, Maaaaaaaaaarwah, you got a smoke?' much to the amusement of Naomi and the staff.

The head teacher of the Arabic Language Department was a tall, lean Egyptian man named Yasser Abdel Ghafar. Despite Yasser's unimposing physical appearance, he instantly commanded attention and I found myself intimidated by his mere presence. He had narrow, angular facial features, a perfectly manicured short beard and moustache framing his thin lips; his piercing black eyes made me feel like I was being interrogated every time I was called on to answer a question in class. He demanded high performance from his students and appeared to take any failure or difficulties we had while learning this rather challenging new language as a personal insult. It was as though our performance was a direct reflection of his teaching abilities, and he was damned sure the Arabic department was going to be considered one of the highest performing departments within the language school. Consequently we worked hard, very hard.

Our language classes were held Monday to Friday, from 8 a.m. to 5 p.m. A typical day would begin with two speaking lessons. After a mid-morning break, we would have individual tutorials until lunch. At 1 p.m. class would recommence with writing, reading and listening activities for the rest of the day.

However, our training would not finish at 5 p.m., when the classroom lessons ceased and the teachers went home; instead, the twenty or so new words introduced to us that day had to be learnt by the following morning. Somehow, during the afternoon and evening, those words would have to be retained so they could be recalled on cue and used in sentences come eight o'clock the next morning. In addition to learning twenty-plus new words a day, we were also confronted with four exams per week, to consolidate our training—and unintentionally increase our anxiety levels!

I found that by 5 p.m. my brain was completely drained and I couldn't conduct even the most basic of functions—let alone consolidate the day's learning—without having a break. The best way for me to switch off from language training was physical exercise. Throughout my life I had enjoyed playing a number of sports at state and national level and fitness was an important part of how I perceived myself. It was only natural that I would turn to exercise as a form of release during a period when I was mentally challenged. I soon developed a routine of hitting the gym or going for a long run moments after we were released from class, in the vague hope of reigniting my mind before demanding more effort from it later on.

Each evening was spent attempting to cram the words into my memory bank, hoping that through repetition they would become permanently embedded in time for the following morning's class. Fortunately, I seemed to have an aptitude for language studies and, aided by the use of palm cards with the Arabic word on one side and the English translation on the other, I soon found I was starting to retain words. My Arabic vocabulary began to grow.

I had previously studied Bahasa Indonesian at the Special Forces Base at Swanbourne in Perth after being given a place on the course normally attended only by Special Forces soldiers. I had been studying Indonesian at the Edith Cowan University in my own time and had already completed the first semester when a spare place came up on the Special Forces course. I was extremely fortunate to have been offered that position. However, learning Arabic made the task of learning Indonesian seem like a walk in the park. The most difficult challenge I faced was articulation of the unique Arabic sounds that are produced in the throat rather than the mouth. These guttural sounds require the use of muscles in the back of the mouth and throat that we simply don't use in the English language. After each day in class, it felt like my tongue and mouth had spent the entire day in the gym. These muscles were literally exhausted and sore from repetition, after having spent 30-odd years dormant in the lethargy of the English language.

Before I knew it, my three months of mental gymnastics and late-night cramming had passed and, armed with enough vocabulary to hopefully get me out of trouble in the Middle East, I graduated from the Arabic language school. Although at the time it was intellectually arduous, in hindsight I am so thankful for Yasser's persistence in getting his students to perfect the nuances of this difficult-to-master language. Yasser's dedication to making us as proficient as possible in Arabic would actually play a role in saving my life in Lebanon just twelve months later.

2 An Unexpected Complication

Eight weeks after I accepted my UN posting, and only a couple of months before I was to leave Australia for the Middle East, came an unexpected complication—in the shape of a man who hailed from the picturesque high country of Victoria.

In early October 2004, I sat nervously in my summer dress amid an excited, buzzing congregation in a small country church in the Snowy Mountains. My army friend Linda Brown was marrying a naval officer. I was anxious because, at Linda's insistence, I'd naively agreed to play my guitar during their wedding ceremony and sing a song I'd written for the happy couple. Why, for the life of me, had I agreed to do this? I was an army officer—a specialist in water transport and amphibious operations—not a songstress.

Moments later I sang the lyrics I had composed to mark the complicated journey Linda and her husband-to-be, Alex Gillett, had endured to make it to the altar. In fact, this was the third attempt they had made to tie the knot. On the previous two occasions, one or both of them had suddenly been deployed overseas on military operations. So, in the days leading up to the wedding, we all had our fingers crossed that nothing would derail their big day this time.

I was relieved to get my 'musical moment' over and done with, so I could relax and enjoy the celebrations. The reception was being held in an outdoor marquee on Linda's parents' farm, in the foothills of the majestic Snowy Mountains. It was a splendid backdrop for a beautiful wedding. Due to the isolation of the farm, most guests came prepared to brave the chilly conditions and camp on the property overnight, to avoid a long drive to the nearest motel.

To my delight I was seated between two of my army girlfriends, Anita Smith and Nicki Bradley, both of whom I first met as a cadet at the Australian Defence Force Academy (ADFA), but had scarcely seen since. The very nature of military life means you are often posted to opposite ends of the country, or even the world. Army postings are designed to be for a three-year period but, from my experience, I was lucky if I ever spent just a year or two in the one place before packing up my life and moving on. During this disruptive and continual transition, it was easy to lose track of your mates.

But the brilliant thing about army relationships is that they are often forged during times of duress—slogging it out in the bush together on 'field training activities' certainly seemed to result in strong bonds between my friends and me! We might not have seen each other for a decade, but the moment we reconnected, it would be like I had seen them only yesterday. We would simply pick up our conversation from where we had left off many years prior, without batting an eyelid. So, during the reception, Anita, Nicki and I barely drew breath as we caught up on each other's news.

The rest of our table was filled with army and navy personnel, except for one charismatic guest who had caught my eye. His name was Clent and he had gone to school with Linda in this little farming community in northeast Victoria, before moving interstate to the city to pursue a corporate career in marketing.

At over 6 feet tall, Clent certainly commanded attention and I was impressed at how well he carried himself in conversations around our table. The military crowd can be quite intimidating for outsiders, especially when you're the only one in the group who isn't in the services. Military people tend to speak in what sometimes seems like a foreign, abbreviated, acronym-filled language; but, despite this, Clent didn't appear to be deterred at all and handled himself admirably. I was intrigued by his confidence and by his ability to strike up a conversation with absolutely anyone.

During the evening I found myself deep in conversation with Clent, learning about his country upbringing on an adjacent farm and his current work in Sydney, where I was also living at the time. Hours seemed to disappear as Clent shared his life story with me. He had grown up on his family sheep farm, 'Keelangie', which was nestled on the opposite side of the hill from Linda's property.

The entire region is a secluded, magnificent part of the world, where the Murray River runs fresh from the snow-capped mountains. Clent described how Keelangie's rolling hills, fringed by the national park, changed colour vividly with the seasons. During his early years, summers were hot and dusty, often over 40 degrees, while in winter, the fog would often hang thick as pea-soup until mid-afternoon in the valleys; this made for an unpleasant walk home from the school bus in both seasons.

Hard work was the norm throughout his childhood—from dawn to dusk and seven days a week. Clent described how the property would come alive during shearing and harvesting: 10,000 merinos to shear, 1500 acres of land to tend, and scores of fattened cattle to nurture before being sold at the stockyards.

During the winter months, Aussie Rules football formed the social hub of the Upper Murray community. Clent recalled with a twinkling smile that everyone was involved—he and his two younger brothers, Brent and Kelvin, all played for the local Cudgewa club. Clent's parents managed everything, from sports medicine to helping in the tuck-shop. In fact, despite their workloads on the farm, they were heavily involved in most parts of the community as volunteers. I imagined his parents as stalwarts of the Country Fire Authority and State Emergency Service, as well as the school council—continually donating their time and expertise for the benefit of others.

Clent told me that, despite their love for the country and their rural community, he and his brothers were drawn to the big city.

They all left home to complete university studies in business in Melbourne. The three brothers were the fourth generation of their family to have grown up at Keelangie, but none of them was compelled to return to take over as their parents grew older, and so take the farm on to a fifth generation. A decade of intermittent drought and below-average rainfall—as well as successive years of devastating bushfires and depressed wool prices that were often well below the cost of production—had convinced Clent and his brothers that this wasn't the path for them. But, as the eldest, Clent felt a strong pang of guilt about the upcoming sale of the family farm and his decision not to 'continue the family legacy' on the land.

It was clear that Clent had a close-knit family and I admired his respect for his parents and siblings. He described family and life values that were the same as my own. In fact, our upbringings were actually quite similar—I too had a dedicated, loving family and had spent my childhood in the country, living on a small hobby farm on the far north coast of New South Wales. But where Clent had relished the snow-clad mountains, I'd savoured the beach lifestyle.

Clent's conversation was captivating. I would be lying if I didn't admit that I was also quite attracted to him. What girl wouldn't be? He was tall, with a lean muscular build, dark-haired, vivacious, spirited and handsome; his Irish heritage accounted for his stunning green eyes, which sparkled with the mischievousness of a schoolboy. He possessed a brilliant smile that was simply infectious and very welcoming, making me feel instantly relaxed, as if we were old friends rather than new acquaintances. Although I hung on every word as Clent painted a vivid picture of his life, I also found my thoughts drifting, wondering if he was attracted to me.

Focus, Matti! I snapped myself out of this crazy daydream. After all, even if my feelings were reciprocated, I was about to be deployed to the Middle East, to work with the UN as a peacekeeper on a one-year secondment. The last thing I needed at this point was to fall in love.

I assured myself that it wasn't possible anyway; after all, for many women in uniform it is extremely difficult to meet men outside the services, especially romantically. As soon as you mention you're in the army, some men become somewhat intimidated by the fact that you are coping in a male-dominated work environment. Then they become even more unsettled by the fact that you can handle a weapon! As cadets, my army girlfriends and I had desperately resorted to concocting fictitious and less confronting professions in order to be less threatening to the opposite sex, at least on the first date. However, I had long ago given up looking for 'Mr Right' and was now focused on my career, so I didn't feel the need to be secretive about my choice of occupation.

Before I knew it, the evening had all but vanished. The handful of remaining guests—those who had not already turned in for the night—decided that it would be much warmer to sleep on the dance floor of the marquee, directly in front of the jet heater. Even though it was spring, temperatures in the mountains often dropped to sub-zero over night, so I didn't take much convincing that the dance floor was a far better option than my original intention—sleeping in my (by now) freezing car.

Clent agreed to help me retrieve my sleeping gear. Being a gentleman, he offered me his coat as we stepped out of the warmth of the marquee and into the freezing cold. The shock of the temperature change seemed to engulf my entire body as if it were a blanket of ice. As I exhaled, my breath formed puffs of steam as soon as it hit the frosty air. It was a bitterly cold night; my car was covered in a thick layer of frost.

Clent placed his arms around my shoulders in an attempt to warm me up, as I was clearly shivering—my summer dress now proving less than adequate for these cold temperatures. As we approached my vehicle, we stopped to take in the stars that were glittering in the clear night sky. There wasn't a single cloud, and the stars seemed brighter than I had ever seen them before. I wondered if the high altitude made the air thinner, allowing the stars to shine through, enhancing their brilliance.

Just as I turned to ask Clent whether my thinking was correct, he gently cupped my face in his hands and kissed me. It was the most delightful surprise. However, my astonishment at his affection towards me must have been evident, because he suddenly looked worried and asked, 'Is it okay to kiss an army officer?' I laughed at his suggestion that we were some kind of protected species and, without replying, I reassured him that his actions were very much welcomed by returning the kiss.

On the drive home to Sydney the next day with Anita, our discussion centred on Clent. I downplayed my excitement, because I wasn't even sure if I would ever hear from him again and, more importantly, I didn't want to build up my hopes. But I received a text message from him asking me to dinner before I had even arrived back in Sydney.

I was thrilled to get Clent's invitation, as I had found myself thinking about him more than I liked to admit. He seemed like the most perfect man. He was corporate and savvy, yet balanced by his country values and upbringing; he was one of the most considerate people I had ever met, yet at the same time was still a man's man and a typical Aussie bloke, who loved nothing more than to enjoy a beer with his brothers and mates at the footy. Too good to be true?

I accepted his dinner invitation, hoping to find a chink in the armour. I needed some negative traits that would convince my heart that there was no chance of a relationship. After all, I needed to concentrate on my preparations to leave for the Middle East, and not entertain the idea of romance with a man I barely knew.

Three days after meeting Clent at the wedding, I found myself sharing a wonderful dinner with him at a friend's restaurant. Sienna Marina is owned and managed by Daniel, a Lebanese immigrant who had become a great friend to me in Sydney.

It was a brilliant night, right up until the moment of our departure. Daniel had mistaken Clent for a tough army officer, not a marketing executive, and, when we were leaving the restaurant, he took Clent aside and gave him some 'fatherly advice'. Daniel informed Clent that I was like a daughter to him and Clent should take exceptionally good care of me—if he didn't, then Daniel would personally hunt him down!

Daniel had dark black, piercing eyes and he shaved his hair tight against his head—he was an attractive man, but he could also be quite intimidating. He thought it was great to 'see how the tough guy handled himself'. I was horrified—I had enough trouble intimidating men on my own, without Daniel's assistance. Clent took it all in his stride and admired the fact that I had friends looking out for my best interests.

Unfortunately for my heart, Clent had proved to be every bit the amazing man my first impression of him had led me to believe. Bugger! Why was this happening now? It seemed to be one of life's cruel jokes—give me the perfect job overseas and then, a nanosecond after I accept it, show me the man of my dreams, who is firmly entrenched in Australia. My life was suddenly becoming complicated.

3 My Heart and Head at War

The culture of the Australian Army has had a substantial influence on my life. I first exposed Clent to the army's unique customs and traditions at a formal military 'dining-in' night two months after we met. It was a Christmas function to which partners were invited. Clent's knowledge of anything military was limited to playing toy soldiers as a five-year-old and what he had seen courtesy of Hollywood, so it proved to be a steep learning curve on that balmy evening in Sydney!

The dinner was an opportunity for the members of the 9th Force Support Battalion to celebrate the year in time-honoured style and let their hair down just a little. The unit had been the 'on-line logistics battalion' that year—on-call to deploy at very short notice to anywhere in the world. I had served as its adjutant (the military version of something like an executive officer in the corporate world) for the past two years. The function was also a chance for the entire battalion headquarters to formally say farewell to me before I left for the Middle East.

Putting Queen and Country as a first priority in life was an unfamiliar and slightly puzzling concept for Clent. To up stumps and leave your family and friends to deploy anywhere in the world for an indeterminate length of time was a crazy, foreign idea to him. I explained that this was the fundamental code and the sacrifice expected of all service personnel. Many of my mates had even missed significant events such as the birth of their child when they were deployed on military operations. It was a culture of service first, and personal needs second, and I hoped this Christmas dinner would give Clent an insight into it.

Clent and I were at the head table. It was an intimidating situation for him, in that we were seated alongside the most senior soldiers present—the commanding officer and the regimental sergeant major, plus their wives. The six of us on the head table faced a horseshoe seating arrangement that had the rest of the dining contingent looking at us.

Clent felt it was like a veritable fishbowl—except that there were none of the ornaments fish can normally hide behind! He knew that every single person in the room was watching and judging him on how he coped during his introduction to the battalion. They would be analysing his every move, assessing if he was worthy of being my boyfriend. Clent fumbled the peas on his fork; he drank wine, then beer, then port, far faster than he might otherwise have done, in an attempt to numb his nerves.

After the formalities of the dinner were over and the soldiers' request for karaoke was well underway, Clent decided to take the boxed framed plaque that I had been presented with as a farewell gift to the car for safe-keeping. He skirted the room, to avoid being pulled up on stage for a song, and attempted to make his exit unnoticed. Unfortunately, at the top of the stairs he tripped spectacularly on an empty ammunition crate that had been placed there to prop open the door and was sent flying, landing squarely on his butt on the concrete metres below. Somehow he managed to keep the plaque high above his head, clasped tightly in both hands for fear of damaging it.

On landing, Clent did a quick take, to see if anyone had witnessed his dramatic plummet. He looked left—no one. He looked right . . . there was a swarm of about 30 soldiers, a few of whom rushed over to ask if he was all right. He bounced back up onto his feet indignantly and thanked them for their concern, then made haste to the car. As he rounded the corner, the crowd burst into hysterical laughter.

For weeks afterwards, Clent sported an enormous bruise that stretched from his neck to his knee. Whenever he was asked about his introduction to army life, he would exclaim 'Tough crowd!' while revealing the gigantic and impressive bruise. Despite his 'war wounds', he had survived his first taste of the tight-knit army community—and passed with flying colours.

Over the next few months I completed all of my military preparations for deployment, including a combat medic course focused on providing emergency first-aid treatment for battlefield injuries. In the Middle East I would be working in teams as small as two-man patrols, in remote regions some two or three hours' drive from the nearest hospital. So we needed to be self-reliant and able to provide a high level of first aid to each other. As a combat medic, I would be qualified to administer strong pain relief such as morphine and would also be competent at venous cannulation.

Cannulation is an art form in itself. It requires the vein to be punctured with a special needle called a cannula, through which intravenous drugs and fluids can be administered directly into the bloodstream. Cannulation can be a critical process in keeping a patient alive, especially if they are losing a lot of blood.

The practical phase of the medics' course tested our ability to find a vein and cannulate a live patient. This proved another massive hurdle for me personally, since I am not particularly good with needles or the sight of blood. In fact I have such a strong phobia of needles that the Red Cross have banned me from donating blood altogether—they even cut up my donor's card after I fainted on repeated attempts to donate! It seemed my veins would collapse at the mere sight of a nurse armed with a needle. Mercifully, it transpired that I did not have any problems inflicting needles on other people; I passed the medics' course without any embarrassing fainting incidents.

Australian Army officers serving with the UN are all qualified combat medics. Unfortunately, the majority of the other 21 nations contributing military personnel for this UN mission did not have the same standard of training. I would be the only Australian working in my patrol area; my international counterparts might not be able to assist to the same level if I were injured. All I could do was ensure that I was prepared to render aid to the best of my ability, and hope that it would not be me who was in need of help.

My schedule to prepare for the UN mission was hectic; but in between training and travelling interstate for courses, I managed to find time to catch up with Clent. It was a ridiculous situation: we both knew the relationship could not continue as I was about to depart the country in a matter of weeks. Common sense said that we were making the inevitable departure more painfully difficult by continuing to see each other. However, despite our attempts to keep our distance or pretend that this was just a casual thing, we couldn't seem to stem the flood of emotions we had for each other. We had both known upfront that there was a clear end-date—but if I had initially thought it would be an easy task to walk away from Clent, I had been deluding myself.

I refused to admit it, but I was falling in love. The more time we spent together, the more we connected and the stronger our bond became. During the times we were apart, I craved for the next opportunity to catch up with him. It was like an addiction that I could not conquer. The pragmatic side of me knew that the sensible thing was to end the relationship and embrace the excitement of my upcoming immersion in the Arab world. We even attempted (more than once) to break up and go our separate ways, but each time it would only last a few hours before one of us convinced the other that we should just enjoy what remaining time we had left.

So we adopted an attitude of 'what will be, will be', knowing full well that it was irrational and naive to expect such an infant relationship to survive a year of separation. But neither of us could bear the thought of cutting ties completely. It was as though we needed some strand of hope to cling to, even though our brains were telling our hearts to abort.

Both Clent and I had experienced the heartache and difficulties associated with long-distance relationships before. Neither of us had managed to make it work. So we adamantly refused to contemplate trying to make it work again, especially given the astronomical distance involved in this case—I would literally be on the opposite side of the world! I couldn't stand the idea of leaving my heart in Australia while I ventured abroad for a whole twelve months—my heart, my mind and my body were inseparable things. But at the same time I couldn't let this beautiful man, whom I now adored, out of my grasp. I was in a dilemma, and feeling torn.

Clent was not the only complication for this imminent deployment. On two recent occasions, I had been admitted to hospital as an emergency patient with an undiagnosed illness. This decline in my health had also posed questions as to whether I was medically fit to deploy. I had first experienced abdominal pain and vomiting while serving in the Solomon Islands two years earlier. Due to the sporadic nature of my symptoms, however, a diagnosis had never been made. I would be symptom-free for months on end and then suddenly, out of the blue, I would have an attack of severe pain under my right rib cage, causing extreme difficulty in breathing. The pain would be completely debilitating and get so bad that it would induce vomiting, and I would need to go to hospital.

The second episode requiring hospitalisation occurred three weeks after the first, during a trip with Clent back to the Snowy Mountains. His parents had just sold their beloved family farm, and we helped them move into town. Four generations had lived within the walls of the Keelangie homestead and so there were quite a few treasures to be sorted, packed and moved. It had been an exhausting weekend. We were about to hit the road when I suddenly felt the cramping sensation under my ribs, a tell-tale sign I was about to have a pain attack. Within minutes I was doubled up on the floor gasping for breath while trying to reassure Clent and his family that I was okay, but would appreciate it if they would call an ambulance or drive me to the nearest hospital.

An hour later, despite having received several doses of morphine, I was still vomiting and in great pain. It was at this moment, in my tortured and feeble state, that I truly appreciated Clent. In between two strong surges of pain I turned to him, as he reassured me and dutifully held my hair back out of my face, and said, 'Well, this has been one heck of a getting-to-know-me process—how do you like me so far?'

Before he had time to answer, I was vomiting again. It was the turning point in our relationship—with such loyalty, I knew Clent was a 'keeper' and I no longer had control of my heart.

Some time later, when I related this story to my parents, my dad concurred that any man who was willing to spend a night in hospital by my side, holding my hair back while I vomited, was worth his weight in gold and was also clearly a man in love. As a result of this second trip to hospital, the army delayed my departure for the UN posting, allowing time for a full medical investigation.

The delay also meant that Clent and I had a couple of unexpected extra months together. During this time I was homeless, having already rented out my apartment in Sydney, since I was supposed to have left for the Middle East. As fate would have it, at precisely the same time, Clent's flatmate moved interstate with his work at short notice. Clent was now looking for someone to share the rent of his apartment near Balmain in Sydney's inner west and I was looking for a temporary residence. It made perfect sense for me to become Clent's short-term flatmate, didn't it?

I was apprehensive about this decision. It had been a long time since I had lived with anyone else and I was somewhat set in my ways. The other glaringly obvious consideration was that this would be taking our relationship to a whole new level, one that I was not sure I was ready for. Living with someone is an entirely new ball game. The very best and worst of our personalities and fallibilities would be exposed, warts and all. But, foolishly, I thought that if I lived with Clent, I would find those chinks in his armour that he had so cleverly hidden up to now. Maybe then I would not feel so torn about leaving him behind. So, with so much going on and without too much more thought, I agreed to move in, knowing that it would only be for a couple of months.

My ingenious plan failed miserably! Instead of finding a smelly, untidy, grotty male, who annoyed the life out of me by leaving his dirty clothes on the floor and not washing the dishes, Clent was the most organised and best flatmate you could ask for. He not only did the washing and ironing (mine included, on occasions) but he was fastidiously clean; in fact, it was me who, in comparison, was the messy one. The only element in Clent's domestic repertoire that was not completely five-star was his cooking. He could whip up tinned spaghetti on toast and was comfortable in front of the barbie, but he was definitely a meat-and-three-veg lad from the country and a fair way from being a culinary genius. But, as it turned out, this too was a Match Made in Heaven as I loved cooking with a passion. And Clent loved eating. Where had this gifted man been hiding all my life? And why had he suddenly appeared in my world now, with the worst possible timing?

I considered myself a relationship disaster. It was the one facet of my life that I just could not seem to get right, no matter how much I tried. All the sensible and caring men who wanted a relationship with me usually became great mates; but I just didn't feel enough spark, or chemistry, for such friendships to evolve into something romantic. Instead, I was always attracted to the 'wrong man'—you know, either the one who needed rescuing (where I could be the hero who resolved all his issues) or the wild one who was the life of the party (and whom I naively imagined I could tame).

I had learnt the lesson of life and love the hard way. At only 21 I had married an attractive man, who on the surface was confident and flamboyant. But scratch the exterior, and underneath was an intimidated and insecure creature who was scarred from an abusive childhood. He would tell me stories of the endless nights he and his mother had spent sleeping in the family car, unable to return to the house because his father had been on an alcoholic binge.

His childhood seemed to have been destroyed by abuse and that accounted, in large part, for his lack of self-worth. I desperately attempted to 'fix' him, by enveloping him in all of my love, because I truly adored him. But it wasn't enough. He couldn't break the cycle of abuse; in time, I too became the victim of his vicious words and nasty behaviour. Although determined to succeed, to make it work, three years later we divorced. It had been a bitter pill to swallow—I had failed to rescue him, and I was now blemished and scarred from the experience.

I think that, as a consequence of my failed marriage, I had put up all sorts of barriers around my heart, to try to protect myself from ever being hurt again. In fact, I later concluded that I may have often subconsciously sabotaged my relationships, to stop things from getting too serious. In a way, my choice of career with the military assisted this pattern of behaviour, by transferring me every few years from one place to the next—an ideal excuse for terminating relationships. I had become resigned to the idea that 'Mr Right' was simply not out there for me.

But Clent was different. Every barrier I had ever built around my heart had been ineffective in keeping him out. Even in the short time I had known him, I felt that he could actually be my soul mate. Despite my fierce urge to continue my normal pattern and run from this relationship too, I truly felt things were different with Clent. But the timing of his coming into my life was all wrong; I was about to move to the other side of the world. I had worked very hard to earn this once-in-a-lifetime posting with the UN and I just had to hope that our feelings would be strong enough to survive a year apart—but that would be a big ask, considering that we had only known each other for such a short period of time.

My biggest concern about the upcoming UN deployment was my undiagnosed medical condition. It had now been a couple of months since I had last experienced a crippling pain attack and yet, although I felt fit and well, there was no evidence to suggest that I would not have another episode tomorrow. I was surprised that the military would consider sending me to the Middle East with no conclusive diagnosis having been made, let alone a treatment plan devised. I made it clear to the doctor that the possible danger was compounded by the fact that I would be operating in remote regions, in two-man patrols, where there would be no medical support readily available. Not only was I concerned about my own health but I also did not want to put a UN team-mate in a difficult position, having to provide first aid to me if I had an attack some three hours' drive from a hospital.

The additional medical tests, which included an endoscopy, were inconclusive—like all the previous tests I had undergone. Perhaps I'd had a gallstone which I had passed, reasoned the doctor. Since my gall bladder appeared healthy and there was no evidence of further stones, he thought it was unlikely that I would have further pain and vomiting episodes. All reasonable tests had been carried out without discovering anything serious, and I had been cleared of any life-threatening illness. So the doctor felt it would be unfair to stop my deployment on this highly sought-after posting that would fast-track my army career simply because of the possibility of another episode occurring, given that I might never experience another pain attack again.

I had openly declared my health concerns but, with the military doctors advising that there was only a low chance of a repeat pain attack, I was given the green light to take up the UN posting. I still had concerns but, in view of their assessment, if I opted to withdraw on medical grounds now, it would in effect be a career-ending move. At the very least, I could not expect to be offered a similar overseas posting in the near future.

I had worked extremely hard to earn this representation role and I was not prepared to risk my career by turning it down. In the end I took the job and left the country, convinced that the decision would also effectively end the best relationship I had ever had.

4 Our Blonde Aussie Lass

It was a teary departure at Sydney airport. I knew I had made the right decision to go, but logic and rational thinking did little to console my heart, which felt like it had shattered into a million pieces. I felt empty and numb. At the same time I chastised myself for being so emotional—after all, I was embarking on a once-in-a-lifetime experience that most of my colleagues would have given their right arm to have. I should have been bursting with anticipation and enthusiasm instead of feeling so pathetically sorry for myself. I needed to push aside my feelings for Clent, embrace the excitement that lay ahead, and focus on the job I had been sent to do.

After an overnight stop in London, I arrived at Ben Gurion airport, Tel Aviv, Israel. Tel Aviv (literally, 'Hill of Spring') is a congested, sprawling and enormous city that only seems to stop because it has reached the edge of the Mediterranean Sea. Modern high-rise buildings loom over the bustling population. Armed guards were everywhere and quite disconcerting; obviously there was a need to search and protect even in the shopping centres. I was relieved to get on the road to the old city of Jerusalem, a little over an hour's drive away, where the UN mission I was about to join had its headquarters.

For the next seven days I learnt all aspects of the mission, which was called UNTSO (United Nations Truce Supervision Organisation) and had a long and complicated history. In 1948,

Israel was declared an independent state and hostilities erupted with her Arab neighbours, resulting in the UN establishing UNTSO to stem the violence. The continued unrest in the region had made it necessary for the UN observers to remain in place ever since, and they will most likely be required for some time to come. This makes UNTSO the longest established of the UN's missions, indeed almost as old as the UN itself (formed in 1945). The UNTSO force consists of approximately 150 military personnel, dispersed between four countries—Israel, Syria, Lebanon and Egypt—and drawn from 22 countries, most of them European and North American, but also including Argentina, Australia, Chile, China, Nepal and New Zealand. This made it a cultural experience in itself! The UNTSO mandate stipulated that we were unarmed military observers and therefore would not carry weapons. This was my first overseas deployment where I would not be armed; it was an unsettling notion for me to have no means of protecting myself while serving in the Middle East.

The Australian contingent to UNTSO was led by a lieutenant colonel, and comprised eleven captains and majors working as UN Military Observers (UNMOs) for twelve months at a time. The Australian UNMOs were 'trickle fed' into the mission, in order to maintain some sense of continuity and to retain mission knowledge within the contingent, so I arrived on my own. We shared the load of observing and reporting on the military activities of the four parties to the 1948 Armistice Truce Agreements (Israel, Syria, Egypt and Lebanon), mostly from border observation posts. Many UNMOs were in their mid-50s, either on their swan song farewell postings prior to retirement or making a career out of the well-paid UN missions. I soon learnt that very few countries sent female officers to UNTSO, because of the close living conditions and the cultural aspects of working in the Middle East.

I was to spend the first six months of my one-year posting in Syria. After surviving a week of UN training and mountains of administration in Jerusalem, my first test came in the form of driving a Toyota Land Cruiser from Israel to Syria via Jordan. Spicing up this challenge a tad more was the fact that this had to be done without the aid of a GPS because, at the time, no GPS navigation systems had been fitted to any of the UN's vehicles. I was also driving on the opposite side of the road to Australia and through countries where road rules appeared to be optional.

There were four other UNMOs who had also been assigned to work in Syria and so, with their families and our guide, we divided into three vehicles to form a convoy. We set out in the early hours of the morning, attempting to avoid peak-hour traffic in Jerusalem; we then headed south through Israel, made our first border crossing into Jordan, and then travelled the entire length of the country before arriving at the northern border crossing into Syria. Once through the formalities of entering our third country for the day, we drove across the barren desert before finally arriving in the evening at our destination—Damascus. It was a massive day and an indication of some of the challenges that lay ahead of me, since what I had just completed was considered a normal, standard day in the life of an UNMO. I was left in no doubt that it was going to be an interesting and hectic year.

I immediately fell in love with Damascus. Not only were the spice cart–filled streets a veritable feast for the senses, but the Syrian people were truly amazing. They were far from what my preconceived Western notions had led me to expect. They were genuine, hospitable and incredibly generous, in spite of their often abject poverty. In a sense, they were some of the happiest people I had ever seen. My immersion into this Middle Eastern culture gave me a new life perspective. I rented an apartment with another Australian UNMO, Major Deb Warren-Smith, in the vibrant, cultural melting pot of the city, not far from the embassy quarter; then, for a week at a time, I worked on the Syrian side of the Golan Heights, a two-and-a-half-hour drive away.

I felt very safe in Damascus as there appeared to be a police officer stationed at virtually every street corner. The penalties for petty crimes were so severe that they seemed to deter criminal behaviour altogether. The prison perched on top of the hill overlooking the city was a visible reminder and warning that acts such as stealing were not tolerated in Syria. However, this initial sense of security was shattered one afternoon during my first fortnight there, when our apartment was broken into.

I returned home to find the front door wide open. I was hit instantly by a sinking feeling in my gut that my privacy had been invaded and anxiety about whether or not the intruder was still inside, unable to escape. Not wanting to enter on my own, I ran to get Muhammad, our real estate agent who happened to work in an adjacent building—this would also allow time for an escape, if someone was still inside.

Strangely, nothing was stolen. Our money, passports and possessions were all in place. The only thing that had been damaged was my camera—I had the latest Sony digital camera, which was small enough to fit into my pocket. Whoever had jemmied open the front door perhaps did not understand how a digital camera worked. The camera had been removed from my backpack and was sitting on the dressing table in my bedroom. Three of the four screws that held the outer casing in place were lying on the floor and the camera was in two pieces.

I immediately called the UN security officer, who told me that one of two things had probably happened: either the person responsible did not understand that the images were recorded on the memory stick rather than film—and so had unscrewed the camera's external metal case trying to obtain the roll of film—or they were trying to install a bugging device. He went on to explain that the Syrian Secret Service sometimes 'checked' the apartments of UN personnel, supposedly for our own safety. They were also interested in monitoring the photos taken by UN personnel, as there was a strict policy in place prohibiting UN staff from taking photos of any Syrian installations. However, installing listening devices within UN apartments or personal equipment had not occurred previously.

This was a strange and somewhat baffling incident, so my camera was sent to the UN headquarters for further investigation. Nothing suspicious was found; however, my camera was broken beyond repair and never worked properly again. It remained a mystery as to who was responsible and why the camera was tampered with.

•

I had been allocated to Team Oasis, which manned the two southern Observation Posts (OP) in Syria—OP 57 and OP 58, which overlooked the UN-enforced 'area of separation' between Israel and Syria, established during the peak of hostilities in 1974. The area of separation was over 75 kilometres in length and ran along the border. No military forces were permitted within this region (with the exception of the UN), effectively creating a buffer between the two feuding countries.

Team Oasis consisted of ten UNMOs, who were rostered in pairs to serve seven days at a time at the small OPs, which were approximately the size of a tennis court. Our routine meant that I would leave the relative comforts of Damascus with one other team-mate for a seven-day patrol, isolated on the Golan Heights; this made for an interesting close-quarters living arrangement. One UNMO would remain at the observation post during the day on their own, while their team-mate patrolled the region by vehicle with an UNMO from another OP. As well as observing from the OP itself, the person who remained at the post was required to conduct a number of other duties throughout the day; one of which

Walk through UN Observation Post 58, Golan Heights, Syria.
http://www.youtube.com/matinajewell

was to prepare an evening meal from food they had purchased locally. This relatively mundane routine at the OP led to it being affectionately known as 'looking and cooking' duties.

OP 58, which became my favourite of the two posts, was perched high on the bank of a spectacular *wadi* (an Arabic term for a valley through which water flows intermittently) and boasted incredible views into neighbouring Israel and Jordan. It was a truly magnificent, yet harsh, landscape.

I was the only Australian, and only female, member of Team Oasis. My other nine team-mates came from nine very different and culturally diverse countries. I would learn so much about not only the Middle East but also the homelands of my team-mates. However, Team Oasis's cultural diversity also caused a few problems over how some members viewed my gender and the roles women should fulfil.

During my first week on the Golan Heights I was patrolling with my Argentinian team-mate, Juan, in southern Syria. Juan had been tasked to teach me the evacuation route from both OP 57 and 58 to Damascus—should we ever need to vacate the position in a hurry. Juan did not seem all that keen to work with me and it took several weeks to earn his respect. From what I could understand, his issue was with my gender. I later discovered that it was only in the 1990s that Argentina started to open up opportunities for women to serve in the Army and that these women had faced many barriers to making careers in the military. So Juan was in unfamiliar territory having to spend the next twelve hours in a vehicle with a girl. The day continued to go downhill from its bleak outset.

Juan was driving while I completed half-hourly radio checks with our headquarters in Damascus and simultaneously attempted to memorise the evacuation route, making notes of the main landmarks as we went. Shortly after leaving OP 58 it became clear to me that Juan had gone off track, an easy thing to do in southern Syria, where there are no signposts and confusing rabbit warrens of dirt roads through tiny villages that all look the same.

The UN-issued road map was literally only a sketch drawing and barely resembled the area we were operating in. The map lacked the appropriate scale or detailed topography and, as a result, I had zero confidence in its accuracy. You wouldn't give your worst enemy a map like that to travel in a benign country like Australia, let alone to depend on during military operations where it was vital to know your precise location at all times. Without GPS navigation systems, UN personnel were forced to be completely reliant on these dodgy maps and to learn about their areas from information passed along by senior team-mates.

I offered to assist Juan in working out where we were on the map, but he flatly refused. As I would learn, some South American men are stoic and proud, and are desperate to save face, particularly in front of women. After an hour or more of driving in circles while I gave best-guess location reports to our headquarters via the radio, Juan finally capitulated and stopped to ask some Syrian locals for directions. He was quite agitated by now and yelled at the locals in broken English, demanding they help him. The locals, who could not understand him, became frightened and ran away. This made Juan even more furious. I again offered to assist, and told Juan that I could speak Arabic and perhaps could get directions from the locals in their native tongue. Juan made it clear that my assistance was not required and that he was in control of the situation. After all, I was a 'junior', and a woman, and I had been in Syria for less than a week. What would I know?

We sped off in what turned out to be the completely wrong direction. Soon, we hit the unmistakable *wadi* that marked the southern border with Jordan, and even Juan admitted he was heading exactly 180 degrees in the opposite direction to where we should have been going. So far Juan had made it virtually impossible for me to learn the evacuation route! He was fuming and got out of the vehicle to make a call on the mobile phone. An hour later we were back at OP 58, where our Irish team-mate, Pat, swapped places with Juan and we started the day all over again some four hours late.

All was going well with the second attempt to conduct evacuation route training, until we got a flat tyre. Pat pulled the vehicle over to the side of the road and assessed the tyre while I radioed headquarters to inform them of our situation. Pat started to gather the equipment to change the tyre. We had pulled up in front of a general store and by now a small crowd of Syrian men had gathered and were watching our movements with interest. Pat was having difficulty and was straining with the spare tyre so, as soon as my radio communication was complete, I hopped out of the vehicle to help him, pausing to say 'Marhabah' to the locals, which means hello in Arabic.

Suddenly the Syrian men jumped to their feet and were at our sides, offering to assist us. In fact they insisted that we sit and have a cup of Arabic coffee—bitter and black—while they did all the hard work of replacing the tyre. Pat was impressed with my influence with the locals and later told the rest of our team that 'if you're going to have any vehicle problems, make sure our blonde Aussie lass, Matti, is in the car with you, then you'll have an abundance of help'.

With our spare tyre in place, we farewelled our new friends and continued our training. But, due to the late start, we didn't finish until much later than scheduled, by which time the sun was already starting to set. All UN observers are supposed to complete patrolling and be back at their OPs prior to sunset. We arrived back at OP 58, to drop Pat off, right on that deadline, which is known as 'last closing down' time.

It was already dark, and yet I needed to drive another 45 minutes on my own to get back to OP 57. Since this was my first week in Syria, I had only driven the route between our two OPs a couple of times and this morning's drive to OP 58 to collect Juan had been the very first time I had driven on my own. Now I would need to find my way back in the dark. My radio transmissions would be broadcast to the entire UN force in Syria, notifying them that Team Oasis had broken orders and were on the roads after last closing down time.

I nervously headed off from OP 58, hoping my memory of landmarks would be enough to guide me home to OP 57 as quickly and safely as possible. But would I even be able to see those landmarks in the dark? The poverty-stricken areas of southern Syria have little electricity, so even the villages are dimly lit; the night sky was cloaked in complete darkness as a result of thick heavy clouds, ruling out any assistance from the moon. The headlights on my UN vehicle only gave a few metres of light on the gravel road in front of me. The atrocious road conditions and wandering livestock meant that I had to drive quite slowly to prevent a collision. I prayed that I would not encounter any local drivers either, because the Arabs in this part of the world don't use their headlights at night, a custom that still remains a mystery to me.

It was such a dark evening that I couldn't even make out the usually distinguishable Golan Heights mountain range. I resigned myself to the fact that not even the recognisable landforms would be of any assistance to navigate my way back to OP 57 that night.

It was not long before I came to an intersection of dirt roads and was unsure exactly which road to take. I felt I had my general bearings of north and south correct, and I knew I needed to stay veering to the right in order to avoid driving into the *wadi*, but the rest was a complete guess. I opted to take the road heading east and soon reached a town which I hoped was the one on my map just south of OP 57. However, there was a detour around the village and I was thrown off-course. I could feel the anxiety starting to churn in my stomach as I tried to reassure myself that all would be okay so long as I could remain calm and apply common sense to the situation.

I was forced down unfamiliar roads and I sensed I was heading off-course without knowing if there would be roads to get me back on track. I thought, *Geez . . . bloody Juan and his ego have landed me in this mess during my first week. What an initiation!* My biggest fear was hitting a landmine. The number-one rule in the Middle East is that you do not go off road, due to the continued threat of unexploded mines; but I seemed to have no option as I was being channelled down dark dirt laneways.

Sensing I was going to get more off track if I continued driving, I pulled the vehicle over and checked my map once again. I was now also starting to worry about my safety. Driving on my own, unarmed, at night as a woman in remote Syria, was probably not an ideal situation. My mind was starting to race with worst-case scenarios and I began to verge on panic, which was not helping. Then I decided to turn around and head back into the village I had just passed through, hoping to find some locals who might help me. Turning the vehicle was difficult because the road was so narrow; it was nearly impossible to remain on the road and complete a full 180-degree turn without putting a tyre off into a potential landmine.

Thankfully, when I arrived back in the village there were some young shepherds returning home with their flock of goats. Swallowing my fear, I tried to sound confident and hoped like hell that they could understand my Arabic enough to give me directions. Al humdulliah (praise Allah)—the boys miraculously understood what I was saying and helped me get back to OP 57.

After an hour and a half of highly stressful driving at night through the southern backblocks of Syria, I finally arrived back at the gates to OP 57, where my Dutch team-mate, Arijan, was extremely relieved to see me in one piece. I was exhausted, but elated that I had managed to follow my instincts and get myself out of a very difficult and potentially dangerous situation. I made my final radio transmission, but to my shock the duty officer at headquarters, berated me over the radio about being out after last closing down.

I was furious. I had been publicly humiliated and blamed for something that was out of my control—a dangerous situation that, as a first-week UNMO, I should never have been put in. If I hadn't been able to speak Arabic and find my way back to the OP, the scenario would have resulted in a search and rescue operation. I felt the duty officer should have been grateful that he wasn't trying to coordinate search parties for the rest of the evening.

Arijan attempted to console me, but his encouraging words did little to calm me down. I decided to cool my heels in the observation tower before calling the duty officer by phone and letting him know the facts about the day's patrol. He apologised profusely, but the damage had already been done.

After the phone call I returned to the observation tower, where I sat in the dark and tried to pull myself together. I had never felt as alone and helpless as I had that night. I had been absolutely terrified during the drive, but I'd managed to suppress my emotions in order to concentrate on the task at hand. Now all those feelings of fear, frustration and anger seemed to be pouring out uncontrollably.

The next morning I sent an email to Clent in Australia, asking him to purchase and post to me a top-of-the-line GPS navigation system, so I could at least give a reference point should a similar situation arise in the future. I was starting to understand the hidden dangers associated with working in a UN force with outdated equipment and, at times, poorly coordinated operations.

5 Souks, Hammams and a Chicken Killer

During my first three months in Syria, I established a routine in which I would undertake back-to-back patrols on the Golan Heights. I had chosen this routine for three reasons: firstly, it consolidated my learning of my new job so I could get up to speed on the issues of our region as quickly as possible; secondly, it enabled me to accumulate leave days, which I intended to take in a block period, so I could travel and explore other countries outside of Syria; and thirdly, it was a feeble attempt to distract myself from missing Clent.

The news from Australia that I feared most was that Clent had moved on and found himself another girlfriend. I was ecstatic when he reassured me that he hadn't and that he still felt as strongly for me as I did for him. His emotional support was vital to me, and he was brilliant at boosting my confidence whenever I felt a bit down and out of my depth.

We had continued to remain in contact by phone and email since my departure from Sydney; my feelings had only grown stronger for him, despite the physical distance between us. Sydney, he told me, was not the same since I'd left. In addition to my absence, he had a new boss, who was making life extremely painful at work, to the point where he felt his work environment was completely untenable and he was forced to evaluate his career options.

During the handful of days I spent on leave in those first three months, I found that any spare time away from work only exacerbated my feelings of loneliness and compounded my desire to be with him. I wished that I could share this cultural experience with him and that we could enjoy together the amazing opportunities to travel to the exotic locations that were on-hand and beckoning to be explored. If only Clent weren't so far away.

One night, while on duty on the Golan Heights, I received the most unexpected good news. Clent called to tell me that he had resigned from his job in Sydney with the aim of doing project work from Dubai. A three-month odyssey around Europe some years earlier had whetted his appetite for further exploration of distant places and now, with me living in Syria, he had an excuse to make it happen again. With Clent living closer to me in the Middle East, he would be able to travel with me and we could explore countries together when I had time off work. I was thrilled. Gobsmacked! I was so taken aback I could barely pull myself together to tell him how happy I was with his news. Our relationship was actually going to get a chance to survive while I completed this once-in-a-lifetime job with the UN.

•

Prior to Clent's arrival, I sought approval for his intended visit from Lieutenant Colonel Noel Beutel, my Australian contingent commander, who also happened to be the chief of the UNTSO force in Syria. The UN mission was an 'accompanied posting' for just about every one of the countries involved, except for Australia. Personnel from all the other nations had their partners and children living with them in Damascus, but the Aussies were often referred to as the mission 'orphans', with families left at home.

This had been an accompanied posting for Australia until five years earlier, but now our army's policy was that military recognised dependants (husband, wife or child) were not permitted to enter the area of operation in Syria, Israel, Lebanon or Egypt. Instead, the army would pay for such recognised dependants to be flown to Rome or somewhere else for a visit three times during the twelve-month mission, or alternatively the officer would be flown home to Australia three times during the year. With the exception of recognised dependants, we were allowed to have anyone else visit us within the area of operation—parents, siblings, friends, family, boyfriends, girlfriends or even fiancés. But not a husband, wife or child. To me, it seemed a strange rule.

On my arrival in Syria I had found that my Australian team-mates had visitors staying with them. My flatmate, Deb, had her father stay with us in Damascus for several weeks during my first month in the country, using our apartment as a base for travels around Syria and to other countries. It was a wonderful opportunity for family members to get a taste of our lifestyle, and to experience Arabic culture themselves. Sadly, Deb's father passed away suddenly a few months later, making their time together in Damascus even more precious.

Lieutenant Colonel Beutel confirmed that Clent was simply viewed as any other Australian tourist and therefore was clearly not subject to the Australian military policy, since he was not recognised as a dependant. He assured me that Clent was free to come and go as he pleased, or even to stay in Syria as long as he wished.

Ian and Rob—two of the five Australians serving in Syria—were married, and had left their wives and children back home. Although Clent's visits were not an issue from the point of view of our Australian commander, I made a special point of ensuring that the other Aussies were also comfortable with them, as the policy seemed to me to be unfair in many ways. Ian and Rob put my mind at ease by confirming that they didn't have any objections to Clent's staying in Syria—in fact, they would welcome any Aussie—and that they would do the exact same thing if roles were reversed and they were in my situation. Since Clent had approval to visit or stay as long as he wanted, and there were no issues with my team-mates, he went ahead and bought his airline ticket to the Middle East.

•

Four months into my deployment, and while Clent's decision to upend his life and move to Dubai was still sinking in for me, he arrived in Syria. Fortuitously, I was rostered on leave and able to collect him from the chaos of Damascus airport and drive him back to my apartment, located at the foot of Mt Kassioun. (Many Syrians believe that the biblical story of Cain killing his brother Abel occurred on this mountain.) I was brimming with a mixture of emotions, ranging from excitement (that Clent had taken such a huge leap of faith in me and our relationship to move to the Middle East) through to fear (that I would somehow stuff it up). There were so many things I wanted to share and show him in this city during his visit. Yet I was conscious that he had just arrived in what was a very foreign place, and the country boy might need time to find his feet. Also, we had not seen each other for several months, and things might have changed between us.

We were beginning to get acquainted again when I received a phone call—my leave was cancelled for the night. I was needed at headquarters immediately to replace the UN duty officer, who had suddenly become ill and been taken to hospital. This was unfortunate timing, but there was nothing I could do. So Clent's first night in Arab lands was spent on his own—no doubt wondering if he had made the right decision to give up his job in Sydney, to follow me to the Middle East and continue associating himself with the unpredictable world of the military.

I had organised for ten days' leave so I could spend this time with Clent, and I had arranged to hire a UN vehicle, to explore places outside the capital. My brother, Mark, who lived in London, had also coordinated his holidays to travel to Syria at the same time and it would be his first opportunity to meet Clent. Mark arrived in the early hours of the day following Clent's arrival, just in time to join in the celebrations of the Finnish Ball, which was held in the magnificently grand Damascene ballroom called The Palais de Noble ('The Noble Palace').

I had intended to start our four-day tour of Syria with Mark and Clent early the next morning, but it wasn't to be. I was struck down out of the blue by another severe abdominal pain attack. It had been eight months since I had last been rushed to hospital with the undiagnosed condition; but now I was in Syria, and the UN relied on the host country to provide medical treatment. Struggling to breathe, I was expected to call a taxi and get myself to the local Damascus hospital.

I spent the next two days in hospital with Mark and Clent by my side—quite a bizarre getting-to-know-you brotherly experience for them during this medical emergency. Syrian hospitals were no place to be on your own if you were really sick, so I was very fortunate that Clent and Mark happened to be visiting me. The nurses, while lovely and incredibly attractive (they all could have passed for models), left me with some doubts about their medical qualifications. Language was also a real barrier when it came to getting effective pain relief. My Arabic language course had focused on military words and general communication; I had not learnt to say 'I need morphine for the pain, please'!

Once I had been released from hospital, the three of us set out on our trip around Syria in a UN-issued vehicle that only I was authorised to drive. Although we were two days late departing Damascus, it was one of the best trips I have ever experienced. I felt privileged to visit some of the most amazingly preserved history in the world, in an area where many tourists don't feel safe enough to venture, with two of the most important people in my life.

We explored the remarkable medieval Crusader fortress, Crac des Chevaliers, perched atop a steep hill, which was built in 1031 and described by T.E. Lawrence as 'perhaps the best preserved and most wholly admirable castle in the world', in spite of the many battles and sieges which were fought amidst its walls. We then drove to the ancient city of Aleppo, which contests with Damascus for the title of the oldest continually inhabited city in the world. Completing our adventurous history lesson, we spent a night in a basic, but more than comfortable, hotel in the town of Palmyra and delved among the spectacular Roman ruins. Palmyra was once a bustling city on the spice trade route, but is now virtually deserted. If it weren't for its magnificent ancient ruins—its temples, citadel, amphitheatre and funerary towers in the Valley of the Tombs, luring a few off-the-beaten-track tourists, it would probably have been completely abandoned long ago.

A highlight of the trip was our interaction with the Syrian Secret Service (SSS) officers, better known in the UN contingent as the 'Not So Secret Service' because they were so easily identifiable. There were four of them—very large men—crammed into a small white car, so they were pretty conspicuous, and they would follow us on foot at whatever tourist attractions we visited. On our first day on the road, they actually approached us at the citadel and offered a big '*marhabah*' (hello) greeting; it was obvious to us that they had spent the previous two days driving around the country trying to find us, while I was all that time tucked up in hospital in Damascus, and so they appeared very relieved to have found us at last.

All UN personnel were guests of the Syrian president, Bashar al-Assad, so, when we travelled outside the Damascus region, we first were required to gain permission from the authorities. We were told the SSS officers followed us 'for our own safety'. We often wondered if there was an ulterior motive for being minded in this way.

Nevertheless, there was an advantage in having the SSS follow us on our trip around the country. If we ever were unsure of which road to take, we had our own personal guides to help show the way. This certainly reduced the risk of getting lost. One time,

View from the citadel overlooking the new and old city of Palmyra, Syria.
http://www.youtube.com/matinajewell

on the highway from Palmyra, I was about to take a wrong turn when the SSS posse started flashing their lights and indicating; then they overtook us and guided me into taking a U-turn so as to get back onto the right road. It was a bizarre experience; in fact, Mark and Clent thought the whole trip and the SSS escort were like something out of a Hollywood movie.

On our return to Damascus, Clent continued his application for a marketing role with a water company in Dubai and later found himself one of the final two candidates in the selection process. In between business trips to Dubai and Europe, he would visit me in Syria. Having Clent around helped in a number of ways. Beyond the obvious emotional support, his presence eased the complication I had faced earlier in the mission when a team-mate's wife protested her concerns about a woman spending a week at a time with her husband on the two-man OPs. Now that I had produced a living breathing boyfriend, it seemed, her fears that I was somehow a threat to her marriage were no longer valid.

●

While living in Syria I desperately wanted to experience the traditional public bathing houses called *hammams*. I had read all about the most famous *hammam* in Damascus, called Nureddin, which was established by the Sultan Nour al-din al-Shaheed in 1169. Nureddin had been operating as a bathing house for nearly 850 years and was one of the oldest public baths still operating in the city—I figured they must know what they were doing. But unfortunately, the Nureddin *hammam* was strictly for men only. Given that Australia is such a young nation, and its towns are only just over 200 years old, the concept of a bath-house existing for over 800 years was absolutely mind-blowing to me.

Some *hammams* opened for women-only bathing sessions on one or two days a week. After a little investigation, I discovered a *hammam* that opened on Tuesdays and Wednesdays for ladies only.

Armed with a basic map and a general sense of where it was located within the old city, I set off on foot to find it.

A large Roman wall, erected some 2000 years ago, surrounds the old city. Behind it lies a chaotic grid of confusing laneways, which twist and turn and create a navigational nightmare. Often these narrow passageways lead hopelessly into a dead-end or, worse still, double back on themselves, making it hard to distinguish them from others. The old city is home to a number of large *souks* (markets), the Christian and Jewish quarters, the citadel (fortress) and several mosques. It is also a food lover's paradise.

As I made my way through the Souq al Bzouriyya my senses were overloaded with an intoxicating medley of every Middle Eastern spice imaginable. Vendors displayed their wares on tables in front of their shops or simply on plastic tarps on the ground. Piles of orange, red and yellow ground spices were constructed with great precision into pyramid shapes. Fresh fruits were stacked uniformly into towers with care and attention to detail, and large bins overflowed with olives, rice, lentils, figs and nuts of all shapes and sizes. The air was fragrant and infused with the smell of roasting coffee and a twist of cardamom, cinnamon and coriander.

The *souk* was bursting with locals, who hurriedly pushed their way through the swarming crowds. Veiled women floated past me in sheets of black rayon material; with only their dark eyes exposed to the outside world, they looked at me, intrigued since my head was uncovered. We were advised not to wear the traditional Muslim head dress, such as the *hijab* or *burqa*, when we were dressed in civilian clothing, despite our desire to blend in and not stand out so much from the locals. It was explained that these were not simply items of clothing, but religious symbols, and to wear them when not following the Muslim faith would be seen as disrespectful to the religion. I was always very conscious of my appearance and deliberately dressed modestly, to avoid any unwanted attention.

Horse-drawn carts, goats and other livestock were also meandering through the crowd. The *souk* was dimly lit; the only illumination was from the shards of light that streamed down from the bullet-hole-riddled iron roof.

My eyes alerted my stomach to the amazing food presented before me. In response, my belly grumbled with anticipation and my mouth started to salivate. Perhaps I had time for a bite of lunch before my *hammam* experience? I gave in to my hunger and headed to a traditional Middle Eastern restaurant called Elissar.

Elissar was set within an enormous old Damascene house, which had an internal courtyard, marble floors, gurgling fountains and two terraced levels of dining. It was a superb setting. I ordered *mezze* (a tasting plate), which came with an assortment of dishes—my favourite being *muhammarah*, which is a spicy roasted capsicum dip with cumin, olive oil and walnuts, topped with scrumptious pomegranate molasses. I washed down my meal with a fresh mint and lemon juice drink that my UN mates had aptly named 'the Kryptonite Drink' as it was fluorescent green in colour (just like the mysterious substance that is lethal to Superman), but it was a delicious balance between sweet and sour flavours.

With a satisfied belly I continued my search for the *hammam*. I soon stumbled upon the almost concealed entrance to the baths. It was a fabulous old Ottoman-style house. The interior was ornate with marble floors and ancient carpets; the front room was a lounge area for post-bathing relaxation and the consumption of tea. A group of towel-clad Syrian women mingled in this lounge room, but they all immediately fell into silence as I entered through the front door. Their piercing stares made me feel like I had rudely invaded their privacy. I felt alone and unwelcome, and suddenly very conscious of my pale white skin. I had the urge to leave immediately, but I fought my instincts as I had made it thus far and I really wanted to experience this tradition.

This was a tourist-free, no-nonsense bathing house where English wasn't spoken. I swallowed my anxiety and asked for assistance in my best broken Arabic. Thankfully, an elderly lady motioned for me to go to her and she explained that the *hammam* package included a steam, soap bath, scrub down, massage, and a cup of *shay* (tea) afterwards. Seemed like a bargain to me, so I paid my 200 Syrian pounds, which is equivalent to four dollars Australian, and headed through the passageway to the bathing area.

I was directed to undress completely and leave my clothes in the changing area, and then to drape myself in a *pestamel* (cotton cloth wrap) and put on a pair of painful wooden clog shoes that had the heads of the nails sticking through the sole. Feeling more than slightly insecure, I was then led into the steam room. This dank, dim room was extremely hot, like a sauna; the air was fogged with steam, making it difficult to see the other bathing patrons.

I found myself a vacant spot on the hard marble seat, which was cool compared to the hot air. As the steam began to clear, I noticed that I was the only bather who wasn't completely naked. I didn't know if I should remove the *pestamel* or not. In the end I decided to leave it on as I had been instructed, although the wet air had made it transparent so I was not sure what the point was to having it swathed around my torso.

Despite my apprehension, I tried to talk with the other women. Before long we were engaged in wonderful conversations and I struggled to keep up with the countless questions they had for me. I quickly learnt that I needed to be extremely careful when pronouncing the word *Ustraalii* (which means Australian in Arabic) and place emphasis on the 'Ust' part of the word. My audience had displayed looks of horror and disbelief on their faces when I first said *'Ana Ustraalii'* (I am Australian) as it sounds very similar to *Israali* (Israeli). I did not want to be confused for an Israeli while alone in the depths of the old city of Damascus.

Without warning, I was promptly snatched from my stimulating conversation by a very large, jolly, naked woman and moved to another room. The lady gestured for me to remove my drenched cotton wrap and invited me to join her on the cold floor next to a large wooden pail of water. She commenced rubbing my bare skin into a lather of soapy suds. With bubbles covering my entire body she then placed on her hand an abrasive glove that looked like something you would clean a cooking pot with, and started to rub my body in a crude method of exfoliation. I felt like a fish having its scales removed by a fishmonger!

The pail of water was ungraciously upended over me, which was the signal that the exfoliation was complete. Although quite hard and rough, the abrasion phase of the *hammam* was strangely invigorating and my skin had never felt cleaner or smoother. Next was the massage—of sorts! Another large woman, with gigantic breasts that hung down below her navel, gathered me off the floor and guided me into a separate room, which had a wooden table in the centre. I was putty in her strong hands and surrendered myself to the pummelling she inflicted while she simultaneously sang off-key in a loud voice. This was definitely not a relaxation massage, but my muscles knew they were alive.

The final step in the bathing process was to wash myself down and rejoin the other women in the large room that adjoined the steam room. Made entirely of marble, this room contained a number of fountain-like basins; I was told to draw my own water from them, using a wooden bucket and ladle. The handful of female patrons in this room sat around these basins pouring water over each other and washing their bodies again with the Syrian olive oil soap bars provided.

Feeling squeaky clean now, I was given a fresh, dry *pestamel* and led back to the lounge area, where I was delighted and somewhat relieved to rejoin the ladies from the steam room in conversation, while sipping my Moroccan tea. My *hammam* experience had lived up to every one of my expectations and, although at times I was out of my comfort zone, I was keen to repeat the process, if for nothing else than to engage with the local women, who had fascinated me with their stories.

After the tea, the women got dressed in their Western-style clothing, which was then covered by several heavy layers of black rayon garments. They covered their faces with their *hijabs*, before stepping back outside into the world. Although I understood this was part of the Arab culture, it seemed peculiar to me that they were happy to bathe completely naked in a group setting (which was confronting for me, as this is not typical in Australian culture), but then would cover their bodies and faces while in public.

•

Back at work on the Golan Heights, there were other cultural experiences awaiting me. One of my Team Oasis colleagues was Captain Thapa Biswa, from Nepal. Biswa was a wonderful man—quick to smile, eager to learn and reputedly a brilliant cook.

He had rarely driven a vehicle before joining the UN mission and, although his driving abilities had improved enormously, he was still not confident reversing. Whenever he needed to turn around, Biswa would ask his team-mate to take over and reverse, before jumping back in behind the wheel and carrying on with the patrol. It was an amusing situation, but Biswa was not embarrassed—he acknowledged his limitations and was not afraid to ask for help, making him even more charming and endearing.

Early in my time in Syria, Biswa had swerved to miss a pile of rocks on the road and rolled the UN four-wheel drive several times before it came to rest in a paddock. The vehicle, a brand-new Toyota Prado, was a complete write-off, but thankfully Biswa emerged unscathed. As a result, Biswa was now a little hesitant driving—and we were rather nervous passengers!

I was ecstatic to learn that I had been rostered on OP 57 for a week-long patrol with Biswa as I was keen to taste his famous cooking. However, my eagerness to experience his Nepalese cuisine had to be weighed against the warning from my team-mates that Biswa did not shower on a daily basis, which made for an uncomfortable stay towards the end of the week.

During night three of our patrol, Biswa called me frantically from outside the accommodation hut. The OP dog, Junior, had also begun to bark incessantly. My team-mate sounded alarmed, so I rushed to the door to see what was wrong. I was greeted by an elated Biswa, who wore a grin from ear to ear and was awkwardly holding a mop away from his body. On closer inspection I saw that there was a live snake dangling from the other end of the mop. 'Get the camera, quick,' he yelled.

I wasn't keen to get close to the snake, but I could see that Biswa was not going to change his mind, so I quickly snapped a photo. Biswa then proceeded to kill the snake, using only the handle of the mop; this proved to be less than ideal as a snake-killing implement. I was later horrified to learn it was a deadly Palestinian viper, the venom of which is fast-acting and often fatal. I attempted to chide Biswa for being so reckless, considering that we were more than two hours' drive from the nearest hospital, but there was no convincing him that he was anything but a hero. I subsequently developed a strange suspicion that the viper ended up as our dinner the following evening.

I had continued my university studies while deployed with the UN and hoped to complete the last two subjects of my master's degree in project management while working in the Middle East. During my week patrol with Biswa on OP 57, I needed to sit a three-hour exam. The university appointed Biswa as my supervisor and emailed him the exam paper on the morning that the exam was to be held in Australia. I had organised for our daily patrol to start a little later than normal, so I could sit the exam from six to nine o'clock that same morning, Syrian time, before getting on the road to patrol for the day.

It was a bizarre and less-than-ideal situation in terms of exam conditions. I set up a table in the cramped observation tower of OP 57 and completed the exam while overlooking a minefield and the area of separation between Israel and Syria. I tried my best not to be distracted by the Syrian soldiers conducting a training exercise on the fringe of the minefield. Despite my efforts, I spent the entire three hours anxiously waiting for my exam to be disrupted by the sound of a mine exploding. I managed to scrape through that exam with a pass.

•

Every fortnight on both the Syrian and the Israeli side of the Golan Heights, the UN conducted an inspection of all military positions straddling the area of separation. As a result of the 1974 Disengagement Agreement, zones had been established with restrictions on the type of military equipment and numbers of soldiers either side was allowed to have in these areas.

During the inspections we would be accompanied by a Syrian military liaison officer and drive our vehicles into each military compound, where we would ask the Syrian commander for the number of soldiers based there and the types of weapons systems they held. We were permitted to drive around the positions, but not to get out of the vehicle. We would account for various types of weapons systems and do our own headcount of the soldiers we could see because many commanders would give inaccurate responses, often underestimating the number of soldiers present on their base. I became known as the Team Oasis secret weapon, able to pull Syrian soldiers out of their foxholes for us to count; many of them had never seen a white woman before, so they were curious to get a glimpse of me.

Meanwhile, I continued to hone my Arabic language skills at every opportunity. During one patrol on OP 58, my broken Arabic helped to prevent a potential international incident. I had left the OP to go on a 5-kilometre run and, as I returned through town, I was greeted by Oscar, our patrol base dog. Oscar was a scruffy, short-haired, black dog with a white blaze down his muzzle and chest; he was always extremely pleased to see us when we returned to the base after a long day on the road. He was also a good guard dog and gave us early warning of anyone approaching our compound.

On this occasion, Oscar greeted me in the middle of town with a dead chicken in his mouth. I made chase after him, but I soon realised he was being chased by a group of angry Arab men dressed in their traditional white robes, who now also pursued me. I decided to make a run for it back to the safety of our OP.

Oscar dropped the chicken just before we reached our post. Safely behind the closed gates of the UN base, I spoke with the irate mob and offered them compensation for the chicken. But as soon as they heard me speak in Arabic, their outright hostility dissipated. As it turned out they were actually impressed—'honoured', they explained—that I had spent the time to learn their language. It defused the situation immediately.

The men went on to explain that they simply wanted me to know that our dog was the guilty party, a chicken killer; later that day they returned to inform me that they 'had eaten the chicken for lunch and that it was delicious'. The following day I visited the chicken owner's house, armed with a bag full of Australian tea and souvenirs for the children. From the front door, I apologised once more for Oscar's indiscretion and was hospitably welcomed inside for coffee. We sat in the formal lounge room and chatted as much as my Arabic allowed. They were genuinely keen to learn more about my life and why I was jogging in this remote part of the world. They explained that people in southern Syria do enough exercise in the fields every day and hence there is no need for them to run to keep fit.

Morning tea at this neighbour's house became a regular ritual. Every time I drove past, they would beckon me to come in for tea and to play with the children. It was important to have good relations with the locals and I thoroughly enjoyed these brief insights into their lives.

I spent Christmas Day on OP 58, but had finished my weekly patrol in time to join a group of UN personnel who were travelling in a vehicle convoy from Damascus to Lebanon to celebrate New Year's Eve in the snow at the Lebanese ski fields of Faraya Mazaar.

Fortunately, Clent was able to organise his business travel so he could fly back to Syria to join us for this adventure. The group consisted of about ten UNMOs and their families; it was a great mix of nationalities, with Lieutenant Colonel Beutel, Clent and me representing the Australian skiers—although we were clearly out-classed by our skilled European team-mates on the slopes.

Faraya Mazaar is part of the huge mountain range that runs the length of Lebanon and is located right on the coast only about an hour's drive from Beirut. It was a spectacular and well-equipped ski field with multiple lifts and superbly groomed tracks. Never before had I experienced the unique combination of skiing through pristine snow while at the same time overlooking the ocean. We could literally ski in the morning and spend the afternoon at the beach! My Dutch team-mate, Arijan, provided the highlight of the trip by successfully proposing to his girlfriend, Krista, on New Year's Eve. It was a wonderful and memorable way to bring in the new year.

My last two months in Syria were brilliant. I was enthralled by my work on the Golan Heights and I enjoyed my days off in Damascus. I travelled abroad with Clent and explored the hidden treasures around the old city, delving into the thriving *souks*. Even after spending half a year living in Damascus, I felt as though I had barely scratched the surface of the true beauty of the city. There were so many more streets and alleyways with opulent produce to explore, but never enough time to absorb it all.

Life in the Middle East continued to be an amazing experience; everything was great, except for my health. Unfortunately, my brief trip to the Damascus hospital with Clent and Mark had not been my last. The Syrian doctors thought I had symptoms similar to a common illness in the Middle East called Mediterranean Fever and they tested for this condition. I would later find out that Mediterranean Fever is a genetic disorder and, since I am not of Middle Eastern or Mediterranean ancestry, it was unlikely that I would have it. The results were negative, but the Syrian doctors still thought I might have this illness and prescribed a daily medication for it.

As a result of my more frequent abdominal attacks and the fact that the Australian army was assessing if I was well enough to continue serving overseas, Clent withdrew his application for the marketing role in Dubai and stayed on in Syria longer than planned after new year. I felt it was very likely that I would be sent home from the mission on medical grounds, so Clent did not want to lock himself into a contract in Dubai only to find that I was heading back to Sydney.

I ended up spending an extra month in Syria while I awaited the verdict from Sydney. Convinced that the Australian command would cut short my mission, I stocked up on souvenirs in case it was a quick departure home. This turned out to be a rash decision because, instead of heading home, I was instructed to pack up my gear (including the newly acquired souvenirs) and move to Lebanon to complete the last half of my mission.

6 Historic Beauty and New Friends

During a year-long posting with UNTSO, it was common to divide the time equally between two countries out of Israel, Syria, Egypt and Lebanon. I wanted to spend both my six-month tours in Arab countries, to fully utilise my Arabic language skills. My wish was granted, and for the second half of my mission I was selected to join the UN observer team based out of the coastal city of Tyre, in southern Lebanon.

Lebanon was a far more active and hostile region than the Golan Heights, with frequent skirmishes initiated by Hezbollah, a Lebanon-based Islamist resistance movement—reportedly supported by Syria and Iran—opposed to Israel's existence. Occasionally, Hezbollah fighters would fire rockets into Israel and conduct small-scale cross-border raids. Their actions would often be followed by swift and deadly retaliation by the Israeli Defence Force (IDF) in the form of aerial bombardment, artillery and tank fire. Although both Israel and Hezbollah agreed that UN personnel and assets should not be targeted, there was a real danger of being caught in the wrong place at the wrong time. As a result of the heightened danger levels, there were five military observers at each UN position, rather than just two as I had experienced in Syria. The UN posts were referred to as Patrol Bases (PB) rather than observation posts, even though they were pretty much the same. The UN teams would patrol their allocated regions along the border in Lebanon every day by vehicle, foot and helicopter.

The UNTSO force in Lebanon was known as Observer Group Lebanon (OGL). It was divided into four teams that manned the four patrol bases along the UN 'Blue Line', which is the proposed border between Israel and Lebanon. These bases were located a short distance from the Blue Line so they had a view of the border and could observe and report border violations; Israel and Lebanon had agreed with the majority of the proposed border with the exception that Lebanon laid claim to the Cheeba Farms region, which was under Israeli control.

The most highly requested and sought-after of the UN teams in Lebanon was Team Sierra, which manned PB Khiam (pronounced 'key arm') and was responsible for patrolling the hotly disputed Cheeba Farms area. The majority of UNMOs desperately wanted to be part of Team Sierra because it had seen the lion's share of military combat in the past. PB Khiam was located in the same village as Hezbollah's headquarters so, if you wanted action, then Khiam was the place to be—'things happened' almost on a daily basis.

I was not 100 per cent fit and had suffered several pain attacks associated with the still-undiagnosed condition while working in Syria. The attacks were so severe that I had been admitted to the Damascus hospital twice. Lieutenant Colonel Beutel, who had been my Australian contingent commander for the first six months of my one-year posting, was replaced by a new lieutenant colonel from Australia, who was employed by the UN as the chief operations officer based at the UNTSO headquarters in Jerusalem. In an initial interview with my new Australian commander in Damascus, I discussed my health situation. He seemed surprised that I had remained serving in the Middle East despite my emergency hospitalisations and stated that, if I suffered one more pain attack, he would recommend my return to Australia. I could understand his point of view—taking over as the national commander, he expected all ten of his Australian officers to be medically fit. In effect I was now a concern and a problem for him.

I really wanted to complete my UN posting, but not if it jeopardised my long-term health. I conveyed this to my new Australian commander and he sent me to Jerusalem, to get a second opinion from a leading medical professor there, but this again proved inconclusive. So I continued taking tablets for Mediterranean Fever and also kept strong pain-relief medication in ampoules in reserve, which would need to be administered as a muscular injection by team-mates during my transit to hospital if I suffered an attack on duty.

At the request of my Australian commander, I also spoke directly with the senior army health staff officer in Sydney. I was further assured that although it was highly unlikely I had Mediterranean Fever, I was to continue taking the daily medication for this condition and complete the remaining five months of my UN deployment—hopefully without the need of another hospital admission. If I suffered another crippling attack, at that point I would be returned to Australia. I appreciated the efforts my new Aussie commander had made to gain a diagnosis and to clarify if I was compromising my future health by sticking out the last few months of the mission; however, the onset of another attack was still a concern.

Since the hospital in Lebanon was located at the OGL head-quarters in Naqoura, I hoped I would be allocated to the team that manned the patrol base closest to the hospital. This was Team Zulu, which manned PB Hin and was also responsible for conducting radio duties at headquarters, a job no one wanted to do. But I was happy to join Team Zulu, despite the less exciting radio duties, if it meant I was closer to medical care. The last place I wanted to be was on the popular PB Khiam, the furthest PB from the hospital—usually around a two-hour drive.

The pain attacks I had previously experienced would start without notice and leave me completely incapacitated in a matter of minutes. I did not want to be a burden on my new team-mates, who would be responsible for providing first aid and caring for me if I ever suffered an attack while on duty. I felt it was paramount that Lieutenant Colonel Rolf Kullberg from Finland, the chief of the OGL, be made aware of my condition. From my experience in Syria, I knew we didn't have interviews upon arrival with our new UN commanders so there was no point waiting for a face-to-face meeting with the chief in Lebanon to discuss this matter. I also thought it would be preferable to raise this issue prior to my arrival, rather than waiting until teams were allocated and then asking for a reshuffle once I arrived in-country.

So, a week or two before I was scheduled to take up my posting, and before we had been allocated to teams and patrol bases, I raised my concerns with Captain Ash Collingburn, the senior Australian officer and the operations officer in Lebanon (and my former classmate from the Arabic language school). Ash agreed it was sensible to raise this issue prior to my arrival and team allocation, so he spoke with Lieutenant Colonel Kullberg.

Unfortunately, Lieutenant Colonel Kullberg saw things very differently. He felt strongly that he should be able to allocate UNMOs to any patrol base because they should all be fit for duty (a not unreasonable notion). He phoned my Australian commander in Jerusalem to ask why he was about to be sent an Aussie who had a medical condition.

My Australian commander called me soon afterwards. It was a short, curt, one-way conversation, with him shouting and me dutifully listening. He advised me the team allocations had now been made and I had been assigned to Team Sierra on PB Khiam. He was furious and made it clear that he felt I had undermined his command, forcing him to justify his decision to leave me on the mission and placing him in a difficult position with another national commander.

Needless to say, this had not been my intention at all. I had not wanted to cause problems for either my new UN boss in Lebanon or my Australian commander—I honestly believed that I had done the sensible thing for everyone concerned in raising the issue.

I certainly didn't think it best for Lieutenant Colonel Kullberg to find out for the very first time about my compromised health while I was actually having an attack and needing emergency treatment in Lebanon. No matter how strongly I felt justified in my actions, however, I realised that I would have to make amends as soon as I could, particularly with my Australian commander.

•

My first week in Lebanon was hectic. Each day consisted of UN training and getting up to speed on the numerous issues associated with Israel and Hezbollah. Operations in Lebanon certainly made my time in Syria look like a walk in the park by comparison.

Lebanon is one of the most spectacular and picturesque countries I have ever visited. With the Mediterranean Sea down its western side, to the east are enormous mountain ranges—here there are snow-capped peaks enjoyed by skiers in winter and prosperous valleys under cultivation all year round. It offers an extremely diverse landscape in a relatively small space. Its capital, Beirut, is slowly regaining its former title as 'the Paris of the Middle East' after years of unrest, and is a thriving city with a recognisably Western ambience and an interesting mix of Arab and European influences. Beirut's prosperity is widely attributed to the generosity of Lebanon's former prime minister Rafic Hariri, who donated a large portion of his own wealth to rebuilding the city. Sadly, Hariri was assassinated in 2005 and his people still mourn their loss.

The UN mission was based an hour's drive south of Beirut, in the city of Tyre. Any area south of Beirut was considered 'Hezbollah country', so most Lebanese never venture south of the capital. I moved into a basic but clean apartment in the Christian quarter of the old city. My flat was right on the water's edge with a small sandy beach that allowed easy access to the warm, crystal-clear, aquamarine waters of the Mediterranean. A short swim from the shoreline, submerged below the water, lay ancient columns and other visible reminders that Alexander the Great had conquered this region in 332 BC. A small section of the fortress wall that dated back to those war-torn times stood preserved in front of my apartment. I was surrounded by a tangible history lesson and felt very blessed for the experience.

One of the reasons I had rented this particular apartment was because of the large terrace that overlooked the beautiful Tyre harbour. It was approaching summer in Lebanon and I could visualise my days off work—lazing on the balcony in the sea breeze, watching the fishing boats coming and going from the sheltered inlet with their bountiful catches. At night, it was a marvellous sensation to fall asleep to the soothing sound of the waves lapping rhythmically against the shore outside my window.

The deep sleep that followed would only be broken by the piercing wail of the Muslim morning call to prayer. It would blast from speakers dotted throughout the entire city, echoing around the concrete buildings and reverberating off the ocean. I certainly didn't need to set an alarm to wake up! Another UN family also lived in my apartment block, which was great from a social and security aspect. It was comforting to know that this Swedish family was only a floor below me if ever I needed anything.

The UN force in Lebanon had not had many female observers in its almost 60-year history. The Australian contingent had only recently changed its policy to allow 'non arms corps' officers (army personnel other than from Infantry, Artillery, Combat Engineers or the Armoured Corps) to work in Lebanon. As a logistician by training, I was one of the first Australian women to serve there.

Lebanon showed me its ugly side very early on. During the afternoon on day two, the deputy chief of OGL, New Zealand

View of Tyre Harbour from Matti's apartment, Lebanon.
http://www.youtube.com/matinajewell

Squadron Leader Karvae Tamariki, requested an informal meeting at his apartment to discuss some finer details surrounding PB Khiam. Karvae wanted to warn me of some issues I could face in the region, particularly because it had been a while since a woman had been stationed at the post. Keen to make life as safe and easy as possible, I headed off to the meeting.

I had been in the Middle East for seven months by this stage and was accustomed to the way women in Arab countries dressed. I was always very conscious of my appearance and deliberately dressed modestly, to avoid any unwanted attention. On this particular day, I was covered up from head to toe in denim jeans, a long-sleeved polar fleece jacket, and a baseball cap held back my hair. It was a beautiful afternoon and the sun reflected off the Mediterranean Sea as I skirted the port and made my way across town.

Soon after I left my flat, I noticed that I was being followed by two men on motorbikes. Within seconds they were by my side, trying to speak to me in English: 'Hey pretty girl, you are so beautiful. Come for a ride on our bikes.'

I thought it best to ignore them and not speak in either Arabic or English; I hoped they would get bored and leave me alone. But I was wrong and they persisted. I decided to short-cut the upcoming corner by crossing a grassed area away from the road and their motorbikes. At first this seemed to work and they sped off out of view.

When I rejoined the road, however, I caught a glimpse of the men as they returned on their bikes and raced towards me again from a different direction. I started to call Karvae on my mobile phone, but it was too late. The men launched both motorbikes up onto the footpath, one in front of me and one behind, in an attempt to trap me between them and drag me onto their bikes. I pushed past the smaller of the two men and started to run up the street, but I only made it a short distance before they caught me and pushed me to the ground. In a flurry of grasping hands they groped my breasts hard, and in a painful frenzy. We grappled. They tried to hold me down as I struggled to my feet.

The larger man then attempted to straddle me. He grabbed my crotch and said with menace, 'I'm going to fuck you.' Instinctively, I kneed him in the groin and kicked him as hard as I could in the shin with my steel-capped army boot. He crumpled to the ground. I was then able to push the smaller man away from me too.

With a short distance now between us, I yelled in Arabic, 'I am a captain in the Australian Army. I am in Lebanon working for the United Nations.'

The men were stunned and asked in English, 'You work for United Nations?'

'Yes,' I responded. Their faces drained of colour as they clambered onto their motorbikes and sped off.

Karvae had heard the scuffle through my mobile phone, which was still on and working, despite being knocked out of my hand as the two men rode me to the ground. Karvae and another Kiwi, Tony Downey, had already started to drive along the route they thought I might have taken and, minutes later, they found me and I got in their car. Back in their apartment, they consoled me and helped me come to terms with what had just happened. I was in a state of shock.

I had just spent seven months in Syria without incident. There, women and children walked alone on the street—even late at night after an evening meal in the restaurants, which stayed open well into the morning. Only 48 hours into my time in Lebanon and two low-life mongrels had assaulted me! I spent the next day giving statements and descriptions of the assailants to the Lebanese police. I was told by other UNMOs that I was not the only woman in the UN contingent who had been assaulted by local men in Tyre, but the others, including female UNMOs, wives and children, had been too frightened to report it.

I spoke with my Australian senior in Lebanon, Captain Ash Collingburn, who was a brilliant source of support and reassurance.

Ash confirmed that he had passed on the details of the assault to our Australian commander in Jerusalem. I heard nothing from him, however. I was conscious that this incident had now created another issue for him, which he would need to formally report back to Australia because the personal safety of an Australian soldier had been threatened.

I attempted to put on a brave face after the assault, but I was actually quite shaken. I gave a sanitised version of events to Clent, who was in Dubai, as I did not want to worry him. He was not planning on visiting me in Lebanon for a couple of months because I had encouraged him to go to Dubai and Europe with his work commitments while I settled in and focused on my new work routine. After this unpleasant episode, though, I felt like I needed his support more than ever. A few days later, I started my first seven-day patrol on PB Khiam. After the rough welcome, I was glad to be leaving Tyre for a while.

•

Israel and her northern neighbour Lebanon have a long and volatile history. Starting in 1948, when Israel was established as an independent state, Lebanon became home to more than 100,000 refugees who had fled their homes in the former Palestine. These refugees increased dramatically in numbers over the years that followed and by 1975 there were more than 300,000 living in southern Lebanon. Several Palestinian refugee camps still exist on the outskirts of Tyre and many more are scattered throughout southern Lebanon. Tension arose between the Palestine Liberation Organization (PLO) and Israel along the Lebanese border, resulting in continual violence from 1968 onwards.

In effect, PB Khiam had been in the line of fire from Israel since 1982, when Israel crossed the border and occupied Beirut, in retaliation for rocket fire from the PLO. After further provocation from the PLO and Hezbollah, Israel attacked across the border again in 1993. In 1996 the Israelis invaded for a third time—in sixteen days they conducted over 1000 air raids and caused hundreds of millions of dollars' worth of damage to buildings, roads, bridges and other infrastructure. Thousands of civilians were displaced on both sides of the border.

Patrol Base Khiam was two hours' drive inland from Tyre in a truly spectacular setting. Perched on the crest of a spur line, the base overlooked a valley that ran up to the foothills of the Mt Herman ridge line, which was the dominant terrain feature of the Golan Heights and housed a number of Israeli military compounds. PB Khiam had a fantastic field of view across the UN's Blue Line. It was also located at the previous junction of three countries—Israel, Lebanon and Syria—making it a strategically important site.

The base was named after the town of El Khiam, as PB Khiam was located within the southern edge of that village, which was also the home of Hezbollah's headquarters. A small base of similar size to the OPs in Syria—about the size of a tennis court—PB Khiam was surrounded by a razor-wire fence, but only a padlock on the front and rear gates prevented access to the post. If anyone really wanted to enter the base, there wasn't much stopping them—a set of bolt cutters would give easy access. This low level of security was always a little unnerving for me, considering we were unarmed observers in a dangerous part of the world. But it seemed to work, as the UN was not a likely target for militia action.

The base was surrounded by three Hezbollah posts, the closest being only 75 metres away. I was surprised the UN had allowed Hezbollah to establish its headquarters, bunkers (places to fight from or to shelter from attack) and storage areas in such close proximity to us; at times, I wondered who was monitoring whom.

Our role was to observe and monitor the UN restrictions on Israel and Lebanon, and to report any violations of the peace agreement to our headquarters in Naqoura, from where the information would be passed up the line to the UNTSO headquarters in Jerusalem and from there to the Department of Peacekeeping Operations within the UN Security Council in New York. Observations were made from a deck at the patrol base and by daily patrols in vehicles, on foot and by helicopter. The routine in Team Sierra offered the option of completing a three-, four- or seven-day patrol; personnel would rotate onto the base on Tuesday and Friday mornings. This schedule, where personnel would trickle feed on and off the post, ensured there was continuity of knowledge of the many events occurring in the region.

PB Khiam was always manned by five people at any one time. One observer would remain at the base for the day, observing the surrounding area from the tower and completing numerous duties, including cooking an evening meal for the other four members, who spent the day patrolling in vehicles. The four members on the move would split up and travel separately in two vehicles, with each team assigned a local Lebanese interpreter for the duration of the day's patrol. These patrols would be conducted in UN four-wheel drive vehicles (a Toyota 4-Runner or, my preferred car, a Toyota Prado). All UN vehicles were clearly marked with 'UN' symbols painted on the doors, bonnet, back door and roof, while a UN flag flew from the rear of the vehicles.

At PB Khiam we also had a third vehicle that we would occasionally use—an armoured vehicle that was easy to drive but very difficult to stop because of the weight of its armour plating. When I drove it, I was always fearful that I would accidentally hit a child if I couldn't brake in time. This would have been very easy to do, since houses in southern Lebanon sit right on the edge of the road—there is often only a metre or less between stepping out from the front door and being on the road.

Team Sierra at this time was made up of eleven UNMOs from nine different countries: Australia, Austria, Canada, Chile, China, Estonia, Finland, the Netherlands and Norway. We called PB Khiam our home away from home. I was the only Australian and the only female in Team Sierra. My team-mates' personalities were as diverse as the countries and cultures they had come from. At one end of the spectrum was Major Zhaoyu Du, or simply 'Du', as we called him. He seemed to take up about one matchbox in space. He was a softly spoken, intelligent, conservative, neat and diligent Chinese army officer. He absolutely loved his family and was terribly proud of China. His face beamed when opportunities arose to talk about either topics or to share photos of his wife and one-year-old son.

At the opposite end of the personality scale was Major Paeta Hess-Von Kruedener, a Canadian Special Forces officer. He insisted on being called 'Wolf' and he was a real larrikin! Wolf was medium height with a strong muscular build and he sported a thick moustache that framed his infectious, semi-permanent smile. He was also a family man with a wife and two children, and was always up for a laugh, spending much of his spare time plotting practical jokes at our expense. Wolf was confident, but not arrogant; loud, but not overbearing; respectful and a natural leader.

Most of my patrols during my first week on PB Khiam were conducted under Wolf's tutelage. He was very excited to have an Australian join Team Sierra and welcomed me to the team, saying, 'An Aussie? Fantastic, someone who will understand my sense of humour!' Wolf and I immediately hit it off, developing a healthy sibling rivalry. After just a day patrolling together, we became good mates. We had spent the entire twelve hours in the vehicle taking the mickey out of each other, a cultural habit that my other team-mates did not fully understand, but one that Wolf relished. At times, some of the members of Team Sierra really did not know how to handle Wolf's sarcasm and teasing because in their cultures giving someone a hard time was a sign of dislike, not acceptance.

My first night on PB Khiam set the scene for my friendship with Wolf and how I would fit into Team Sierra. After dinner the entire team was in the kitchen to help clean up. We turned up the music and everyone was allocated a job; mine was to dry the dishes. As kids, my brother and I had been responsible for drying up and we regularly enjoyed flicking each other with the tea towel (when Mum and Dad weren't looking). With the advent of dishwashers, it had been a long while since I'd flicked a tea towel at an unsuspecting brother. I finished drying the plates and, before I hung up my now damp towel, I spied Wolf with his head underneath the range hood, cleaning the top of the stove. Without giving any thought to my actions and their potential consequences, I flicked the towel in Wolf's direction, intending to just miss him.

To everyone's surprise, especially mine, I missed the side of the oven and hit Wolf fair and square on his backside, giving off an almighty crack like a whip. Wolf jumped as the towel connected, and hit his head on the range hood. 'Who the hell was that?' he bellowed. My team-mates were trying to make themselves scarce, or pretending to wash more dishes.

When Wolf turned around, he saw me in apologetic shock and nervously laughing. I explained, amid my mirth, that I'd intended to give him a fright and not actually collect him, but I was obviously out of practice and not such a good shot any more. Wolf responded knowingly, 'Of course it was you. Well I guess you're not going to be the quiet new girl who just sits in the corner.' Wolf then gave me a high-five in congratulations for 'getting him a good one'.

His response confused my team-mates. They just didn't understand that this skylarking was an Australian and Canadian way of breaking the ice and showing friendship.

•

The UN had two military forces working in southern Lebanon. I was an unarmed observer with UNTSO. The second UN force was called the United Nations Interim Force in Lebanon (UNIFIL), which was made up of two armed infantry battalions, one from Ghana and the other from India, about 2000 soldiers in total. The UNIFIL force occupied positions along the Blue Line as a buffer between Israel and Lebanon. The Indian battalion was the closest unit to us. My first week on PB Khiam culminated with lunch at the nearby Indian company headquarters.

I was told that prior to my arrival at Team Sierra, the team had never been invited for lunch with the Indians. My team-mates teased me, saying how great it was to have a girl join the team—the benefit had already materialised in the form of a free lunch with the Indian commander. This made me feel a bit uncomfortable, but I had to admit the Indian force did seem quite intrigued with me, simply because many of the soldiers had never seen a white-skinned woman with blue eyes and blonde hair before.

After lunch the Indian commander took us for a tour of the base including the food storage room. The UNIFIL force were provided meals by the UN, however the UNTSO contingent were expected to purchase food locally. As a result, when Wolf spied a 20-kilogram bag of rice his eyes lit up and he searched for something to exchange. With nothing to swap, Wolf jokingly offered to give me to the Indians in return for the bag of rice. The Indian commander, who also enjoyed practical jokes, later agreed to help get back at Wolf; this plan involved a special bowl of ultra-spicy soup for him the next time we visited for lunch.

The jokes made for good times and a bit of fun; reinforcing our mateship and camaraderie in what was a very serious part of the world.

7 Danger in Ghajar

I thoroughly enjoyed patrolling with my new team-mates and getting a grip on the myriad of complications and challenges associated with work in the El Khiam region. I quickly settled into life on the patrol base and was comfortable and happy with my new surroundings, up until midway through my second patrol.

This was the first time I had manned PB Khiam on my own during the day, while my team-mates conducted vehicle patrols of the surrounding region. I was working through my list of duties when I remembered I had been asked to burn a number of confidential documents. With the papers in hand, I headed to our 'fire point', which was simply an empty 44-gallon drum in a sand and gravel pit located inside the barbed-wire perimeter fence.

Suddenly, our patrol base dog, Gwynn, started barking, alerting me to the presence of a local man who was building a rock wall around the civilian house just in front of PB Khiam. The man, in his mid-50s, had a scruffy appearance with an unkempt moustache and a stubbly beard. He was dressed in soiled pants and an old woollen jumper riddled with holes. He wore a strange cloth-style hat and a cigarette was dangling from the side of his mouth. He had stopped work and approached the fence of our compound. He was gesturing for me to come to him and was speaking in an Arabic dialect that I didn't understand.

Gwynn was going berserk, barking and growling at the man. I had a strange, awkward sense that this man's interest in speaking with me was not good. I patted Gwynn and tried to calm her down. When I turned back towards the man, he started licking his lips and touching his genitals suggestively. Repulsed, I waved him on and continued with my duties, turning my back on him.

My attempt to ignore him became futile, because he moved to a part of the fence where he was only a few metres away from me at the fire point. To my horror, the man then started masturbating in front of me! I was completely shocked and dismayed—this was the second incident of a sexual nature in only two weeks. What the hell was wrong with these guys? I was dressed in my Australian army desert camouflage uniform, which is the most unflattering, non-provocative outfit imaginable; I was on a clearly marked UN patrol base in the middle of the day. Yet this nutter thought this was somehow an invitation to relieve himself in front of me.

I had been monitoring the locations of my two patrol teams and I knew that our most experienced Lebanese interpreter, Eddie, who lived in El Khiam, was in Kilo patrol. This patrol also had my Norwegian team leader, Yngvar Dypvik, in the vehicle and was only fifteen minutes' drive away. I called and asked them to return to PB Khiam immediately, as I needed Eddie to have a chat with this local villager who was acting inappropriately. After I finished my phone call I climbed up the ladder to our observation deck with my digital camera in hand, hoping to take a photo of the perpetrator as evidence, if he was still there. I was stunned to find that the man had finished masturbating and had simply returned to building the wall as if nothing had happened.

The photo I snapped of him back at work came in handy an hour later when the Lebanese gendarmerie (police) came to investigate the situation, after Eddie lodged a formal complaint with their office. From my photo, the man was identified straight away as a resident of El Khiam who had a history of sexual offences. The gendarmerie apologised profusely and insisted that this type of incident would never occur again. They were embarrassed that a UN army officer had been exposed to such an event in their neck of the woods and they were doing everything in their power to ensure that I was okay. They even arranged for the town mayor to visit me in an attempt to smooth things over, as they were very keen to make sure the UN continued to support their region.

Naturally, I assured them that this incident would not cause a problem with the UN and they need not worry. For me personally, though, this second episode in a fortnight made me question my own safety. After the gendarmerie departed, I reassured my concerned team-mates that I would be all right on the base on my own, so they too could leave and continue their patrol. Although I put on a brave face, I was terribly shaken.

In the back of my mind, ever since the first assault in Tyre, I had been reminded of an incident years earlier. Colonel Higgins, an American officer who had been the chief of the UNTSO force in Lebanon at the time, was abducted from his UN vehicle on his way between Tyre and the headquarters in Naqoura. He was held captive for two years, during which time he was tortured, and he was subsequently murdered. This violent incident reminded me that we were never completely safe, especially since we were unarmed. Adding to my angst was the prospect that anyone with a set of bolt- or wire-cutters could easily get into the base.

I decided to keep a shovel (the only thing I found in the shed that might be of use to defend myself) within arm's reach, although I was not sure what good that was going to do me if I needed to use it against an intruder. I was thankful that we had two dogs on the post; if nothing else, they were good company—Gwynn, in particular, sensed my anxiety and wouldn't let me out of her sight. Both Gwynn and the puppy, Ghajar, were good guard dogs, providing early warning of any movement around our base. I also hoped the dogs' presence would be effective in deterring any further unwanted visitors, as our Lebanese interpreters had told me that many people from an Arab culture are afraid of dogs and see them as dirty animals.

I called my Australian contingent commander to inform him personally of the incident. I did not want to put him in a potentially embarrassing situation, finding out for the first time about the event at the daily operations brief that took place each evening, where he might lose face in front of his headquarter colleagues if he was not able to answer questions about the incident. I was a little nervous making this call because my last conversation with him, about being allocated to PB Khiam, had not been pleasant. He had already been briefed by Ash on the first assault in Tyre, so I hoped that he would understand my sensitivity to this second incident and provide me with some much-needed reassurance and support, particularly since it had occurred within a UN compound. However, he responded abruptly, saying, 'It's part of the cultural experience, Matti—I suggest you get over it.'

His response shocked me and I didn't know what to say. The conversation ended and I hung up the receiver feeling worse than before; I was gutted and felt let down. It struck me that he really didn't seem to understand the gravity of the situation or my concerns for my safety and wellbeing, which I felt were validated given the history of the mission.

Assaults can happen to both men and women in any work environment and in any country of the world, and I knew it was beyond my commander's (and the UN's) control to prevent such events from happening. I was committed to sticking out the rest of my twelve-month assignment with the UN regardless; although I had hoped for a little support and encouragement from my commander.

I felt that the first two phone conversations we had had, regarding my health and team allocation in Lebanon, had got us off to a bad start, but now our relationship had gone from bad to worse. From his point of view, I imagined that I had created extra work for him—he would need to write reports back to Australia detailing my medical condition and, now, two sexual assault incidents. Years later I discovered that neither incident was actually reported back to Australia at the time. I then asked my Australian commander about this and he confirmed to me that he did not believe that the incidents were significant enough to report. I certainly did and made reports to the local Lebanese police at the time and later to the ADF military police.

Thankfully, my team-mates at PB Khiam provided amazing support and rallied round me, for which I was immensely grateful. But on my days off work in Tyre, as much as I tried, I couldn't simply 'get over' the assaults. I was afraid to walk down the street on my own, for fear of being attacked by some of the local men, who continued to stare at me like I was some sort of exotic animal on display at the zoo. I had thought that perhaps my blonde hair was the cause of the unwanted attention, so I went to the hairdresser with the plan of dyeing it black; but three different hair salons convinced me not to. They explained that it was actually my blue eyes that were the cause of the attention. If I dyed my hair dark, my eyes would stand out even more and possibly create even bigger problems. I was deflated, as there was nothing I could do about my eye colour, except try to hide my eyes behind dark sunglasses.

I started to retreat indoors. The phone conversation I had had with my Australian commander played over in my mind—it was probably not his intention, but his words had made me feel pretty terrible about myself. It was not just a question of my wanting to establish a better relationship with my reporting officer—this was part of the widely accepted military culture of team work, loyalty and respect up and down the chain of command. I had always experienced good rapport with my previous bosses throughout my entire career. In fact, I had never before faced a situation like this with a superior officer, and I did not know how to handle the frosty association that had developed between us. We were working in different countries, so there was no opportunity to sit down and resolve the problem face to face. I felt like I was never going to gain his respect, let alone his support.

After two days on leave and in hiding, I realised that it was a ridiculous situation and it could not continue for the next five months. I needed to make a change. I had been sent to represent my country and do a very important job, which I could not do concealed behind closed doors. I was damned sure I was not going to let a handful of deranged men prevent me from fulfilling my duties and stop me from enjoying my time in Lebanon. Although I knew it was not going to be easy, I needed to face my fears and get back out among the community. Perhaps once people knew who I was, things would settle down.

One of the two male Australian army officers then serving in Lebanon was Captain Anthony Birch. I had known Birchy for over ten years, since we were classmates at ADFA and Duntroon. So I called him to ask for his help to take back control of the situation. I asked if he would mind escorting me for a walk through the Tyre shops and markets. He was happy to help, so we headed downtown. But even Birchy's presence (he is a well-built, solid man, towering at over six feet tall) did not deter some men from staring at me or making offensive remarks—Birchy was appalled by their provocative offers of various sexual acts.

After the walk, Birchy and I had a beer at his apartment and he apologised for not previously being aware of the daily ordeal I was facing in the community. He knew that some Arab men were deeply attracted to Western women, while others were repulsed, because they viewed them as harlots due to their dress and perceived permissiveness. But he had not realised how confronting this was for me until he experienced it first-hand. Even though Birchy had put his arm around my shoulder during our walk, giving the impression that we were a couple, the local men still stared and asked straight out, 'Do you want to have sex with me?'

But it was a small step towards getting back on my feet, as I had at least taken control of my emotions. Although I would remain very wary of some of the local men in southern Lebanon during the rest of my tour of duty, I made a pact with myself that I would not let them get the better of me. I was determined to complete my assignment and enjoy the amazing opportunities offered by this spectacular country.

•

I learnt a great deal about the Khiam region and quickly graduated to the status of a senior in the team, helping teach new UNMOs their roles and responsibilities. Our team composition changed each month as members were posted to other mission areas or returned to their home countries, and then new people arrived to replace those who had been reassigned. It was a constantly changing melting pot of people and cultures; juggling the ever-rotating team dynamics was an aspect of our daily lives almost as important as patrolling.

Like all military 'families', Team Sierra had its issues. This was not surprising, considering that we consisted of eleven confident military officers from ten very different and culturally diverse countries. Of course there would be teething problems, but I relished working in such a dynamic group.

Major Hans-Peter Lang from Austria took over as the team leader when Yngvar returned home to Norway. Hans-Peter was a very professional officer—a no-nonsense kind of guy with a direct and somewhat authoritarian style. He would have been perfect at commanding soldiers; but his style was a little abrupt for leading peers—we were all officers of equal or similar rank.

I had a good relationship with Hans-Peter, as I seemed to have earned his respect on my first day by politely challenging his decision on a particular patrol through the town of Ghajar. Hans-Peter appeared to admire me for having the confidence to ask questions and challenge his thinking as to why things were done a certain way, rather than blindly following. I enjoyed patrolling with him because he was highly dependable and conscientious, which gave me confidence that I was in safe hands when working with him. We had each other's back. He was the sort of guy who you wanted around if things went wrong and rounds of ammunition started to fly.

Wolf's relationship with Hans-Peter, however, was a little tense. Wolf was also an alpha male personality type, and his military experience and skills standards were second to none in Team Sierra. In many ways Wolf was the natural leader, despite Hans-Peter holding the appointment title. Many of the team members looked to Wolf rather than Hans-Peter for advice and decisions, and this in itself created considerable tension in our camp. Watching those guys interact was like watching two rams butting heads in a paddock.

When Hans-Peter clashed with a couple of our team members who felt he was discriminating against them, Wolf stood up to him. The situation then deteriorated to an extent that became unworkable and a team meeting was called to resolve the friction. After a long, tense discussion, the air was cleared by everyone getting issues off their chests and by speaking freely (a confusing situation for Du, whose experience in the Chinese system was that you simply never questioned the hierarchy, under any circumstances). Life became good again in Team Sierra, but, by no coincidence, Wolf and Hans-Peter were rarely assigned on PB Khiam at the same time.

Despite this, or maybe because of it, we actually became a tighter bunch. While spending 24 hours a day up to seven days at a time in a confined space with my colleagues, I felt that I got to know them all very well. In fact, in many ways I considered them like brothers. I developed a strong bond in particular with five of my team-mates: Wolf, Du, Tore Rosseid from Norway and two Finnish officers, both named Jarno (to distinguish them, we nicknamed Jarno Limnell 'Smiley' and Jarno Mackinen 'Big Mack'). I did the majority of my patrols with these five guys and even spent my days off-duty hanging out with them while exploring the historic ruins at Tyre or snorkelling in the waters of the Mediterranean.

Clent also became good friends with them during his visits to Lebanon. On one occasion, when Clent flew into Lebanon the day before I finished my duty at PB Khiam, my off-duty team-mates took it upon themselves to look after him. This started with a few beers, which invariably turned into a few more beers and resulted in a big night out at the local tavern. Clent became great mates with Wolf, Smiley Jarno and Big Mack, in particular, together with the three Australian officers who were also stationed in Lebanon—Brad Smith, Amanda Johnston and Birchy. It was terrific for Clent to get to know the guys and he enjoyed their company as much as I did.

The work routine with Team Sierra continued to be hectic and at times dangerous. The one element I dreaded the most was our daily patrol of the town of Ghajar. This town had a complicated and troublesome history, starting with the events of the Six-Day War in June 1967, when Israel was at war with Egypt, Jordan and Syria. During that conflict, Israel captured the Golan Heights from Syria. As a result, the original junction of the borders of Syria, Israel and Lebanon was moved, and the Syrian town of Ghajar was now no longer in the country of Syria. Thus, not only were the Syrian residents of Ghajar isolated from their homeland, but the town itself straddled the new border, with half of it in Israel and the other half in Lebanon. Neither of the two countries particularly cared for the Syrians, whose village had become of huge strategic importance both to Israel and to those Hezbollah fighters operating in southern Lebanon.

Making the situation even more explosive for Ghajar's residents was the Israeli Technical Fence. This was a massive security fence that stretches right along the border between Israel and Lebanon. The fence was monitored by heavily armed Israeli Army patrols, and if anyone touched it, a sensor would be set off and a Humvee patrol full of armed Israeli soldiers would be at the scene within minutes. The UN had insisted that Israel not construct the fence through the town of Ghajar, which would have isolated the Syrians even more from one another. As a result of Israel's compliance with this, the fence abruptly stopped on the western side of Ghajar and then recommenced immediately on the eastern flank of the town, before continuing up the Golan Heights ridge line.

This break in the security fence had led to Ghajar being known as 'the hole in the Israeli national defence system'. This in turn made Ghajar a key town for Hezbollah to infiltrate into northern Israel, where they would attack Israeli patrols and try to capture soldiers, whom they would take back into Lebanon to be used as political bargaining chips. Israel has a long record of exchanging Hezbollah and PLO prisoners for any of its soldiers who are captured; this continues even to this day.

As a result, Ghajar was always on high alert and a bustling, tense place. Twice a day, Team Sierra was tasked to patrol between the Hezbollah bunker and the Israeli defensive compound, both located on the northeastern flank of the village. The Hezbollah bunker was renowned for being occupied by martyrs-in-waiting, who were willing to die in the name of their Islamic cause.

The road that led from the Hezbollah compound to the Israeli base was narrow, with a bitumen surface that had been damaged by previous bombing, and had completely disintegrated in several sections. It was wide enough to drive a vehicle down, but Hezbollah refused to allow the UN to take its vehicles down this road. Instead, we were forced to park our four-wheel drive just before the Hezbollah bunker and to proceed down the road on foot, unarmed and with no protection apart from carrying a bright blue UN flag.

There was also a simple mesh wire fence that ran along the bitumen road between the Hezbollah bunker and the Israeli compound. It was on the side of the road surrounding the civilian houses; I presumed that it had been erected by the local Syrian population, perhaps in an attempt to keep the Hezbollah out of their town—or to keep their children from playing on the extensive minefield that was on the other side of the road.

This foot patrol would take half an hour or so to complete; throughout the entire time, my heart would be pounding and adrenaline surging through my veins. All of my senses were on high alert and working overtime. I was on the lookout for any sudden movements and was prepared to dive for cover at any moment. My mind would be racing and scrolling through my options should any one of the myriad of possible eventualities occur.

If the peace agreement was broken and fighting erupted during our foot patrol, the options were pretty poor and our chances of survival slim. There was no protection or cover if there was gunfire. It would be a dangerous 500-metre dash back to our vehicle; but getting to the car would pose enormous risks, given that the Hezbollah bunker would be a high-priority target for Israel. Compounding the problem was the minefield—going anywhere near it was definitely not an attractive option during a fire fight, or at any time for that matter.

The only viable option would be to cut through the fence surrounding the town of Ghajar and take our chances within the buildings there and among the local population. But I always worried that the Syrians living there would not welcome UN personnel—as individuals, we were not personally responsible for forcing them to continue to live in this disastrous situation, but the townsfolk might well have blamed the UN as an organisation for their plight. In the end, I just focused on doing the job that was asked of me, and hoped like hell that the UN blue flag would be enough protection.

To get to this problematic bit of road, we first had to negotiate the chicanes at the rear of the Hezbollah base. On my first day patrolling in Lebanon, I was greeted there by a nervous young Hezbollah soldier, who levelled his gun at me. He had obviously never seen a female in the UN patrol before and was thrown by my presence. Our Lebanese interpreter attempted to reassure the soldier that I was simply a new team member and we should be permitted to conduct our normal patrol. The young soldier was not easily convinced. I held my breath and attempted to hide my own anxiety while he radioed to seek clarification on what he should do. After a few nervous minutes, he received approval from his senior commander and we were granted access to the road.

I was very relieved. I hoped that this would be a one-off event—a rude introduction not to be repeated—but I was wrong. On several more occasions over the months that followed, many of my team-mates had weapons levelled at them. In one terrifying incident, two of them were even dragged out of their vehicle by

Hezbollah gunmen and held at gunpoint while their cameras were confiscated after they photographed a Hezbollah position on orders by UNIFIL.

We were often stopped in the chicanes behind the Hezbollah position by their soldiers and questioned about our activities. We would then be allowed to continue our foot patrol, or sometimes we were refused entry. On each occasion that we were refused access, we would submit a 'restriction of movement' incident report through the UN. This simply noted that Hezbollah had stopped our patrol and restricted the areas we could inspect.

My attitude and motto was 'The Guy with the Gun Makes the Rules'. No matter how much approval and freedom of movement the Lebanese government had granted the UN, Hezbollah was clearly in charge in southern Lebanon. In any confrontation, I would acknowledge Hezbollah's intentions, make the appropriate reports and attempt to continue our patrol with as little fuss as possible. There was no upside in pushing our legal position with Hezbollah while we were unarmed.

I experienced many tense and terrifying moments during the Ghajar patrol. Hezbollah would often play games in our presence and while we were in view of the Israeli Army. On one occasion, when we were patrolling on foot down the road in front of the Israeli defensive compound, a Hezbollah soldier on a motorbike went speeding past us and continued towards the Technical Fence, which was only metres in front of the Israeli base. Just before the fence that marked the border, he skidded to a stop in what appeared to be a provocative attempt to draw fire from the Israeli position. I can only hazard a guess that Hezbollah did this to try to bait Israel into illegally firing across the border, in clear view of our patrol. However, he clearly endangered our lives in the process. My heart was racing in those few split seconds, as I waited for any reaction from the Israeli position. Luckily for us, they did not respond.

The Hezbollah soldier then stopped on his way back to his base and attempted to shake our hands. I definitely did not want to shake his hand; instead, I wanted to chastise him for being so reckless, with no sense of responsibility for the safety of UN personnel. He was ready to die as a martyr, but I was not. I assume that his attempt to shake our hands was done with the aim of trying to show Israel that the UN was friends with Hezbollah and that we were biased to their cause, which was clearly not the case. Unsuccessful in both his objectives, he rode back to his Hezbollah compound.

Hezbollah was not the only group posing danger for the Ghajar patrol. The Israeli post operated an unusual weapons system. In 1980, under the Geneva Convention, the UN had attempted to prohibit the use of certain weapons considered inhumane or indiscriminately causing excessive injuries. Israel had never agreed to these prohibitions and therefore does not abide by these international weapons restrictions. As a result, while serving in Lebanon, I saw first-hand a number of weapons that I had never seen before.

The weapon being used at this Israeli position was apparently a laser weapon. The Australian Defence Force uses lasers, but only as range finders or for targeting systems, not as weapons on their own. On many occasions while patrolling the Ghajar road, the Israeli laser was aimed at us. I do not know what was intended or what physical damage may result from these lasers, but at the very least this action intimidated us. At first, Israel denied it had lasered us, but I was informed that, after several protests by the UN, Israel admitted that at least one such accident had occurred and pledged that it would never be repeated.

Despite Israel's assurances, the large laser (which was spherical, and slightly larger than a basketball) continued to burn bright red, throwing a beam in our direction during our subsequent patrols. The UN requested access to their post, to investigate this unidentified weapon and to determine whether there was a physical risk to UN personnel patrolling in such close proximity to it. Israel refused the request. Disturbingly, for me and my colleagues, it is still not known if there will be any long-term physical side-effects from our exposure to emissions from this device.

Ghajar was definitely the most treacherous part of the Team Sierra area to be patrolled each day. However, it was not a case of being able to switch off for the remainder of the day, as the entire region was unpredictable. Hezbollah forces, for example, had several times forced UN personnel from their vehicles at gunpoint and had even severely beaten some of them.

Hezbollah aimed to remind Team Sierra personnel that it was never to be taken lightly. In one of our patrol areas, Hezbollah had dug three graves, which were still gaping during my time in Lebanon. My team seniors told me that Hezbollah had threatened previous Team Sierra UNMOS that two of the graves were for UN observers and the third was for a Lebanese interpreter. The graves were not for any particular UNMOs or interpreter; they were for any Team Sierra patrol that they were able to capture if we were to upset them by coming too close to their activities. If the UN continued to interfere with their activities, Hezbollah threatened that these graves would be filled with our dead bodies. It was a daily visual reminder to me as to who had control in the south and that I should always keep my wits about me.

One of our Lebanese interpreters, Nuhad Rashid, knew only too well how dangerous patrols in the Khiam region were and just how quickly a normal patrol day could turn into a nightmare. In January 2005, just seven months before my commencement on the UNTSO mission, a member of Team Sierra, French UNMO Commandant Jean-Louis Valet, was killed while patrolling the border region of the Golan Heights. He died instantly when he was hit by fire from an Israeli Merkava tank during a response to a Hezbollah attack. Commandant Valet's UN team-mate was very lucky to survive, having sustained shrapnel injuries to his shoulder and head. A round had pierced his UN beret, scathing his skull, but miraculously it had not been a fatal hit. Nuhad also sustained light injuries that day, but he gallantly dragged the injured UNMO to shelter behind their vehicle as Israel continued to fire in their direction.

At that time, southern Lebanon had been mostly peaceful for about five years and local communities were getting on with their lives in the relatively benign environment. The death of Commandant Valet was a sobering shock to the UN peacekeepers and a reminder that, although peaceful at times, this was still a volatile combat zone.

Thankfully, the constant stress of patrolling the Khiam region was balanced against lots of great moments shared with my team-mates. Team Sierra would refuel our vehicles at the Indian battalion headquarters, a little over 5 kilometres from our base. Wolf had befriended a young, skinny little Indian corporal who was responsible for the allocation of fuel. The corporal had a brilliant, white, beaming grin that stretched from one side of his face to the other whenever we entered his compound. He had invited us repeatedly to share tea with him, but we never seemed to have time as we were always in a rush to either get back to our base before sunset or start our list of duties for the day's patrol.

One afternoon, Wolf disappointed the soldier once again by turning down his offer, but promised that he would definitely take him up next time he refuelled. So the following day, when I was patrolling with Wolf, we planned our patrol so as to leave ourselves with enough time for tea with the Indian corporal.

As soon as he saw Wolf, the soldier leapt with glee and informed us that he would rush to make preparations for our tea. We were to meet at his office once we had refuelled the vehicle. Wolf and I then found ourselves sitting together at his request on a small lounge inside the dimly lit hut that was his office. It was very hot, and the humid air was stale and musty because there was no air conditioning. We were graciously presented with large cups of warm, milky, sweet tea. It was so sweet that it tasted like an entire can of sweetened condensed milk had been the main ingredient, rather than boiling water. We found out much later that the sweetness of the tea was a sign of respect, and the soldier had signified our importance by lacing our cups with lots of sugar.

Wolf and I struggled to drink our insanely sweet tea, because we didn't want to offend our host.

After some time we realised that we were sitting on our own, with no sign of the corporal. It seemed strange that he was not joining us for this long-awaited cup of tea, after he had been so enthusiastic when we had finally accepted his invitation. We waited and waited, becoming more and more confused by his absence as time passed by.

Increasingly frustrated, Wolf went to find the soldier; he soon returned, bursting with laughter. The corporal, he said, was just outside the door, together with a crowd of Indian soldiers, who had come to see the foreign officers drinking tea. I asked Wolf why the corporal would not join us, if he was just outside. Wolf explained that the soldier said it was against the Indian military rules. We were later informed that respect for rank and hierarchy in the Indian army is so very strong that soldiers will not share a tent or eating area with an officer; nor will they sit during conversations, instead choosing to remain standing as a sign of respect. If asked by an officer to sit, they will at first politely refuse to join the officer, but if ordered to do so, they will sit on the floor rather than on a chair next to the senior rank. So the soldier who had welcomed us for tea was not actually permitted to join us for this ritual—he wouldn't dare think of sitting at the same table as officers. However, it was great kudos for a soldier to host foreign officers for tea, especially when one of them was me—the intriguing white woman from Australia!

For the next twenty minutes, while Wolf and I struggled to drink the sickly sweet concoction, every now and then a turban-covered head would briefly appear around the door for a sneak peek at us, before retreating. By the time we'd finished our tea, there were over 30 soldiers huddled outside the office, patiently waiting to catch a glimpse of us. They even formed a tunnel for us to walk through back to our vehicle—just as football fans do when their team runs onto the field.

As we went through, the soldiers requested that we shake their hands and pose for photos—they even asked for my autograph! It was a hilarious situation that would make Wolf and me laugh for weeks afterwards.

8 And Then Came a War

It was the start of July 2006, and my time in Lebanon was rapidly coming to an end. I had a little over a month to go of my UN posting before I was due to return to Australia via a luxurious holiday in England, America and Fiji with Clent.

I felt so very fortunate for the many amazing opportunities I'd had during my year living in the Middle East. I had worked with a bunch of incredible people from all over the world, who had become lifelong friends. I had also lived in some of the most spectacular, beautiful and challenging environments on the planet. I knew I would return to Australia with a different life perspective as a result of my experience working with the UN. I was now far more appreciative for all the blessings we take for granted in our bountiful, peaceful country. Sometimes I think we simply do not understand just how very lucky we are to live in Australia.

My parents were also nearing the end of an overseas trip. At the time, they were travelling with Clent through Turkey. They still lived on the picturesque property on the outskirts of a town called Alstonville in northern New South Wales where I had spent my childhood. It was a small farm nestled in the subtropical hinterland, a short drive from the beaches of Byron Bay. Mum and Dad had limited experience of travelling abroad, but they were very keen to visit me in Lebanon, despite its dangerous reputation. My Australian commander gave approval for my parents and Clent to spend a week with me, staying in my apartment in Tyre and exploring other regions in Lebanon. The thought of my mother being confronted by armed security guards at Beirut airport made me thankful that Clent was accompanying them. He escorted them from Turkey into Lebanon and then helped navigate them through the many military checkpoints between Beirut and Tyre, with the assistance of the local Lebanese driver I sent to collect them from the airport.

It was wonderful to have this time to catch up with them and for them to experience first-hand the unique Arab culture that had been my life for the past year. We explored the Lebanese countryside in a UN vehicle that I was able to hire for four days. Mum and Dad loved sitting up in the back of the car, being 'chauffeur driven'. My only concern was that driving on the roads in Lebanon, particularly around Beirut, is very hazardous. Being on the roads is literally taking your life into your hands.

There is an Arabic mantra that is frequently invoked—'*Inshallah*', meaning 'God Willing'—and Lebanese drivers seem to drive with this as their motto. If God (*Allah*) is willing, they will survive the drive, but if it is not God's will, then they will die. It is as if they have no control over the situation, and, as a result, no one takes responsibility for their actions behind the wheel. This makes driving a dangerous pursuit. The road rules are not obeyed—by anyone! Although drivers should remain on the right-hand side of the road, that rule rarely seems to be applied in reality. Speed limits seem to be merely suggestions, and the use of the horn is an absolute must at all times. Australian drivers honk the horn to warn of danger, but Lebanese drivers don't seem to be able to drive unless one hand is on the horn constantly.

Over the next four days, I drove us from Tyre to Beirut, north to Jounieh and then on to the historic port town of Byblos. It was a drive that took us across the huge snow-capped mountain range that divides the country from its northern neighbour, Turkey, right through to its southern border with Israel. East of the mountain range is the Bekaa Valley, home to the fortress and temple ruins of Baalbek. It is also reputed to be an area sometimes used as Hezbollah's training ground.

Lebanon's complex and turbulent history dates back over 5000 years. The country has been occupied by the Phoenician, Greek, Roman, Byzantine and Ottoman empires, as well as the Crusaders. At the end of World War I, Lebanon was placed under French mandate and did not achieve independence until some 25 years later, in 1943. The French influence is still very evident in Lebanon, particularly in its food and wine; many Lebanese speak French, the second most widely spoken language there, after Arabic.

The Mediterranean climate in Lebanon combined with the fertile soils of the Bekaa Valley creates perfect conditions for growing grapes. Under French guidance, the Lebanese developed the most amazing high-quality wines. I was surprised to learn that this is actually one of the oldest wine-producing regions in the world; indeed, the ancient Romans built a temple in the Bekaa Valley and dedicated it to Bacchus, their god of wine.

On the last night of our trip, we stayed in the town of Kefrayah at a vineyard called Cave Kouroum. The winery enjoyed incredible views across the valley to the Syrian border and was managed by a French winemaker. It was the only vineyard I had ever seen where vines are left to grow on the ground, without a trellis. The manager explained to us that grapes are only grown on trellises where they are machine-harvested, but these grapes were all handpicked by Syrian and Lebanese workers, who were paid only a few dollars each day. The vineyard had not gone to the expense of building trellises, given that the labour force was a much cheaper alternative. The wine from these hand-picked grapes was truly exceptional—and it wasn't difficult to overindulge!

On our return to Tyre, my favourite local restaurant, La Phoenician, organised a boat trip for the four of us to the rocky outcrop in Tyre harbour for lunch. The restaurant owner and his entire staff pitched in and planned the day as a special surprise for us, their valued customers and friends. We were deeply honoured and touched by their overwhelming generosity, especially considering the trouble they had gone to and the exorbitant cost involved, which they really couldn't afford. We offered to pay for the lunch, but they wouldn't hear of it.

We were taken by boat to a rocky outcrop at low tide, where they had set up tables and chairs under a tent on the rocks, with the warm Mediterranean water surrounding us. It was a beautiful summer day and we all enjoyed a swim while our enormous seafood banquet lunch was being delivered by boat to our 'water picnic' venue. The water was so crystal clear and refreshing—until a local man decided to start fishing nearby, with dynamite! This is a local custom enjoyed by the people of Tyre, but of some concern to us foreigners. The abundant hospitality displayed by our Lebanese friends provided my parents with the most unique and memorable of lunches, and an insight into the generosity of the Lebanese people.

The afternoon was spent exploring the hidden treasures of the ancient ruins of Tyre, which date back to Byzantine, Crusader and Roman eras. The most significant and well preserved of the ruins is the hippodrome, which was used for chariot and camel racing. The Tyre hippodrome is the largest in the world—even larger than the Colosseum in Rome. It was made from stone rather than brick, and could seat 20,000 spectators. It was incredible to sit in the grandstands overlooking the racetrack, as people centuries before us had done.

Our four-day trip was over in the blink of an eye. We had enjoyed lovely summer days while touring the wineries and coastal regions, and it had been great for my parents to spend some more time with Clent. They all got on really well and my parents were

The ancient hippodrome where gladiatorial battles raged, Tyre, Lebanon.
http://www.youtube.com/matinajewell

pleased that I had found someone special in my life. They realised the personal sacrifices I had made in order to succeed in my career and understood how tough military life was on relationships. But somehow Clent and I had managed to make it work—thus far.

Having farewelled my parents—they were heading off to visit my brother in London, before taking a coach tour around Europe—I left Tyre for PB Khiam. This would be my last seven-day patrol; I only had four weeks or so to go before I was scheduled to return to Australia. Clent stayed on in Tyre this time as we planned to travel to Egypt shortly after I had completed my week at Khiam. While I was away he could work on project reports during the day, with the material delivered by email so it arrived first thing the next morning in Australia. At night, he enjoyed catching up with my off-duty team-mates and indulging in the sights and smells that wafted through the city's narrow streets.

As had been the case in Syria, as an Australian tourist Clent was free to come and go from Lebanon as he pleased. However, the Australian commander had introduced a new rule that required his permission before anyone from outside our eleven-man Aussie contingent was allowed to stay in Australian accommodation. He explained in an email that he introduced this rule on advice from the director of entitlements in Australia that he could be personally liable if anyone from outside our contingent was injured while staying at our accommodation, because our rent was reimbursed by the ADF and was therefore regarded as Commonwealth property. The new rule required changes for the entire Australian contingent, but I presumed particularly for Ash, who had recently become engaged to a wonderful local Lebanese girl he had met while working in Tyre, whom he later married after he returned to Australia.

Out of courtesy to my Australian commander, and since I did not want him to feel that he was in a legally difficult situation with Clent's visits, from that point on, aside from one stay that was approved by the Australian commander, Clent sought alternative accommodation in Tyre. There was a vacant one-bedroom apartment in the same building as mine. In fact, it was on the top floor and right next door to me. The rent was so inexpensive that it was financially a much better option for Clent to rent it on a monthly basis, rather than stay in a hotel whenever he visited between work commitments. I called the Australian commander to discuss the policy and ask whether he would be comfortable with this alternative option, and he agreed.

So for the last couple of months, in the few times that Clent was in Tyre, he had stayed in his own apartment, which shared similar views of the harbour to mine. The other Aussies serving in Lebanon welcomed Clent and enjoyed having a mate to go to the gym or to share a beer with. Prior to Clent's visits, I would always inform the appropriate UN personnel on each occasion and, as a courtesy, email my Australian commander to ensure there weren't any issues. Clent would also check the latest security risk assessments for tourists on the Department of Foreign Affairs and Trade's travel advisory website and inform the Australian embassy in Beirut of his location and intended length of stay. During my rotations on PB Khiam, Clent would use the time to do project work in the UK or Dubai, or to travel to other parts of the world.

It turned out to be a very busy week on PB Khiam. The aspect of UN work I enjoyed the most was liaising with local officials to provide humanitarian aid that would substantially improve the quality of life of people living in the poor rural communities. The UN's engineering projects provided fresh water to several villages in the region and its mine clearance program literally saved lives every day. Once a week, Team Sierra would meet with town mayors and *mukhtars* (village chiefs) to discuss the specific issues being faced in their towns and villages. As a woman, I might have expected to be shunned at these meetings but, because I could speak Arabic, I was graciously invited to sit next to the elders at the table and participate in the conversation. In fact, it was sometimes my male colleagues who were a little neglected at the meetings.

I was often told by my Lebanese interpreters about the positive impact UN women had on the local women in southern Lebanon, simply by serving on this mission (and I had also experienced this on the Golan Heights in Syria). The local women were amazed to see a woman working in the military and even more surprised to see women driving cars with male passengers. These normal activities, which we don't give a second thought to, were important and inspirational to the communities we served in.

Since it was my last long tour at PB Khiam, I aimed to visit as many of the towns as possible, to say goodbye to the town elders and the locals who had enriched my life so much. The warmth I had received from the mayors and *mukhtars* had overshadowed the difficulties I had experienced earlier in my tour. As in most things in life, it was the people who had made my time in the country so special. We often don't fully appreciate what we have until it comes to an end—my time in Lebanon was no different. It was sad to say goodbye as I knew I would probably never see these people again.

●

On the morning of 12 July I woke with a buzz of excitement and anticipation in my belly. I was counting down the hours until the following morning, when I would finish my tour of duty and hand over to another UNMO before heading into Tyre, where Clent was waiting for me. Then we were off to Egypt to scuba dive in the warm waters of the Red Sea. The thought of Clent's excitement about diving at Egypt's famous Sharm el-Sheikh brought a smile to my face. It had been a roller-coaster twelve months, with a mixture of both tough and terrific times, but it was now coming to an end. Our trip to Egypt would be our last chance to explore the Middle East before my year was up and we would head home.

I was tasked to lead a normal fortnightly patrol, where we would exchange information with UNMOs from our closest neighbouring patrol base, PB Mar, so our teams could reinforce each other in a crisis. I was patrolling in a vehicle not far from PB Khiam while at the same time teaching Captain Theo Den Hartog, from the Netherlands, about the Team Sierra region. Major Karl Mellberg, a Swedish UNMO based at PB Mar, had picked up Big Mack, my Finnish team-mate, and they were heading towards PB Mar so that Big Mack could learn about their area and exchange information.

Suddenly, an urgent message came over the radio: 'All UN patrols go to the nearest patrol base immediately. There has been an incident on the border.'

During a daring attack on an Israeli Humvee patrol on the border of Israel and Lebanon, Hezbollah gunmen had opened fire. They had killed four Israeli soldiers and captured two more, taking them back into Lebanon and sparking full-scale war. The Israelis were about to smash Hezbollah targets all along the border in retaliation for the ambush. As a result, the UN was hunkering down.

My heart was pounding and my mind racing as I assessed our situation. I knew that Israel would take out the Hezbollah head-quarters and compounds around PB Khiam at the first opportunity. Although PB Khiam was our closest UN position, getting back to it would be very dangerous now that Israeli artillery shells had started to fly across the border. Even so, Khiam was the best option we had, so I drove at top speed and made a run for it to the patrol base.

As we hurtled through the steel gates of our post, sending up a cloud of dust, I heard the *crump-crump* sound of artillery fire. We were in for a busy day in the office! Du was on the gate and held it open for Wolf and my Irish team-mate, Commandant Pat Dillon, who drove in shortly after us. Big Mack and Karl arrived soon after them. We were now up two UNMOs, and PB Mar was down two. PB Khiam was designed for a team of five observers. Our cosy team of five had now become a crowded seven.

My stomach was churning with nervous energy about the uncertainty and danger of what lay ahead. There was an amazing sense of exhilaration and a buzz of apprehension in the air. My UN

team-mates and I were all revved up and on high alert. After days
and weeks of routine patrolling, reporting and domestic duties,
we were now in the thick of the action. Our job was to observe
and report violations of the UN sanctions, which were starting to
occur at a rapid rate around us.

There was normally sensitivity about the use of cameras during
UN patrols; at our UN induction training we had been directed
not to take photographs of Israeli, Syrian or Hezbollah installations
unless under instruction to do so. However, once hostilities erupted
and violations of the peace agreement occurred, we were encouraged
to take photos and videos as evidence of the violations and the
breakdown of the peace agreements. Taking video footage was also
not a normal activity during Australian military operations, but as
UN peacekeepers, it was our duty to observe, record and report.

Wolf directed Du to take the UN video camera, and for me
to grab my own personal camera; from the observation platform,
we took turns at recording violations of the ceasefire treaty in
the form of Israeli air and artillery strikes, as well as Hezbollah
Katyusha rocket launches.

The banshee scream of fighter jets pierced the sky overhead and
Israeli gun batteries on the Golan Heights ridge line to the front
of PB Khiam began to fire continuously at Hezbollah positions
in the towns and villages around our base. I could imagine the
sheer terror, chaos and bloodshed in the places that I routinely
visited, shopped and chatted with the locals. I perhaps felt closer
to the local community than my other team-mates because I could
speak a bit of Arabic and talk to the locals in their own language.
I cringed at the thought of rockets exploding in the town centres,
indiscriminately killing people and destroying their homes.

The Israeli army firing artillery and Merkava tank fire into the
Hezbollah position SP6, Ghajar, on the border of Lebanon and Israel,
Lebanon War 2006.
http://www.youtube.com/matinajewell

The Israeli fighter jets were a formidable sight as they soared high in the sky, preying on Hezbollah targets below. The jets delivered their lethal loads of bombs with pinpoint accuracy as artillery fire concurrently hit targets around us. Every now and then there was a *whooshing* sound and a smoke trail across the sky as Hezbollah fired a Katyusha rocket into Israel. Katyusha rockets are long, thin cylinders some 2 metres in length and of varying diameter, upwards of 10 centimetres, depending on their required range. They can be mounted on a truck and fired in multiple rounds, but in southern Lebanon they were usually fired from improvised static launchers—sometimes consisting of little more than a few wooden boards propped up to aim the rocket in the direction of its intended target.

Oh shit! I suddenly remembered Clent had a toothache and had booked a dental appointment in Tyre today. I needed to quickly call his mobile phone and warn him—this was not a day to be out and about.

Clent took a while to answer and I heard him fumble the phone, which would have rung loudly next to his bed. He should have been up by now, but I had woken him from a dead sleep with a cracking hangover after several beers with the UN boys the night before, he managed to tell me. His head was thumping, and he seemed to struggle to process what I was saying.

Israeli 1000-pound aerial bomb fired by a fighter jet into Hezbollah position SP3 and Israeli artillery fire impacting Hezbollah position SP4, Lebanon War 2006.
http://www.youtube.com/matinajewell

Hezbollah fighters firing Katyusha rockets into Israel in the lead up to Lebanon War 2006, Patrol Base Khiam, Lebanon.
(Video courtesy of Major Yngvar Dypvik).
http://www.youtube.com/matinajewell

'Don't go outside today, Clent.' I rarely call him Clent—usually just CJ. So I hoped he could tell I was serious by hearing me speaking this way. 'Tell me you will not go to the dentist,' I continued sternly. 'There's a lot going down here.' I left it at that because of my concern not to give away information that might be sensitive or of concern from an operational security point of view. 'Love you. See you tomorrow.'

'Love you too, babe,' he replied.

Moments later, another Israeli 1000-pound aerial bomb, fired by a fighter jet, exploded in the town of Marjayoun. These bombs are laser-guided onto their targets, either by pilots using the onboard computers in the aircraft or by troops on the ground laser painting the target to be hit. Our Lebanese interpreter, Nuhad, and his family lived in Marjayoun, so Wolf called him to check that he was okay as yet another bomb exploded near his house. Nuhad confirmed that the bombs had destroyed the nearby Hezbollah building, but thankfully he and his family were safe for the time being, albeit very shaken.

Our UN headquarters, located on the coast in the town of Naqoura, a 45-minute drive south of Tyre, confirmed that all UNMOs were accounted for at the four patrol bases along the border. It was a great relief to know that we had all made it back to our bases safely. Shortly after, a 'code red' order was issued by the higher UN headquarters in Jerusalem. This stipulated that all UN personnel were now to remain at their patrol bases—no one could move without approval from higher headquarters.

The first hour of the war passed quickly. The Israeli fighter jets dropped bombs on Hezbollah bunkers and their artillery hit other targets continuously. Only now and again was there a smoke trail in the sky as the occasional Katyusha rocket headed towards Israel. It was a disproportionate battle, and the Lebanese people were once again caught up in a war not of their making.

Unexpectedly, the UN water truck arrived at our front gates, ready to refill our water tanks. The two Indian soldiers driving the truck seemed oblivious of the war going on around them. We notified both the UNIFIL and our UNTSO command chain about the arrival of the water truck; the soldiers were ordered to remain at PB Khiam until it was safe to return to their home base. Our crowded team of seven had now grown into a congested team of nine.

I instructed the Indian soldiers to get their body armour from their vehicle and put it on, because we had already experienced some dangerously close hits to the post. When they returned to the observation platform, however, we discovered that their flak jackets didn't have any Kevlar plates—they were simply material vests and would be useless in providing any protection from shrapnel or bullets. The Indian soldiers had either never been issued with Kevlar plates or had removed them to reduce the weight, believing they would never be in a situation where they would need armour plating. It wasn't safe for them to stay on the observation platform, where there was no overhead protection, so they took shelter in the bunker for the rest of their time at Khiam.

Rockets and bombs continued to crash down onto Hezbollah positions all around us. But then suddenly everything stopped and there was silence. I had a lump in my throat, making it impossible to breathe, and it felt as though time was standing still.

What happened in that split second seemed to occur in slow motion. At my eye level, a mere 30 metres away, travelling towards us, was a 1000-pound laser-guided aerial bomb—of a type that could destroy a five-storey building—which had been fired from an Israeli fighter jet. I didn't have time to be afraid. The bomb was flying close to our position, heading relentlessly on target towards the Hezbollah bunker located only a little bit more than the length of a standard swimming pool away, just 75 metres from us. The bomb was over 3 metres in length and 30 centimetres in width, making it look the size of a bath tub. It passed so close to me that I could clearly see the stabilising fins at the rear of the projectile.

Kaboom! There was an almighty explosion as the bomb hit the bunker. I just had time to warn my team-mates to get down as the compression blast wave hit us and an enormous fireball ignited overhead. Large pieces of steel, star piquets and concrete shrapnel scythed into PB Khiam as I buried my head between my knees. We were terribly exposed. There was no roof on the observation platform—an obvious design flaw, as shrapnel was now raining down on us. We all curled up in the foetal position and desperately hoped that a big chunk wouldn't crush one of our exposed arms or legs.

There was a moment of anarchy and panic. I could feel my heart beating faster than I would ever have thought possible as adrenaline surged through my veins. My ears were ringing from the explosion, but Wolf's voice broke through: 'Bunker! Bunker! Go! Go! Go!'

My team-mates reacted quickly to Wolf's command and filed one by one down the exposed spiral staircase that was our only exit from the observation platform to the bunker three storeys below. Yet another design flaw!

I let them go first because I felt I had a slightly more protected position on the observation platform than they did, squeezed as I was between the water tank and the platform wall. They moved as fast as humanly possible, but they seemed to take forever. I was a bit jittery, but kept telling myself not to panic: *Keep your cool, Matti, there will be time for us all to get to the bunker.*

I was the last to move. Just as I started to descend the narrow spiral staircase, I saw a second Israeli fighter jet coming in on a low approach. It was either going to strafe or drop another bomb. *Shit, shit, shit!* I rushed back up the ladder, to shelter in the corner of the platform, hoping the walls would provide enough protection. I knew I was moving as fast as I could, but it felt like I was exposed for an eternity on the ladder in a trance-like state. I made a dive for the corner.

Thankfully, the jet was only dropping 'chaff', a confetti-like shower of silvery material designed to attract anti-aircraft rockets. The jet screamed overhead and pulled away abruptly. The low altitude and incredible speed of the aircraft created pressure in the atmosphere; I literally felt the jet as it swooped terrifyingly close overhead. It was trying to entice the Hezbollah bases surrounding PB Khiam to expose themselves by firing anti-aircraft rockets; these would then attract the lethal attention of following Israeli jets. I saw an opportunity to move, so I took it and scrambled down to the bunker to join the rest of the team.

Moments later, with my heart still pounding like a thoroughbred racehorse, I was crammed in with the others in the small operations room of the bunker that housed our radio and reporting equipment. Wolf and I were both trained combat medics, so we instinctively started to check for casualties. To our complete amazement the group had not sustained any fatalities or even minor injuries—not a scratch on any of us! It was an absolute miracle, considering the amount of shrapnel that had blasted into our base and the lack of protection we had.

I reported what was termed a 'firing close' by radio while Wolf used the mobile phone to make it abundantly clear to the UN duty officer that the Israeli bomb had come dangerously close to PB Khiam. Surely the UN would be able to alert the Israelis, and it would not happen again?

Slowly, the reality of what had happened started to sink in. The UN peacekeeper handbook deemed that a 1000-pound aerial bomb impacting within 1 kilometre of a UN position is classified as a 'firing close', a near miss endangering the lives of UN personnel.

Aftermath of a 1000-pound aerial bomb fired by an Israeli fighter jet; direct hit on Hezbollah base SP1, only 75 metres from PB Khiam, Lebanon War 2006.
http://www.youtube.com/matinajewell

So this type of aerial bomb impacting a mere 75 metres from us was 'firing *damned* close'!

I wondered how the Israelis could have been so callous and reckless about dropping bombs so dangerously close to unarmed UN peacekeepers. But, from the Israeli point of view, their retaliation was part of a long history of fighting for national survival and the UN hadn't rectified the problem of the Hezbollah establishing their bases so close to UN compounds. My mind also flashed back to the Qana atrocity of April 1996, during Operation Grapes of Wrath, when Israeli artillery shelled a UN compound where 800 Lebanese civilians had taken refuge. The attack resulted in 106 Lebanese people being killed and 116 injured; four UN soldiers were also seriously injured.

Recalling the brutality of Israel's retaliation policy in previous conflicts, I wondered whether our near miss was deliberate, or a mistake. Regardless of their intention, we now had a decision to make: either to cower in the crowded bunker or to go back up the stairs and do our job of observing and reporting violations of the UN sanctions. We chose the latter.

As I climbed the ladder back to the observation platform, I felt a bizarre mixture of emotions: elation from still being alive, shock from having witnessed such an incredible event at such close range, and trepidation about what might be coming next.

9 Near Miss

The local television news station, Al-Manar, confirmed that Hezbollah forces had captured two Israeli soldiers during the ambush. This announcement resulted in several celebratory bursts of small-arms fire from another Hezbollah position that was located within the old prison, just 100 metres from PB Khiam.

Each close-range crack of rifle fire into the air made us duck because we didn't know which direction they were firing, or where their rounds would land. With the shooting celebrations continuing intermittently, I remained quite jumpy.

For the remainder of the first day of the war, we observed and reported hundreds of violations of the peace agreement from the observation platform on PB Khiam, using a UN mobile phone and radio. During the lulls between barrages of fire, I would talk to Clent using our personal mobile phones. It was a surreal conversation as we suddenly found ourselves in the unfamiliar situation of a war zone. Clent understood that my number-one priority was my duty as a peacekeeper, but—like the majority of UNMOs serving in Lebanon, who also had family and loved ones in Tyre—I was obviously very concerned for his safety. I was also extremely thankful that my parents had left Lebanon the week prior and were not caught up in this too.

The need to confirm each other's wellbeing was now a high priority. We would comfort each other with talk about life after the conflict during these brief phone calls—hoping to keep our minds positive and focused on the future once this bloody battle was over. We discussed plans to simply postpone our departure for Egypt by a few days—this war, we thought, would be like all the other recent conflicts and last for only a day or two. So we still hoped to be diving and dining at the Red Sea in the not too distant future.

This was not to be. The second day of the war took a destructive and unexpected turn as Israel stepped up its aggression. In just 24 hours the Israelis destroyed Beirut airport and established a naval blockade on the Mediterranean Sea. They targeted all roads leaving Lebanon, in an attempt to stop their captured soldiers from being smuggled out of the country. This also meant that it was virtually impossible for anyone else to flee the war in Lebanon without risking their lives. Clent was stuck in Tyre. There was no way of getting him out, and there was nothing I could do about it. For the time being he would just have to hunker down.

At the same time, the threat of Israeli attacks on Tyre increased dramatically as the television news reports speculated on the location of the two kidnapped Israeli soldiers. There were suggestions that the two soldiers might have been taken into the Hezbollah-controlled town of Tyre to be held captive as political prisoners. My heart sank as I heard the news. Suddenly Clent and the UN families in Tyre were in the direct line of fire as the Israeli Defence Force turned its attention to the town.

My mind ploughed through all the different scenarios of what could be happening in Tyre and how I could help prepare Clent for the events that might unfold in the hours and days ahead. Israel was amassing a large force on the border, an hour's drive south of Tyre; it was predicted that Israel would commence a ground invasion, to search house by house for the missing soldiers. I prayed this wouldn't happen as Israel would be expected to use a great deal of force prior to sending in its own ground troops by bombing the town relentlessly to reduce opposition, which in turn would reduce the number of Israeli casualties.

Urban warfare is an incredibly dangerous, hand-to-hand combat situation and the decision to fire or not needs to be made in a split second. The Israeli soldiers, some of them part-time reservists, would obviously be extremely anxious and ready with their finger on the trigger as they burst through doors into houses. Their priority would be to protect their own lives first and ask questions later.

At my urging, Clent and Magnus—the Swedish UNMO who lived downstairs—prominently decorated their apartments with UN, Australian and Swedish paraphernalia, as well as placing stickers of their national flags on their front doors and the front door of my apartment. They also placed national flags on the roof of the building and spray-painted a large UN symbol there, so it could be identified from the air. If worse came to worst and Israel invaded Tyre, the young Israeli soldiers clearing the building would hopefully realise that UN families lived in this particular apartment block and would perhaps be a little more cautious before using their weapons.

My greatest fear was that Clent would be killed. I couldn't bear the thought of him perishing in this war when the only reason he was here was because of me. His sole reason for visiting Lebanon was to give our relationship a chance, and now he might pay for that decision with his life. I would never forgive myself if something happened to him. What words could I possibly find to break the news to his family?

I tried to push these negative thoughts from my mind and focus on the positives. Clent was in the same building as a Swedish UN family—Magnus, Eva and their two young boys lived on the floor below my apartment. Two of my Australian team-mates, Brad and Amanda, were off-duty in Tyre and had also been looking out

Securing country flags and marking 'UN' on rooftop of apartment block, Tyre, Lebanon War 2006.
http://www.youtube.com/matinajewell

for him. Although I could not be with him, at least Clent wasn't on his own during what was no doubt the most terrifying event of his life.

Wolf attempted to make light of the dangerous situation Clent was in by asking me if I put all of my boyfriends through this type of testing process—dropping them into a war zone to see what they were really made of and how they coped under pressure. He thought it was a great way of testing out eligible partners before I made a significant commitment to them. Only Wolf could make me burst into laughter in the face of such a dire and serious set of circumstances.

The situation was only getting worse for us at Khiam too. It was 13 July, day two of the war, and I was supposed to finish my patrol now and be replaced by my team-mate Tore at PB Khiam. But the ferocity of the battle across the border resulted in all team rotations being cancelled for the day. My rotation was rescheduled for the following morning, when I would return to Tyre and hopefully help organise Clent's evacuation through the Australian Embassy.

The hostile military activity around our base was not our only source of concern. There were also significant problems with the functioning of the UN in Lebanon. The OGL headquarters had a nucleus of three key appointments: the chief, the deputy chief and the operations officer. The chief was visiting PB Mar when the war erupted and, since a code red had been instigated from the higher headquarters in Jerusalem, he was stuck at that post, unable to move back to the headquarters at Naqoura.

The deputy chief and the new operations officer (who had replaced Ash Collingburn when he finished his mission and returned to Australia) were both on leave overseas. Because Israel had bombed the airport and blocked any entry and exit from Lebanon, they were not expected to be able to get back into the country, let alone pass through roads that had been destroyed by bombing and make it to the border where the headquarters was located, in southern Lebanon. As it turned out, these two key people were out of action for the entire conflict. With the benefit of hindsight, the incumbents of these two positions should never have been granted leave at the same time since they were supposed to cover each other's role in a crisis.

As a result of this, the three key players leading the UNTSO force in Lebanon were not at the headquarters; this left a huge void. The OGL contingent in Lebanon was surrounded by an escalating level of violence, with effectively limited command or control. It was an unthinkable and untenable situation.

Undermanned and in disarray, the remaining staff at our Naqoura headquarters valiantly attempted to plug these three key roles and worked around the clock, but it still wasn't enough. The staff of captains and majors could barely keep up with the sheer volume of reported violations of the peace agreement coming in from patrol bases, let alone provide appropriate guidance or direction back to those of us on the ground observing the border.

Some of the radio operators were non-native English speakers. This created some frustrating situations, where we had to repeat our reports of violations and near misses several times, just to be understood—taking up time we could ill afford in what was a very dangerous, difficult and stressful environment. Tempers were starting to fray at the frustration of dealing with our own dysfunctional organisation. It was clear to us on PB Khiam that the conflict developing around us was shaping up to be far more than the usual 12- to 24-hour skirmish, and our headquarters was struggling to cope.

The UN appeared to be unprepared for such a protracted war. It could be argued that the UN had become somewhat complacent and was simply not ready or rehearsed to respond to an outbreak of hostilities that lasted longer than a few days.

Those personnel remaining at headquarters now had to start developing a plan for an ongoing war. There were limited contingency plans and no standard operating procedures for rotating team members and resupplying food and water to the patrol bases. Ad hoc arrangements had to develop on the fly.

•

It was the second night of the war and I was planning to put my head down for a few hours of vital sleep. I had not slept the first night, due to the intermittent military activity around us. Suddenly, Hezbollah fighters started firing Katyusha rockets from the valley directly behind PB Khiam southwards into the Israeli town of Metulla. The Hezbollah fighters were hiding behind us in the low ground, causing the Israeli artillery guns mounted on the Golan ridge line to respond instantly with ferocious consequences.

We were now immediately under the direct trajectory of artillery rounds. We assessed that the Israelis were firing a mixture of high explosive and smoke rounds. These artillery shells were roughly one metre in length (1550 millimetres in diameter at their base) and had a cylindrical metal casing that contained the explosive charge—they looked something like gigantic bullets as they flew through the sky. The first sound I heard was the distant *crump-crump*. Then came the unforgettable noise and feeling of what I can only describe as something similar to the sensation of an express train travelling directly overhead; what followed was a thunderous explosion as the round hit the ground close by.

I had returned to the observation platform with Wolf and Karl (one of the UNMOs from PB Mar), ducking behind the parapet as each artillery round hurtled through the air, many only 10 to 50 metres over our heads. We were sitting ducks in the pitch-black night, with no protection other than our light-blue body armour and helmets (the UN's identifying colour). We were powerless to get the Hezbollah to move, and our UN headquarters staff were unable to get the Israelis to stop firing so close to us from their gun batteries 10 kilometres away. Artillery fire is accurate, but never precise, especially when firing at close to maximum range.

Knowing the distance these rounds were covering and that we were caught right in the middle of their path was of grave concern.

Then the inevitable happened. An artillery shell dropped short of its intended target and exploded just 5 metres from the rear gate of our tiny compound. Debris and shrapnel sprayed into the air towards the observation platform where Wolf, Karl and I had hit the deck just in time. My heart was pounding. I squeezed my eyes shut as tight as I could and lay curled up against the platform wall, waiting for the raining clods of dirt and debris to stop plummeting down.

I cautiously got to my feet while my whole body started shaking and my ears were screaming in pain with a constant buzzing sound. Surely this had to stop? I knew I needed to get to the radio in the shelter and alert the UN to the barrage of close hits we were receiving from Israel. So, before the next *crump-crump*, I managed to scramble across the platform and down the ladder to use the radio in the bunker. As I reported the near miss, I tried to sound calm, professional and controlled. But I'm sure the trepidation in my voice was obvious.

Boom! Another artillery round exploded. The building shook and shuddered as two large sections of artillery rounds smashed into the T-wall (so called because these mobile concrete walls look like the letter T inverted) and a plume of fire and smoke billowed from it. Dirt, smoke and debris sprayed into the air. At the time we believed we had sustained two direct hits inside our perimeter fence, because the impact and explosion had been so significant and we had fire coming from the wall just in front of the entrance to the bunker. I grabbed the radio and reported that the patrol base was now receiving direct hits from Israeli artillery.

We were squashed into the operations room of the bunker. I was still partially deaf from the blast and my mouth was as dry as sand as I noticed the angst and uncertainty in everyone's eyes. I did a quick head-count—two men short. The realisation hit me that there were only seven of us—Wolf and Karl were not in the bunker. I had thought they were just behind me when I came back to use the radio. I could feel the fear rise from my stomach as my mind grappled with what to do next. If they had still been on the spiral staircase when the last round hit, they could be dead or wounded outside.

Wolf was like a big brother to me. Taking my chances and without a second thought, I shot out of the bunker to find him. Once more I negotiated the exposed stairs to the roof top that I now loathed with a passion. Moments later, I found both Wolf and Karl on the observation platform. They were gallantly continuing to report the incoming shells.

It had become far too dangerous to continue observations from the roof. I implored them to move to the safety of the bunker. 'Another drop-short could land on the observation platform, killing us all,' I urged.

Wolf agreed. We started to move to the bunker—but too late. *Crump-crump!* Another salvo was inbound. We made haste to descend the ladder just as there was a large flash of light and another horrendous explosion at the perimeter fence. I glanced up as a bright flash of startling electric-white light, which seemed to be immediately on top of us, engulfed the entire night sky. Its intensity was almost indescribable, as though all the lights from a football stadium were focused on us.

The bright light had come from another artillery round that had dropped short and screamed in, clipping the roof of the civilian house just in front of our position and then changing its trajectory so it impacted merely metres in front of us. I watched the round clip the roof gutter just before I dived for cover.

It all seemed to happen in vivid slow motion. Exposed, we hit the deck near the bottom of the stairs. Shrapnel at such a close range should shred anyone near it to pieces.

Afterwards, I didn't want to open my eyes. They were clamped shut as I lowered my arms, which had instinctively protected my face, and began to pad down my body and legs. At that moment, I expected to encounter profuse bleeding and to feel horrific stabbing and shooting pains engulf my entire body as a result of being riddled with shrapnel. But then I realised there was no bleeding. I tested if I could wiggle my fingers and toes—all good!

There were no cries of pain from the guys either. Were they alive? It seemed that the air had been filled with dirt and debris, rather than deadly shards of steel. Miraculously, there was barely a scratch on Wolf, Karl or me.

The three of us darted back to the bunker, rattled but okay. I was confused and in a state of shock. It did not seem possible to survive what we had just experienced. We had literally watched an artillery round explode only 20 or so metres in front of us, but we had survived without injury.

Wolf celebrated the moment with his trademark brilliant smile. As we took stock, he slapped me a high-five, remarking, 'Kiddo, it's better to be damn lucky than damn good. Man, that was a close one!'

Once again we had escaped a dangerously close hit without taking casualties. But for how long could our luck continue like this?

Israeli artillery rounds continued to fire, some falling close to our base. Despite our repeated calls to our headquarters duty officer and his assurance that he was passing on our reports to the Israeli Defence Force liaison officers, the bombardment continued; it went on for probably only twenty minutes, but it felt more like hours. Little could settle my nerves as we crouched in anticipation, barely a word uttered between us.

The underground bunker had a dirt floor and was divided into four small rooms, with a narrow corridor down the middle. We would enter the bunker using a small flight of stairs at the southern end of the building; the first room on the right was the operations room; adjacent to it was an accommodation room which had two bunk beds which the Indian soldiers were using. On the other side of the corridor was the stores room, with a small supply of water and army ration packs; opposite the operations room was another small room with a single bed under which our two patrol base dogs were taking refuge. Gwynn and Ghajar were terrified of the high-pitched noises of incoming shells and had spent most of the war hiding.

Huddled in silence in a steaming hot concrete bunker with artillery rounds falling so dangerously close was a horrendous form of torture. With each near miss, the three-storey building above us audibly groaned, almost as though the very foundations and support beams were protesting against the stress they were under. Dust seeped through the cracks and settled on our helmets.

To compound our sense of hopelessness, we were not receiving information or situation reports from either our own headquarters in Lebanon or the UN headquarters in Jerusalem. It was as though we had disappeared into an information vacuum; sad to say, the best source of information, other than what we could see ourselves, was CNN on television.

Any moment could be our last, if there was a direct hit. Despite this, no one panicked or displayed any signs of negativity or fatalism. Instead, we attempted to support each other and maintain our morale with black humour. It's an unwritten rule in the military that, when things get tough, you can't afford to display any negative emotion. Keeping team morale high at times like this is vitally important, so that the right decisions are made at the right time to improve the chances of survival.

Time inched forward. The waiting game was the worst part, as we attempted to reel in negative thoughts and remain optimistic. It may sound bizarre, but telling jokes was the best form of distraction.

Strangely, the Indian soldiers were not as perturbed by our situation as I was. Wolf teased me as they stared at me with glancing, glossy-white smiles. Despite our predicament, it seemed that they were happy to be at our base. Wolf believed that in their minds they had hit the jackpot by being stuck at PB Khiam with me!

At last the artillery barrage targeting the valley behind us ceased, but the Israelis continued to fire intermittently at other targets throughout the night. Little did we know at the time that some of our reports of near misses were not getting through to the headquarters in Jerusalem to be recorded in the operational log. It is unknown why this happened—one possible reason is that Israeli electronic jamming may have blocked the transfer of information between the UN in Lebanon and Israel. As a result, the chief of staff of the UNTSO mission, Major General Clive Lilley, may not have been properly alerted to the true dangers and circumstances we were facing at the time.

During one of the lulls in firing, I decided to check my emails for anything about the threat assessment or operational activity in the area. I saw that I had received two messages from my Australian contingent commander in Jerusalem.

The first email had been sent late that evening, several hours after the artillery strike around our post, including the shell that virtually landed at my feet. I was eager to read it, expecting a morale boost and encouragement to keep our spirits high and focused, despite the number of times we had miraculously escaped serious injury. I hoped to share the message with my team-mates since, up until then, I was the only person at the base who had not heard from their national commander. In contrast, Du had received dozens of calls of support from his commander and fellow nationals in the Middle East and even from officials back in China, all concerned about his wellbeing.

My team-mates had jokingly teased me by saying: 'You Aussie orphans—no one cares if you guys live or die.' Although in jest, there was an element of truth in the taunt—I had not received a single phone call from the Australian headquarters staff in Jerusalem. I had defended my commander's lack of contact with me, rationalising that he probably had not had a chance to call the four Australians stationed in Lebanon (Birchy and I were manning patrol bases and the other two, Brad and Amanda, were off-duty in Tyre) because of his role as the UNTSO chief operations officer. I figured that he would have been incredibly busy in the UN headquarters in Jerusalem, now that his operational responsibilities had escalated significantly; and he would also be working to address the problems in our OGL headquarters in Lebanon as Amanda had alerted him to the situation already.

Because I had so adamantly defended my Australian commander, I was surprised to find that his email didn't enquire about my welfare at all. Nor did it refer to any of the near misses and life-threatening incidents we had survived over the previous two days at Khiam. In fact, it was not about the war at all. Instead, it was about the administration of my holiday leave entitlements. It left me feeling completely bewildered.

This email became an unintended kick in the guts, at a time when I was under extreme stress. It was written in a dispassionate tone, informing me that, because of an administrative error, I would lose one of my entitlements for free travel out of the mission area. Most likely my Australian commander had sent this email in haste, addressing a quick administrative issue during what had become an extremely busy day for him, without considering the timing and its impact on me.

While this was a disappointing outcome, which I would have coped with quite well on an ordinary day, its pettiness was magnified by my circumstances. I was focused on fulfilling my duties to the best of my abilities and making the right decisions to keep my team and myself alive. At the rate things were going with near misses, I figured I might not need any travel entitlements at all!

After reading this email, I began to question whether the entire UN command and control system had broken down completely. Perhaps he was not aware of what had happened at PB Khiam over the past two days? But how could the chief of operations not be aware of the war going on in Lebanon and the periods of intense battle around the UN patrol bases? My mind was spinning and trying to absorb the situation. It didn't seem to add up or make any sense. If my Australian commander was aware of the war situation and had time to write emails about my leave entitlements, why didn't he have time to phone his two subordinates in the line of fire and offer some much-needed information and support? Despite this, I figured he must have a good reason for his lack of contact.

I was angry with myself, as I had been fighting to keep it together emotionally, but this one email from my Australian commander had momentarily derailed me at a time when it was critically important for me to remain focused on the task at hand and to stay safe.

Wolf entered the operations room and saw the look of confusion on my face. He demanded to know: 'What's wrong, kiddo?' Reluctantly I showed him the email and he was wild with anger; he also questioned why Australian administration issues were being dealt with while we were taking hits from Israeli artillery pieces into our base. He was frustrated that there was still no situation or intelligence reports from either our headquarters in Lebanon or the higher headquarters in Jerusalem. Wolf wanted to ring my boss and give him 'a reality check'. It took a concerted effort to convince him that we had enough problems to deal with on the home front, with Israeli and Hezbollah forces continuing their battles around us, and this could wait to be resolved after the war.

I then opened the second email from my Australian commander, to find that I had been copied in on a situation report he had sent back to the higher Australian command in Sydney. The report included a short summary of the war. Wolf and I were thankful that my Australian commander had provided this information to me, as it was the only update we had received. But we also wondered if this critical information had been shared formally through the UN headquarters to the OGL staff, who needed it on the ground in Lebanon. We had been requesting situation reports from our headquarters in Naqoura by email and phone for the past two days, but they had been too short-staffed to provide them. The information in this email would have been of great benefit to the OGL headquarters staff, so there appeared to be a communications breakdown between the UN headquarters.

I knew that, for the second night in a row, I was going to struggle to get any sleep as the near miss artillery round replayed in my mind, over and over. We kept round-the-clock watches throughout the night and everyone was rostered to complete a shift between 10 p.m. and six o'clock the following morning. The other guys had all managed to get their heads down for some sleep, albeit broken.

With the additional personnel at PB Khiam, we did not have enough bunks for everyone, so I was trying to sleep on the lounge near the kitchen. I just couldn't seem to drift off; the distant *crump* of artillery fire kept disturbing me as my restless mind churned. I started to get quite frustrated, because I was tired and knew my body needed rest, but I couldn't settle my thoughts. Eventually, I gave up on the idea of sleep and went to the operations room, even though my shift did not start for another three hours, at 4.30 a.m.

Pat was just finishing his shift and went to wake up Wolf, who was next on duty. When Wolf arrived in the operations room, he insisted that I get some sleep in his now-vacant bunk as I would be next on shift after him. Knowing this was good advice, as I would need to have my wits about me and be sharp tomorrow, I agreed to try one more time and headed off to settle into Wolf's bed. This time, the cosy sleeping bag did the trick and I was asleep shortly after my head hit the pillow.

The next thing I knew, I woke with an instant stab of fear. It was 6 a.m. and I could hear a radio operator from UN headquarters calling urgently: 'PB Khiam, radio check, over.' No one in our operations room was answering. Where was Wolf? Why had he not woken me an hour and a half ago for my shift? Was he hurt? The rest of my team-mates were all still asleep in their bunks.

I leapt out of bed, not even bothering to put on my body armour, and went in search of Wolf. The radio operator continued to call in vain. As I moved through the kitchen on the ground floor underneath the main operations room, the phone rang. I answered quickly, before continuing my search. It was headquarters and I simply said: 'Wait out, I need to find Wolf.'

He was not in the bunker or the operations room. What had happened? My heart was beating fast and I was starting to panic. Where was Wolf? I scrambled up the ladder, two steps at a time, to the observation platform. To my relief, I could see Wolf outside our perimeter fence, checking the sizable crater left from the artillery round that had nearly taken us out the night before.

I was very relieved that Wolf was not hurt, but I was not sure whether I wanted to hug him—or to punch him for putting me through several minutes of utter distress. Wolf, in his usual brotherly protection of me, had not woken me for my morning shift, but instead had covered for me, allowing me to catch up on some sleep. I yelled to Wolf to turn up the volume on his radio and use it to contact headquarters, to report that we were all safe and accounted for. I then joined him at the crater and thanked him for his selfless act.

On closer inspection in daylight, it was evident that the 155-millimetre artillery round, which had landed just 20 or so metres in front of us, had not detonated and exploded properly. The outer casing of the shell had split into three large pieces of steel, which were extremely heavy and large enough to be difficult for one person to lift.

It was now also clear to us that the two direct hits we had reported were actually extremely close near misses that had hit just 2 and 5 metres outside our base. Large sections of those artillery shells had hurtled into our compound. Of the three canisters we found that contained the explosive charge, two of them had been propelled into our compound and were relatively intact; they were still smouldering and contained some white powder.

These partially ignited canisters were what had caused the smoke and fire at the T-wall that we had seen and reported as two direct hits. Their fuses should have detonated and shattered the outer steel case of the rounds, causing about 2000 hot, sharp fragments to splinter at high velocity into our base. It appeared they had ignited, but they had not fully exploded as they were designed to do. Extremely lucky, given we had been just metres away and still moving to the bunker.

Wolf called headquarters and corrected the previous night's report of two direct hits to near misses with two 'splashes' of artillery pieces into our compound. Wolf and I discussed whether the artillery round's firing mechanism might have become disabled, causing it to malfunction, when it clipped the roof of the civilian house in front of us. He said experts expect to have only one artillery round out of 1000 or so misfire, and it seemed we had scored that one malfunctioning round. No matter what the cause of the misfire, we were bloody lucky to be alive.

For the first time, it sank in that I might actually die during this war. The ramifications of that also started to register. I would never see Clent again. Never return home to the Byron Bay region, and my mum, dad and brother. I still had so much I wanted to do in my life!

I vowed there and then to talk to Clent in Tyre whenever I could, so long as it didn't affect my duties. I needed to know that he was safe; and he needed to know that I loved him—just one more time, just in case it was the last time.

10 Lack of Logic and Logistics

Sporadic periods of intense fire continued across the border over the following days. The nature of this war was different from what one might imagine from World War I or World War II—the Israelis maintained pressure by randomly firing artillery at predetermined target areas and then overwhelmingly responding to any form of attack from Hezbollah forces. Hezbollah fighters moved among the Lebanese people, firing rockets back into Israel; this in turn attracted Israeli artillery fire, rockets and aerial bombs that caused hundreds of civilian casualties. My heart went out to the Lebanese people, who were innocent bystanders in this war. They were simply living in the country from which Hezbollah, reportedly backed by Syria and Iran, had chosen to wage its conflict with Israel. Yet it was the Lebanese people who were paying the highest price in terms of human casualties.

Israeli jets and their aerial bombs had been very effective in disrupting the road networks around Tyre and the Lebanese borders, with the aim of preventing the movement of the kidnapped Israeli soldiers. The destroyed roads also made it extremely dangerous and difficult for civilian and UN movement throughout the region.

Hezbollah ignored Israel's demands for the return of the two soldiers, whose fate received worldwide attention. As a result, Israel increased the intensity of its bombardment all along the border, in preparation for a ground force invasion of Lebanon. The media speculation on CNN and BBC television, that the two captured Israeli soldiers had possibly been moved to Tyre, continued; and, in response to this speculation, the Israeli bombing of the town intensified.

With the increased attacks on Tyre and the heightened levels of danger, the UN headquarters in Jerusalem started to make plans to evacuate to Cyprus all UN civilian employees and UN families in Tyre. Clent tried to kept abreast of UN radio communications via Magnus downstairs, or via the two off-duty Australians, Brad and Amanda, who lived in an apartment close by. I was relieved that Brad and Amanda were passing on appropriate information to Clent—it seemed that the three of them had bonded even more in adversity. They could also hear my distinctive voice over the radio, reporting the continued near misses to PB Khiam. Clent was deeply disturbed by the danger of the situation my team-mates and I faced at Khiam.

Israel electronically jammed all telecommunication networks before and during their bombing raids, to stop Hezbollah forces from communicating with each other. This also significantly reduced the communications within the UN and the phone contact I was able to have with Clent, Brad and Amanda. Despite this, I was told that our Australian commander had given a direction not to allow Clent to take refuge in any Australian apartment. This flowed on from his new accommodation policy. It was explained that my commander had made this directive because he did not want the Commonwealth or himself to be personally liable if Clent were injured in an Australian rented apartment during the conflict.

Although I respected my commander's desire to protect the Commonwealth and himself from litigation, and understood that Clent was not his responsibility, I was disappointed that Clent's safety was not being given more consideration. Clent got himself to Tyre under his own steam and we understood that it was his responsibility to get himself to safety, perhaps aided by the efforts of the Australian Embassy, if necessary, rather than the UN. But the Israelis had destroyed the airport; travel by car was fraught with danger as Israel continued to target and systematically destroy the entire road network throughout southern Lebanon; and the Australian Embassy had closed its doors for the safety of its staff and to allow them to plan a large-scale evacuation effort of Australian civilians.

Knowing Brad and Amanda, I suspected they would continue to support Clent in any way they could, regardless of the directive. However, Clent and I didn't want to put them in a difficult position, so he took refuge with Magnus and Eva, the Swedish family on the floor below. This way he would still have the support and companionship of a UN family, while avoiding the legal issues my commander was concerned about. By all reports, when Clent was with Magnus and Eva, he'd often help burn off energy with their two young boys and act as a sounding board as they talked through the various scenarios that might play out.

Brad and Amanda visited Clent to update him on the situation in Lebanon, for which he was extremely grateful. At one point they even dropped off a large box of food and supplies they had bought during a dangerous grocery run to the other side of town. These provisions were invaluable in their own right, but they were also indicative of the friendship and generosity of spirit that Brad and Amanda extended to Clent during an incredibly difficult time.

During the evenings, if things were quiet in Khiam and Tyre, I would speak briefly with Clent by phone. I tried to mask the concern and utter exhaustion I was feeling, even though I knew Clent could see straight through my best efforts to play down the severity of our situation.

Clent was holding up remarkably well, considering he did not have any military training to draw on, in what I am sure was the most foreign and frightening situation he had ever confronted. His level-headed thinking and ever-positive approach to the situation kept him in good stead. It was comforting to hear his voice and have him as a sounding board, especially since we were receiving little information from UN headquarters. We felt extremely isolated and vulnerable on our post. If nothing else, Clent was able to provide information to us at PB Khiam about what was happening on the ground in Tyre.

Clent told me that he could see the Israeli warships off the coast and hear the helicopters as they hunted for Hezbollah in the dark of night in and around Tyre. The choppers seemed to be in the air a lot of the time; in the early hours of the morning they would sneak up unexpectedly and fire rockets into parts of the town. At this, Hezbollah's roaming jeeps would return fire, sometimes from directly outside his apartment. Clent was honest enough to admit that they frightened the life out of him; I worried that the terrifying sounds would become imbedded deep in his memory. He described the missiles as being like 100 trains travelling at high speed, with a whistle that pierced the stillness of the night.

Alone, in the pitch black of a moonless night and with his senses tingling, Clent at one stage stuck his head over the balcony wall to assess what was happening. The thunderous noise of the helicopters reverberated off the water and the concrete-clad city, but he couldn't see a thing. On the other hand, he wondered, *Can they see me?*

Knowing that Israel would be using cutting-edge night-vision technology, he realised he might be a little red target moving around, easy to spot and shoot. I rationalised with him that, realistically, the Israelis could just take out the entire apartment block if they wanted to; but, even so, it was a good idea to stay away from the balcony, windows and doors.

I am sure the worst emotion for Clent—being untrained and unsure about what to do in a war—was his sense of being completely trapped and powerless to leave Tyre. I also knew he was terribly concerned for my safety at Khiam. It was surreal, and neither of us had ever felt this vulnerability and lack of control before. I was fearful that he would die in this futile war and I prayed that, if one of us should be killed, it would be me. I could not live with the alternative.

Israeli helicopters were also active in the Khiam region. Wolf and I were on the observation platform, and I had just brought him a fresh cup of coffee, when two Israeli Cobra attack helicopters suddenly appeared over the Khiam ridge line and fired two missiles in quick succession. The first thing we heard was the now familiar whirring scream of incoming rockets. Two missiles hurtled either side of the observation deck, causing us to dive for cover. Every muscle in my body braced in anticipation of the explosion, and the atmosphere seemed to pause, like the lull before a storm. One missile slammed into the school in El Khiam, a short distance away, and the second hit the road leading to our base. Both missiles were serious truce violations, breaches of the Geneva Convention and dangerous near misses to our compound.

When the missiles hurtled past us at eye level, we instinctively ducked behind the parapet walls. In the process, Wolf spilt his coffee all over his uniform and exclaimed, 'Damn air force weenies!' before turning to me with a cheeky grin: 'But how cool was it to see that?' We got just a glimpse of the helicopters as they dropped back down below the ridge line, having dispensed their rockets of destruction. The entire event happened in the blink of an eye. It was yet another surreal experience.

We were right in the thick of this war and witnessing state-of-the-art military aircraft and their weaponry at work. Wolf was elated; I was astonished by their speed and precision. Having witnessed such mighty weapons at work at such close range, however, I was becoming more nervous about the escalating number of near misses to our base. Was our luck running out?

I established a triage area in the small room with the single bed opposite the operations room in the bunker, using my Australian-issued combat medic's kit. I had set it up to give intravenous fluids and pain relief should we sustain any casualties. After the sheer number and intensity of firing events close to our position, I feared that these medical supplies and my recently acquired combat medic's skills might actually be put to use.

In my entire fifteen-year army career, I had never seen fast jets or attack helicopters firing their weapons; their astounding capabilities had only ever been something described in tactics lessons in the safe environment of a classroom. As a logistics officer, I had never imagined I would be observing these incredible aircraft in action, let alone at such close range or at the receiving end of the bombs! Yet in the past few days, I had witnessed first-hand Israeli F-15 and F-16 fighter jets laser-guiding their aerial bombs, which could completely raze a five-storey building, onto targets that were at times less than 100 metres away from me. It was difficult for me to comprehend. But, despite the obvious danger, I felt a physical response to the sensations of being in a war, a sense of exhilaration, awe, and the adrenaline rush that sparked a hyper-aware state of body and mind.

To me, war is a horrific and destructive last-roll-of-the-dice situation that results from a failure of diplomacy and, ultimately, human compassion; anyone who has experienced the horrors of battle should never glorify war. The sense of exhilaration I felt was because I was actually getting to put more than a decade's worth of training into action, in a gruelling and testing environment. Although this was not a situation where I was actually leading a team into combat—instead, I was in the unfamiliar situation of being a UN observer, playing a non-participatory, observing and reporting role—I still felt this experience was testing my training and character.

There are few bigger pressure tests than a war zone. In the army we train and train for years on end, repeating procedures so they become instinctive in the fog of war. Throughout those years of honing my skills in the safety of a training scenario, I had always harboured an element of doubt in the back of my mind as to whether I would be able to cut it in the heat of battle. Simulations are just that—simulations. When it came to a real and dangerous situation, would I be able to put my training into action and lead my team to safety, or would I freeze and be ineffective? It had remained a question unanswered until now, and I was relieved that all those years of training and hard work seemed to be paying off.

As a Transport Corps officer, I couldn't have imagined I would one day find myself with a front-row seat to a war as an unarmed observer, reporting the effects of the full gamut of state-of-the-art weapons systems impacting dangerously close around me. I am sure plenty of my compatriots in the direct fighting units of the army would have jumped at the chance to have been in my shoes to gain this unique battlefield experience. The Israeli Defence Force was certainly excelling itself in providing me with the ultimate military tactics lesson—it was a powerful war machine working with precision against a technologically inferior enemy.

In addition to the battles around us, we also faced a significant logistics problem on PB Khiam. From the outset of hostilities, we had had nine UN personnel at the post, which was almost double the intended quota of five UNMOs for our base. We didn't have enough beds to sleep everyone, and we were running out of food, water and fuel for the generators. Because we normally bought food locally on a daily basis, we only had a one-day supply of fresh food at the compound. We had been placed on a code red order almost immediately, which did not permit us to move from the base; therefore, we had been unable to resupply our rations ourselves.

We informed OGL headquarters of these problems but, due to their manning issues, they told us, 'We will add it to the list of things we are working on.' They were so occupied trying to keep up with the operational aspects of this war that they simply did not have the resources to overcome the myriad of problems associated with our need for resupply. Although our food crisis was high priority to us, it simply fell off the list of priorities for headquarters.

We did have a seven-day supply of army ration packs in the bunker, but this was only for the five people usually on the base, not nine. We were keen to hold those rations in reserve, in case we were trapped in the bunker for an extended period, if a ground invasion should eventuate. An Israeli incursion seemed increasingly likely to us as we closely monitored their preparations to cross the border. Israeli troops had placed bridge-laying equipment across the river near Ghajar, which would allow swift transit across the border and into Lebanon.

We tried to overcome our food shortage ourselves with the aid of our Lebanese interpreter, Eddie, who lived in El Khiam. On the second day of the war, Eddie bought kebab rolls for lunch for our entire group from a shop in El Khiam run by one of his friends; he then delivered them by car to our compound. This system worked reasonably well the first time we tried it, but when we attempted to repeat it the next day, Eddie attracted the attention of the Israeli Defence Force, and they responded with artillery fire. He refused to complete the risky resupply run for us again—which was fair enough!

Food and water continued to pose a significant problem for us as the conflict continued. Water was normally provided to our compound by UNIFIL every two or three days—for showering, running the generators and general use. Although we had the water truck driven by our Indian UN colleagues at our base, we had used most of its contents on day one of the war for fire-fighting. When the closest Hezbollah position was destroyed by a fighter jet, a fire had erupted which threatened our base and we had been lucky to have the water truck on-hand to put out the flames. The Hezbollah base was a logistics compound that was used to store ammunition and explosives. The area continued to smoulder for several days after it was destroyed and this ongoing heat caused the ammunition stored there to ignite in what we call 'cooking off', creating unexpected and random explosions right next to us for several days and nights. While we observed the war from the roof top of PB Khiam, these sporadic and unscheduled explosions just metres behind us made us understandably jumpy and on edge.

We normally purchased bottled drinking water for personal consumption from a shop in El Khiam and had a small supply for emergency use held in the bunker, but our stash was nowhere near enough for nine personnel should the conflict continue for any more than a few days. The rapidly depleting supply of water led to our decision to conserve water for the two highest priorities: for drinking, and for cooling the generators that powered the compound. This meant no more showers, making for uncomfortable, sweaty conditions: it was the middle of summer, and, in the sun on the exposed concrete roof on most days, temperatures reached into the high 30s.

We had been conducting 24-hour 'piquets' (rostered shifts of duty) on the observation platform since the war started. For me, the extreme discomfort was exacerbated by the need to wear my heavy Kevlar jacket and helmet whenever I went outside, resulting in my uniform becoming quickly drenched in sweat. There was no shade on the platform, so sunscreen was now paramount to avoid being burnt to a crisp. I was the only one who carried sunscreen in my kit bag and, since I only had a small bottle, it wasn't going to last for more than a few days when shared between all of us. It was strange that an item as insignificant as sunscreen could have such importance at a time like this.

On day three of the war our logistics problems increased dramatically. A plan had been formulated by UNIFIL to return the extra four people now at PB Khiam to their home locations at PB Mar and the Indian battalion headquarters. The UN had obtained a 'tactical pause' agreement from Israel—they would cease bombing in our area so we could move the two UNMOs from PB Mar and the two Indian soldiers and the water truck. The UN decided to send two armoured personnel carriers (APCs) to PB Khiam to escort the two groups back to their home bases.

During this window of opportunity, Israel agreed not to bomb certain identified road routes during a specified period of time, allowing the UN APCs to transit safely. However, the Israelis broke that promise and one of their fighter jets dropped a 1000-pound aerial bomb on the nominated road just as the UN APCs were approaching our base. Fearing the crews had been hit, Wolf and I grabbed our combat medic kits.

Although the bomb had exploded only 200 metres or so from our position, it was on the leeward side of the ridge line and, due to the fall of the hill, we couldn't see the actual impact from the observation platform on PB Khiam. The explosion once again shook the base; its sheer impact and sound were incredible. We hurriedly made contact with UNIFIL headquarters. Thankfully, the crews hadn't been injured in the blast.

Shortly afterwards, the APC convoy arrived at our rear gate. This was the opposite direction to the intended and agreed approach to PB Khiam. The Indian crew commander explained to us that he had not been able to find the assigned road, and they had ended up on the wrong road and the wrong side of the ridge line. This was actually a stroke of good fortune as it turned out. By sheer luck, they had not used the designated road targeted and destroyed by the Israeli bombing.

For us, the Israeli attack was a serious breach of trust and we lost confidence in the Israeli Defence Force's ability to coordinate all elements of their personnel. This was proof that we couldn't rely on Israeli guarantees not to hit assigned roads near UN vehicles during any agreed window of opportunity to move. As a result, the two APCs and their crew of fourteen Indian soldiers were ordered to remain at PB Khiam.

Our very serious logistics problem was now exacerbated: our overcrowded team of nine had expanded to a bulging 23 people taking shelter at the compound. This was an unsustainable situation. We informed headquarters that we would run out of water and food by nightfall.

The Israeli bombing continued in and around PB Khiam, resulting in a rather crowded and uncomfortable time for the 23 people crammed in the bunker. Thankfully, and by sheer chance, the ration packs we held in the bunker were Hindu rations and therefore suitable for our new guests, who seemed to enjoy our hospitality, not to mention the opportunity to be close to a white-skinned woman for probably the first time in their lives. The irony of the soldiers' grinning during an artillery barrage was wearing thin for Wolf, who barked at them to stop staring at me. Despite being an awkward situation for me, at least they were smiling.

Later that afternoon, a new negotiation with Israel for another window of opportunity to move was sought and the approval was granted for the extra personnel at PB Khiam to move back to their bases. Before their departure, the Indian APC crew commander found some ration packs in his vehicles to replace the ones consumed in our bunker by his soldiers. The transit went ahead this time without incident. It was a relief finally to be back to our old team of five at Khiam. But we had now completely run out of fresh food.

11 Disempowered and Disillusioned

Despite the remarkable efforts of those UNMOs struggling away at headquarters, the logistics problems we were encountering at PB Khiam were unlikely to be resolved for several days. I was quickly learning that, when operating in a multinational UN force, things were done very differently to how the Australian Defence Force operates. In fairness to the UN, such a level of efficiency is difficult to maintain when a force is constantly changing. Officers on the UNTSO mission were rotating in and out from their respective countries every month and were also swapping between the four UNTSO countries (Syria, Lebanon, Israel and Egypt). This made continuity difficult. Moreover, UNTSO observers come from different military forces with different styles, different technologies and different levels of operational experience. I was frustrated by the absence of many basic procedures that we would take for granted in the ADF—such as having a logistics plan in place that had been developed, tried and tested. Despite these challenges, we made do and got on with the task at hand as best we could, and tried to resolve issues as they arose.

Wolf and the others felt we needed to resolve the logistics situation for ourselves by driving into El Khiam to find food and water. Although this would be breaking the code red order, Wolf reasoned that, if Israel invaded southern Lebanon in the coming days, which we fully expected from our observations, now might be our only opportunity to get supplies. Such a situation had actually occurred during previous battles involving Israel. I had seen scratched into the wall of the bunker on OP 57 in Syria the fifteen days marked off during which two UNMOs had been trapped while Israel occupied their compound in 1973.

Wolf felt strongly that we couldn't rely on OGL headquarters to resolve our food and water shortage. It was obvious that there were command issues in the absence of key staff and there also appeared to be a lack of coordination between the two UN forces in Lebanon, UNIFIL and UNTSO, which made us even more anxious. We felt like we were sitting in isolation at PB Khiam, with little information.

But, despite the logic Wolf was espousing, I was not comfortable with the idea of breaking the code red order when we still had some food, in the form of ration packs, on our post. It was the only time that Wolf and I did not agree on an operational issue. I felt that the risk of injury outside the patrol base was just too great and that we needed to give headquarters more time and opportunity to fulfil their role of resolving the resupply situation. I voiced my opinion, but I was outvoted.

Wolf, Du and Big Mack made two dashes into El Khiam on two separate days to grab vital supplies of food and bottled water. They were nervous and anxious waits for Pat and me at the base. In truth, I'm not sure which was worse—to wait, or to go with them. I prayed they would return unscathed. Just moments after the boys left the village's general store on the second run, it was destroyed by Israeli artillery fire, killing the shop owner. With the shop decimated, that was the end of our self-initiated resupply. Wolf, Du and Big Mack were extremely lucky that it hadn't cost them their lives too.

Bunker of UN Observation Post 57, Golan Heights, Syria.
http://www.youtube.com/matinajewell

When they returned to the compound with their bounty of food and water, having scraped through yet another near miss, I rushed to their vehicle and hugged each of them tightly. Wolf knew I was torn about his decision to leave the base for food. I was very relieved they had survived their brave efforts to ensure we had the essential supplies we would need in the bunker if we were to be trapped down there for any considerable length of time.

In the midst of all this commotion, Eddie, our interpreter, made a daring sprint to PB Khiam, thinking that he would be safer at our patrol base than hunkering down in his own house in El Khiam. Eddie was shocked to find that we were no less at risk of injury or death at our compound. He had hoped that the UN would have been spared bombardment by Israel at all costs and was stunned to see how close the Israeli shells had fallen to us. Eddie was now also stuck at our position, so we were back to the situation of having an extra person to feed and account for. We now had six people at Khiam.

On day four of the war, I received an email from the Australian commander with an update on the overall situation in Lebanon. At the same time we also received an assessment of Israel's intent from OGL headquarters. After days of markedly increased tension between the Israeli government and Hezbollah, Israeli forces were now preparing to launch a major assault against Lebanon, to attempt to eradicate Hezbollah militants permanently. This report confirmed that it was likely that the Israeli force would move into southern Lebanon over the coming days.

Late that afternoon we had another near miss, this time from an Israeli Merkava tank. The Merkava is a ferocious-looking piece of machinery—the sheer presence of the armour-clad, 65-tonne tracked beast is said to create shock and awe in its opponents. It certainly was a terrifying and powerful vehicle in action. In just moments, the main gun fired a round which completely destroyed a Hezbollah bunker only 25 metres from our post. It scared the hell out of us all. Because the round hit so very close to us, it sprayed sections of the destroyed bunker—concrete, steel pickets and bricks—into our compound. Even after four days of battle, and despite the number of near misses we had already survived, we were quite jumpy—to the point that any noise had us hitting the deck for cover. Our survival senses had been sharpened and were now working overtime, making our reactions quicker than normal to keep us safe.

The tank round had sent us all sprawling onto the deck of the observation platform. Our equipment and gear were haphazardly abandoned as we dived for cover and hoped this explosion wasn't 'The One' that would bring us unstuck. Afterwards, there was a quick check of each other—it seemed to be another miracle and somehow we were all okay.

We relied heavily on open-source media—the internet and cable television in particular—as these were our best sources of information on what was occurring in the war. CNN reported that Israel had code-named this war Operation Just Reward. I was appalled and furious. There was nothing just or rewarding about the disproportionate response I was witnessing from the Israeli Defence Force. Having been under bombardment from Israel ourselves for several days, it was hard to keep a sense of what was happening on the other side and therefore at times it was difficult to remain objective. However, the loss of so many innocent Lebanese civilian lives, plus thousands more casualties, was not 'Just Reward'.

By mid-afternoon on day five of the war Lieutenant Colonel Kullberg, the chief of OGL, had managed to return to the head-quarters from PB Mar. This was welcome news as we knew his presence at Naqoura headquarters would get things coordinated and under control. Shortly after learning this piece of good news I received a phone call from Birchy, my Aussie team-mate at PB Mar. Birchy explained that he had called our Australian commander in Jerusalem to raise the issue that we needed his support and contact during the war. We had both narrowly survived numerous near misses already and things were shaping up to only get worse when

Israel crossed the border. The commander explained to Birchy that he was simply too busy in the headquarters to phone us, but he would instruct Amanda, who was our senior Australian in Lebanon and off-duty in Tyre, to call both of us each day to check on our status. I was relieved to hear that Birchy too had not received a phone call from our commander, and that it wasn't just me. And it was reassuring to know that Amanda would be in daily contact. But I was a little disappointed not to have direct contact with my commander.

Some may wonder why I desired contact from a man who I didn't have the best relationship with. In retrospect, this feeling stems from the widely accepted military expectation that, when faced with such a dangerous situation, it's reasonable to expect your superior to provide direct contact, guidance and encouragement. This need for contact also resulted from his role as the UN chief operations officer—I had hoped that my Australian commander would not only give me support from a national perspective but also reassure me that the UN headquarters had the situation under control. It was an instance in which I felt that no news meant that it was not good news. But at the time I rationalised that perhaps my commander not only had a lack of time but might also be experiencing communication problems across the border; if this was the case, I was appreciative that he had established a support network for us with Amanda.

I tried to call Clent to give myself a morale boost, but I couldn't get through. The phone gave a constant engaged signal and this could only mean one thing: Tyre was under attack from Israel and they had jammed the network again, to prevent Hezbollah forces communicating. I really hated these periods of silence—not knowing what was happening intensified my concern to fever pitch and it took all my strength to prevent myself from thinking the worst.

I soon learnt the reason for the blocked phone network: Israel had dropped a 1000-pound bomb on the newly established part of Tyre, hitting a civilian apartment building that possibly housed Hezbollah communications. The bomb had destroyed five storeys of the building, killing an off-duty UN civilian and his wife. The explosion had sent shrapnel into several other apartments, including those of two off-duty Team Sierra UNMOs. My team-mates Tore Rosseid, and his wife and two children, as well as Hans-Peter Lang, had all narrowly escaped injury. These events in Tyre intensified my fears for Clent's safety and made the danger seem even more real.

As a result of this latest attack, many of the UN families decided to leave their apartments and move for safety to the UN rear-duty headquarters, which was located in Tyre and had UNMOs on duty supporting the main headquarters in Naqoura while also supporting the nearby UN families. It was housed within the Lebanese resort called The Rest House Resort, on the opposite side of Tyre from the old city. However, because the UN was not prepared to accommodate these families at the rear-duty headquarters, later that same night an order was given that all families, with the exception of those whose apartments had been substantially destroyed in the bombing, must return home to their apartments, which were dispersed throughout the city. There seemed to be a lot of confusion, frustration and fear within the UN community in Tyre.

Magnus and Eva invited Clent to stay in their apartment. Clent, having two younger brothers of his own, got on well with their boys, aged six and nine, providing them with daily rewards if they remained on their best behaviour in what was a nightmare situation for their parents. Eva later told me that Clent was a great support and at times a much-needed circuit breaker. That didn't surprise me at all—Clent is really just a big kid too! He was conscious of the tensions running through the family and would spend time with them throughout the day, when appropriate, but sleep in his own apartment by night. I just can't imagine how terrifying it must have been for parents to have young children in such a dire situation.

When the phone lines were back up and running, I briefly spoke with Clent to reassure him that I felt he was probably actually safer in the apartment block they were in than they would be in the UN headquarters. Our apartment block was in the Christian quarter of Tyre and, to my knowledge, this precinct had never been targeted by Israel in previous conflicts, which was one of the reasons I had chosen to live there. Clent told me how he had witnessed the Israeli Defence Force dropping pamphlets over the city of Tyre that afternoon, just prior to the bombing of the apartment building. The leaflets were delivered by Israeli unmanned aerial vehicles (UAVs) and contained cartoon drawings and Arabic messages to the Lebanese people from the Israeli government. In military circles, we call this type of activity psychological operations (psyops) but I had never seen it used in any of my previous operations. The cartoon drawing showed people being bombed and depicted Nasrallah's face, the leader of Hezbollah, as the head of a snake. The Arabic text written on this cartoon pamphlet translates as 'Is the resistance protecting a homeland or is the homeland the victim of resistance!!!'

إلى السكان اللبنانيين

سيزيد جيش الدفاع الإسرائيلي من اعماله في لبنان ضد الأعمال الإرهابية المستمرة لحزب الله المطلق العنان بغية الدفاع عن مواطني دولة إسرائيل.

من اجل سلامتكم ولرغبتنا بمنع الحاق الأذى بالمدنيين غير المتورطين عليكم الامتناع من التواجد بالأماكن التي يتواجد فيها ويعمل منها حزب الله ضد دولة إسرائيل.

بما في ذلك:

• أماكن إطلاق الصواريخ باتجاه أراضي دولة إسرائيل
• أماكن تواجد مخازن الذخيرة والعتاد العسكري لحزب الله
• مراكز حزب الله في جنوب بيروت والمناطق التي تحت سيطرته في جنوب لبنان
• ضاحية بيروت الجنوبية مركز الإرهاب

يدعو جيش الدفاع الإسرائيلي السكان اللبنانيين والجيش اللبناني إلى الامتناع عن تقديم المساعدة سواء كانت مباشرة أم غير مباشرة لعناصر حزب الله كل من يفعل ذلك سيعرض حياته للخطر.

اعلموا ان استمرار الإرهاب ضد دولة إسرائيل يمنع عنكم العيش بمستقبل أفضل.

دولة إسرائيل

The second psyops pamphlet reads:

To the Lebanese Population
The IDF will increase its operations in Lebanon against the ongoing Hezbollah's terrorist acts in order to defend the citizens of the state of Israel. We want to prevent any harm caused to civilians who are not involved with Hezbollah, so for your safety you must refrain from being present at places where Hezbollah is present or where Hezbollah operates against the state of Israel.

This includes:

•   Places where missiles are launched on the territory of the state of Israel.

•   Places where ammunition and military equipment owned by Hezbollah are stored.

- Hezbollah centres in Southern Beirut and areas under its control in Beirut.
- Beirut's southern suburb, which is the epicentre of terrorism.

The IDF is calling the Lebanese people and the Lebanese army to refrain from providing assistance, directly or indirectly to the elements of Hezbollah. Anyone who does so will put his life in danger. We assure you that the continuation of terrorist acts against the state of Israel is robbing you of a better future.

The State of Israel

•

I had been keeping in contact with Clent's family back in Australia by phone, giving his parents and brothers updates on our situation, to try to allay their fears. The communications network in southern Lebanon might be destroyed completely, so I tried to prepare them for this situation. It would have gone against every emotional instinct, but if we were unable to communicate, I hoped that they would not think the worst. Instead, I assured them if something terrible had occurred, then the Australian Army would be in contact very quickly—in other words, no news is good news. I was thankful that Clent's entire family, like many country folk, had been heavily involved in the emergency services as volunteers. They had experienced crisis situations and were very pragmatic, sensible and level-headed during our entire ordeal. Their calm approach was reassuring, and Clent's two brothers, Brent and Kelvin, would cheer me up, often making jokes about the crazy situation we were in. They were a brilliant support team.

Psychological operations pamphlets falling from Israeli unmanned aerial vehicle into Tyre, Lebanon War 2006.
http://www.youtube.com/matinajewell

I had also been calling my brother, Mark, in London, offering him the same advice regarding communication. I assumed our parents would contact Mark immediately after they received the news of the war in Lebanon while travelling on their tour around Europe. I had appealed to Mark to downplay the situation to Mum and Dad as I knew they would be sick with anxiety.

Thankfully, my parents did not hear or see the news until the last day of their European trip, when they were heading to my brother's house in London. I was able to speak with Mark, Mum and Dad that afternoon, which was day five of our confinement at PB Khiam. When I first heard the sound of their voices, full of fear and concern, I wanted to cry and to tell them how much I dearly loved them. I fought back my tears, however, as I desperately wanted to spare them anxiety and worry, by minimising the real danger. Yet, at the same time, I wanted to savour this precious phone call in case it was the last, soaking up their encouragement, love and support.

I was fine and away from the battle, I assured them, but just then, the Israeli artillery guns started firing in our area again, causing me to cut short our conversation. The sound of shells exploding outside the bunker gave them a hint of the real story. My mother heard the unmistakable blasts and burst into tears, sobbing uncontrollably. My words of reassurance did little to comfort her, but she apologised for being so upset when she knew I needed her to stay strong. Although only brief, it was the most difficult conversation I have ever had. I cannot begin to imagine the suffering and uncertainty that my parents went through over the following days.

I knew my parents were regretting the day they had supported my decision to join the army. I wished I could have been more convincing in downplaying the intensity of activity around Khiam, as my parents' worry and their not being able to sleep were not going to help the situation. I wished I could have done something more to ease the concern I knew they would endure until they knew I was well and truly safe.

Matina on a force protection exercise on the *Kanimbla*.

Matina fast-roping
from a Navy Sea King
helicopter.

L-R: Wolf, Matina and Du on the observation platform of PB Khiam.

Bridge destroyed by an Israeli aerial bomb, southern Lebanon. *Source*: Yngvar Dypvik. This photo was taken a few months prior to the July war 2006.

Matina with Indian and Ghanaian crew in front of an APC, Rest House Resort, Tyre.

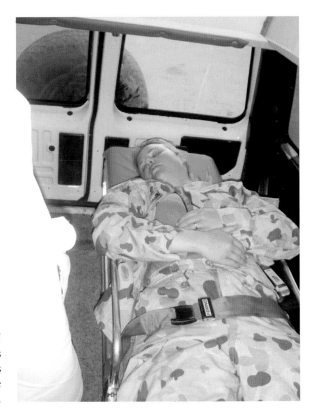

Matina inside a UN ambulance. She was dropped out of this ambulance during the evacuation from Tyre.

PB Khiam before the bombing.

PB Khiam after being hit by a 1000-pound aerial bomb. *Source*: Tore Rosseid.

Transfer of fallen team–mates. *Source*: Tore Rosseid.

UN Ceremony for
the team–mates who
died at PB Khiam.
Source: Tore Rosseid.

Matina and Clent Jewell's wedding at Lennox Head.

ANZAC Centenary Commission

Matina now serves on the Anzac Centenary Commission. She is seated between former Prime Ministers Bob Hawke and Malcolm Fraser.

Photo L–R front: Rear Admiral Ken Doolan (retired), The Right Honourable Malcolm Fraser, Major Matina Jewell (retired), The Honourable Bob Hawke

Standing L–R: Kylie Russell and Warren Brown

As the war continued and the near misses to all of the UN bases along the border increased, I wondered why we had been left at our posts. We were unarmed peacekeepers whose mandated mission was to observe and monitor a peace agreement. There was now clearly no peace to keep. The UN had not predicted such a violent and ferocious event; although the unarmed UN personnel working at the border had bravely reported hundreds of violations of the UN sanctions, we were simply not sufficiently equipped or organised to continue operating while surrounded by full-scale war. The fact that the UNTSO force did not have even the most basic operating procedures in place—like how to supply food and water in an emergency, or a plan for safely relieving and changing team personnel during such a crisis—was a clear indication to me that we were not intended to remain in this highly volatile and dangerous situation. Why then had there been no decision to withdraw the unarmed peacekeepers?

I wondered if the option of withdrawing the UNTSO peace-keepers had been recommended. There may not have been anyone in the OGL headquarters authorised to make such a big call while the chief was absent on PB Mar. We had not seen any communication from our higher headquarters in Jerusalem either and, from the email I had received from my Australian commander about my leave travel entitlements, it appeared to me that they were also a bit out of touch and unaware of the severity of the situation we faced on the patrol bases in Lebanon.

Withdrawing a UN peacekeeping force was a massive decision, which could not be made lightly, as it would have significant and important flow-on consequences. There would be pressure on the UN by some parties, such as the Lebanese government, who would not want the UN to withdraw and leave them somewhat isolated from world public opinion through an information blackout about Israel's conduct. Such a decision needed to be made at the highest level, but I questioned whether the top echelons of the UN were fully aware of the situation.

My feelings of disempowerment and disillusionment reached a peak when I received a couple of phone calls from the local Lebanese mayors and *mukhtars*, asking us to help evacuate their citizens to safety. These were the same people we had regularly met with to liaise and discuss ways the UN could assist them. They were now asking for our assistance but we, the UN, were unable to provide it. I felt completely powerless.

These local communities were pinning their hopes of survival on us and we could not insulate them from the indiscriminate Israeli attacks. Even if we had been given permission from UN headquarters to move from the base to respond to these requests, how could we evacuate entire villages with only three vehicles? Having told the mayors and *mukhtars* that we were unable to help them, I then had to observe and report as their towns were bombed by Israel, no doubt resulting in many casualties to innocent people. It was a cruel punishment, and I felt somehow personally responsible for their fate.

Even though I was feeling this way, I strongly support the need to have a UN force in place in southern Lebanon; I also feel the UN undertakes beneficial work all over the world. I am of course aware that the UN has its failings, but, with no better alternative, I support the remarkable job UN personnel perform by monitoring activities and aiding in the maintenance of at least some form of peace in these volatile regions. At this particular point in time though, given that we could not help desperate people in their time of crisis, I questioned the value of my presence in the country and, indeed, the value of the UN's presence there. Later during the war, the UN established a system whereby town mayors could request UN support through the Lebanese government, and on several occasions the UN helped evacuate entire communities close to the Israeli border.

•

My shift on the observation deck was complete so I headed to the bunker; I needed a break. My nerves were shot from near misses and I was emotionally wrought from seeing such carnage inflicted on blameless people. I was jumpy and on edge, and starting to question the high risk of injury or death associated with reporting more violations from both Israel and Hezbollah from the exposed observation platform on the roof top.

As I sat in the bunker with the dogs nuzzling their faces into my body, listening to the explosions outside, I had an eerie premonition of my own death. I had a vivid sense that my time was up and that I was going to lose my life during this war. It was strange, in that I didn't feel that my team-mates would suffer the same fate—just me. Making the sensation even more bizarre was that I didn't feel panicked or fearful of this destiny. In a way, I immediately reached a level of acceptance of this outcome and my only concern was to ensure that everything was in place to make my passing as easy as possible for my family, friends and Clent.

Despite the physical and mental fatigue, I took a very pragmatic and logical approach to the premonition. From the bunker of PB Khiam I called my friend and colleague Captain Linda Gillett back in Australia and simply said that things were looking a little bad at my end. Linda immediately understood what I meant. I asked her to support Clent and my parents through what was clearly going to be a horrific situation for them should my circumstances deteriorate. It was a terrible request—such an awkward thing to ask of one of my best friends.

Linda was shocked on a number of levels. Firstly, that she was receiving a phone call from me, having seen the news reports and knowing that I was in the thick of war. Secondly, that she could hear explosions outside. And thirdly, that I was so calm about my situation. It must have been so horrendous and bizarre to hear me asking her to ensure that my loved ones were supported through the aftermath of the war and that I didn't think I was going to make it.

Linda was rattled by my request, so I tried to snap her out of her emotional state by telling her that I needed her to keep it together and be strong for me. It was an unfair and appalling thing to do to a friend, but I trusted Linda innately and knew she was strong enough to cope with my absurd request. It was actually at Linda's wedding that I had met Clent—she was the mutual friend that had brought us together. I knew, as she was the strongest and most dependable person I had ever met, she wouldn't let me down.

12 Rotation, Rotation

It was 17 July 2006, day six of the war and Israel was poised to invade southern Lebanon. The UN believed Israeli forces would start their advance into hostile territory through three crossing points on the border; one of these access areas was the Khiam region. This theory seemed justified as Israeli activity had rapidly increased around PB Khiam and we could see their tanks and ground forces starting to position themselves to prepare for an assault across the border.

On the patrol base we were bracing ourselves, knowing that one of Israel's first objectives would be the Hezbollah headquarters in the town centre of El Khiam, not far from our base. We anticipated Hezbollah would provide strong resistance and we had started to prepare, physically and mentally, for the likelihood of spending extensive time in the bunker. My nerves were raw and my gut was constantly churning after so many near misses during the past week.

All the UN posts along the border were in the middle of intense battles and it seemed only a matter of time before the invasion began in earnest. I told myself to strap in for another danger-induced adrenaline rush.

Meanwhile, we received a message from headquarters that there was an amendment to the team rotation plan. Tore would no longer be coming to PB Khiam to replace me. Instead, it would now be Hans–Peter, since Tore had his wife and two children with him in Tyre preparing for evacuation. Hans–Peter was thrilled with this change as he was keen to get out to where the action was.

The other change was that my Irish team-mate, Pat, was also now to rotate off the post with me, instead of Big Mack, who aside from me had spent the next highest number of consecutive days on the base and was, therefore, the next team member due for rotation. Lieutenant Colonel Kullberg had made this decision because Pat's wife, Marion, was in Tyre preparing to evacuate and Pat was also a junior UNMO in a situation that demanded experience of the region. This was only the second patrol Pat had completed at Khiam, while Big Mack was an old hand, having served regularly on the base for over six months and being our team's deputy leader. It was a sensible decision.

Headquarters also surprised us with the decision to reduce the manning on PB Khiam from five UNMOs down to only four, meaning Pat would not be replaced by another Team Sierra member. We were confused by this and could not understand the thinking behind the chief's decision to reduce our manning at a time when our workload had escalated substantially. With the war intensifying at a rapid rate, the base would need to continue keeping watch around the clock; fewer people meant more watch time and less rest for an already weary team. Wolf voiced these concerns to headquarters, but it was a done deal. PB Khiam would reduce to four UNMOs.

The biggest concern we had with the rotation plan was that OGL headquarters had directed that the team rotation be conducted using our soft-skinned vehicles—a standard Toyota Prado or 4-Runner—without any armed escort from UNIFIL. Considering the rotation would take at least four hours to complete in total (two hours each way between Tyre and Khiam)—all of which would be close to the border where Israel was preparing to invade Lebanon—the whole thing seemed like a very bad idea. Our sense of humour by now was somewhat warped by any normal standards, so we named it a suicide run.

In light of all the military action that was continuing and the heightened danger levels of moving on the road, it seemed absolutely absurd to consider a move in anything less than an armoured vehicle. We strongly questioned the lack of protection this plan offered. Thankfully, after much discussion and reconsideration by UNIFIL, which had previously stated that it could not provide armoured vehicles for the move, our suggestions were heeded—UNIFIL allocated two APCs, with a crew of fourteen soldiers. The rotation was due to take place that same day at 12 o'clock.

On each day of the war, the UN had attempted to complete our team rotation, but, due to the ferocity and unpredictability of the surrounding hostilities and several other logistical factors, this hadn't been accomplished. I should have been replaced on PB Khiam on day two of the war; this uncertainty and daily postponing of the rotation of personnel had been difficult to deal with and now I wondered how Big Mack must be feeling, knowing that he wasn't on the first rotation list any longer.

The process to rotate out of PB Khiam and travel to Tyre was so fraught with danger that it seemed far safer to remain on Khiam, where at least there was a bunker to shelter in. I had managed to survive this long. But at the same time I yearned to get to Tyre, to ensure Clent was safe and to help get him out of Lebanon.

I had run out of clean uniforms on day one of the war and, since I had spent twelve days on duty, an extra five days at the base on top of the seven-day patrol I had just completed, I was also now starting to get low on the medication that had been prescribed by the Syrian doctor for my abdominal condition. I had brought additional medication with me to cover seventeen consecutive days but, like the UN, I had never imagined I would need more than an extra ten days' worth of treatment, so I too had been caught out by the ferocity of this war. With the nearest UN hospital in Naqoura—a two-hour drive away—running out of medication was an additional concern that I had alerted Lieutenant Colonel Kullberg to.

Sure enough, when the scheduled time for the APCs to arrive ticked around, day six was no different from the others—it was too dangerous and the rotation was once again cancelled, to be rescheduled for the next morning.

I should have been back in Tyre five days earlier and our plane tickets to Egypt and the Red Sea dive holiday had long since lapsed. I tried to call Clent on his mobile phone, to let him know the disappointing news that I would not be in Tyre again tonight, but I couldn't get through to him. The mobile phone network was jammed, giving a constant engaged signal, revealing that Tyre was once more under attack. I again played the anxious waiting game, trying to distract myself and my concern for Clent by conducting an audit of our depleting stores.

Only a short time later, a message from headquarters informed us that the team rotation was now back on and that Hans-Peter had already left Tyre and was moving in a UNIFIL convoy of two APCs. As well as replacing team members, the convoy was also bringing much-needed food and water supplies, and medication for my abdominal condition to PB Khiam. Despite my best attempts to avoid letting myself get too excited, only to be disappointed yet again, I thought this was a great sign. Pat and I hurriedly started packing our gear to be ready for the transfer back to Tyre.

But again, the rotation came up short. An hour after Hans-Peter set out from Tyre, Israeli forces crossed the border and invaded southern Lebanon, pushing a kilometre into foreign territory at one section of the border. There was an enormous battle raging and Hans-Peter's convoy was forced to take shelter at a UNIFIL position called 9–1, about 45 minutes' drive from Khiam. He was stuck just over halfway. The team rotation was cancelled again.

I was devastated. I had just finished mentally preparing myself for navigating the dangerous drive into Tyre; I was also full of hope of seeing Clent. I summoned all my mental strength to push those feelings aside and refocus on the issues at PB Khiam, because I would be staying put for another night and hostilities in our region had now intensified. In some ways I was relieved to be staying within the relative safety of the walls of a clearly marked UN base, given how treacherous any movement on the roads would be, now that Israeli ground forces had invaded. If it hadn't been for Clent being stranded in Tyre and that I was running low on medication, I would have been somewhat reluctant to leave the base. I knew that travelling on the roads was extremely risky.

Just when I had accepted that I would spend another night on Khiam, the convoy with Hans-Peter onboard unexpectedly started rolling again to complete the transfer. Pat and I once more hurried to get ready, realising that it would be a very 'hot' (quick) handover with Hans-Peter. Israeli fighter jets were pounding our region with rockets and bombs. We would not want to spend any time dilly-dallying around at the front gates of our base, transferring equipment and personnel while shells were flying in such close proximity. The transfer needed to be swift and efficient, to reduce the risk of injury.

Wolf was very worried about my safety during the transit to Tyre. The stakes had increased dramatically since Israel had commenced its invasion. He repeatedly asked me if I was sure I wanted to travel, given the risk; he even urged me to stay at PB Khiam.

I was torn. Wolf was right—it was safer to stay at PB Khiam, but I couldn't escape the fact that I was low on medication; I didn't want to suffer another abdominal pain attack and become a burden to my team-mates, who would have to treat me as best as they could without the necessary medication or skills. My team-mates already had their hands full monitoring the war; the last thing they needed was the additional stress of a medical emergency. Despite my reservations about my safety during the transit, in the end I had been ordered to move back to Tyre and I was required to follow that directive, albeit taking my chances on the road.

About an hour later, we could see the two armoured vehicles as they started to weave their way through the narrow streets of El Khiam. Israeli fighter jets had been swooping above us incessantly for the last hour, dropping precision 'smart bombs' on Hezbollah targets all through our area. The definitive whirring sound of an aerial bomb perforated my ears as it exploded in the town of El Khiam; while I could not see the actual impact, it had hit just in front of the leading UN armoured vehicle carrying Hans-Peter. He later explained that the vehicle lurched into the air with the blast, and smashed down on the opposite side of the road. Miraculously, all inside were unharmed and the driver pressed on. Both vehicles arrived at the main gate of PB Khiam a few minutes later.

I rushed to the convoy and found Hans-Peter visibly shaken and in shock. The near miss certainly wasn't inspiring me to swap with him! Despite his distressed state, he directed me to sit at the front of the lead vehicle, as commander of the convoy, since I was the most senior UNMO in the crew. He explained that the vehicle crew was being led by a corporal who didn't know the way, so I would be required to navigate and report our position every ten minutes to headquarters.

Our handover was suddenly interrupted by a high-pitched shrieking noise, like a banshee scream—it was the sound of another inbound 1000-pound aerial bomb. My eyes moved from Hans-Peter to frantically search for cover, but there was nothing substantial around. In what seemed like slow motion, and in a dazed trance, I stupidly wandered in a circle, as if I had plenty of time to make a decision (this was time I didn't have and I still discovered no shelter). Opting at last for the armoured vehicle itself, I slammed myself hard against its front tyre, in the sheer hope that the bomb would impact on the other side.

Kaboom! Another massive explosion! The bomb detonated a mere 300 metres or so away—thankfully, on the other side of the vehicle to me. Debris pierced the air around us. Astonishingly, not one of the dozen UN soldiers who were taking cover near the vehicles was injured. Dodging 1000-pound bombs was starting to become an unhealthy habit for us!

I wanted to get on the road immediately but, in the anarchy of the moment, Pat had misplaced his helmet. While he searched, dashing back into the accommodation hut, I said a final and difficult farewell to Wolf, Big Mack and Du.

Wolf, in a more serious mood than his customarily magnetic self, sternly instructed me: 'Take care, kiddo, and, for God's sake, stay safe.'

Trying to lighten the mood, I replied: 'Don't worry about me—I'll be fine, and I promise to have a cold beer ready for you and the guys when you get into Tyre too in a few days' time.' I also made the same promise of cold beers for a reward on their safe return to Big Mack, knowing how much it would appeal to both men.

I asked Wolf to hold off reporting the latest two aerial bomb near misses to headquarters until my convoy was well on its way, because I didn't want us to be ordered to hold at PB Khiam. If that had happened, we would have had the same situation as on day three—an overcrowding of 21 people on the base, draining the limited stores and supplies.

As I prepared to get on my way at last, my team-mates' faces said it all—a look of dread, extremely fearful at the prospect of my making the journey. And, though it went unsaid, there was a sense that our tight-knit team, which had worked so effectively together, was now disbanding, and changing those dynamics and routines that had kept each of us safe. They hugged me tightly. They hugged me as though this was our last goodbye.

Then I clambered into the lead vehicle with a nonchalant 'Don't worry, she'll be right; we'll make it through to Tyre' over the drone of the supercharged engine. I'm not sure whom I was trying to convince, but my words did little to ease the concerns of my anxious team-mates remaining at Khiam.

·

I was now in charge of two armoured vehicle crews and a group of armed Ghanaian and Indian infantry soldiers providing protection for the convoy. There were sixteen of us in total in the two vehicles. This next two hours would no doubt be the toughest test of my military career. Navigating a convoy of armoured vehicles through southern Lebanon during a war was a big ask, and I hoped I had the skills and experience equal to the challenge.

I had little time to ponder this situation, which was outside of anything I had ever anticipated. I was a logistics officer whose specialist skills were in amphibious operations and beach landings; I was now in the middle of a war-torn furore and certainly out of my comfort zone.

I was surprised to find that there was no GPS in the UNIFIL armoured vehicles. I had stopped carrying the personal GPS that Clent had bought for me when I was serving in Syria because our UNTSO vehicles in Lebanon did have GPS fitted. I would again be completely reliant on a less than adequate UN-issued map. As in Syria, these maps lacked too much significant detail to be of real use. Still, I had to make the best of it, because it was all I had; I knew that my exact location at every moment was critical and punishment for any error could be fatal.

At handover, Hans-Peter had also alerted me to the issue of communications. The radio system in the UNIFIL armoured vehicles we were now travelling in could not communicate with our UNTSO mission radios—they were programmed on different frequencies. I was expected to report in to my OGL headquarters in Naqoura every ten minutes during this two-hour transit. But, to do that, I could only use my mobile walkie-talkie radio, which had limited range. Beyond that, the only other option was my personal Lebanese mobile phone, but this was very unreliable, due to the lack of mobile coverage in southern Lebanon and the Israeli use of jamming devices during the invasion. *You have to be kidding me!* I thought. How could we, the UN force, be totally reliant on bloody mobile phones and walkie-talkies in the middle of a war? This was amateur hour and completely crazy.

I was fortunate that at least I still had some credit left on my mobile. In Lebanon, phones operate with a pre-paid card-charge service—you purchase a mobile phonecard from a provider store and then enter its code into your mobile for credit to make calls. Soon after the war began, I had started to run very low on phone credits and, because we were on code red, I was unable to get to a shop to purchase a new card to top up my credit. We had also been told by Eddie, our interpreter, that there was a shortage of phonecards in southern Lebanon because everyone in the south had been making calls since the war started. At that time, it had taken some thinking outside the box for me to be able to recharge my credit.

I had previously accompanied Lyndall Sachs, the Australian ambassador in Beirut and an incredibly accomplished and charismatic woman, at formal events and had even escorted her on a tour of the Israeli border region. Because I had got on well with her and the embassy staff, I had felt able to phone her office on the fifth day of the war, requesting that her staff purchase four phonecards in Beirut (one for each of the Australian UNMOs working in Lebanon) and then text through to me the recharge numbers that we could use for our phones. Had I not done this, I wouldn't have had any credit on my phone to communicate with my headquarters during the drive to Tyre. These communication problems should have been resolved at a higher level, but the OGL headquarters was struggling to pull lots of issues together on the fly, so we solved whatever problems we could ourselves to reduce their workload.

Wired on adrenaline and in charge of a group of Indian and Ghanaian soldiers, I got the convoy rolling and headed towards Tyre. My heart was thumping and I was urging myself on: *Come on—do a good job, Matti!*

So many elements were running through my head. The myriad of eventualities we might face during the two-hour journey ahead swirled in my thoughts. I would need to make decisions quickly and to have contingency plans at all times, in case my first option fell through. I also knew I would need to keep focused, to make the right decisions at the right time to keep this convoy and the sixteen lives in it out of harm's way. The thought of getting the convoy safely to its destination in Tyre and to ensure Clent was evacuated out of the country and out of danger gave me inspiration and spurred me on.

13 A Treacherous Journey

Just out of PB Khiam's gate, we drove past the remains of the bombed Hezbollah position, 75 metres from our base. For the first time, the full impact and blast effect from those lethal 1000-pound aerial bombs became clear to me. The building and its fortifications were completely destroyed. Debris and shrapnel littered the road and were scattered down the hill. I asked myself again how it was possible that we could have survived that near miss on the very first day of the conflict. It was clear that if the Israeli fighter jet had come in from any other angle, the blast would have ripped into our patrol base. Had that occurred, all of us on the observation platform would almost certainly have been killed there and then. I wondered how many of my nine lives I had left for this trip to Tyre.

I was sitting near the front of the leading armoured vehicle, side-on at 90 degrees to the windscreen. My seat was a hard, unpadded wooden bench, making for a very rough and uncomfortable ride in the six-wheeled beast. Just in front of me and slightly to my right were two padded leather seats, side by side, for the driver and the vehicle commander. I don't think it was normal for a passenger to sit where I was; usually the vehicle commander

Matti inside UN armoured personnel carrier during transit, Lebanon War 2006.
http://www.youtube.com/matinajewell

would be doing the navigation but, because the UNIFIL crew did not know the way, I had been directed to sit here so that I could guide the Ghanaian driver, who was a metre or so to my right. The Indian corporal, who was the vehicle commander, was standing on his seat, also just off to the right from me, observing with his head out the turret of the vehicle. I could reach forward and tap his leg if I needed his attention.

The wooden bench seat that I was sitting on ran all the way back to my left, through to the troop-carrying area and the back doors of the vehicle. A few metres away from me on my bench seat were five smiling, turban-clad Indian soldiers. There were no windows in their section so they couldn't see what was happening outside. My team-mate Pat was travelling with five more Indian soldiers in the rear compartment of the second vehicle; as a consequence, I was not in communication with him; nor did I have the opportunity to discuss decisions with him.

I was telling the Ghanaian driver which roads to take. His brilliant-white gleaming smile and subtle sense of humour was in stark contrast to the all-enveloping gloom that hung heavy over the war zone and infused everything with the stench of smoke. There were no seat belts or harnesses in these UN vehicles because APCs are typically used in combat situations; the theory is that seat belts slow the exit of infantry going into battle. However, in this particular situation the APCs were being used to transport UN observers. The absence of seat belts made for a very uncomfortable trip as armoured vehicles aren't renowned for their suspension and the driver often needed to swerve and veer around bomb debris strewn across the roads. Despite every attempt I made to brace myself with my hands and feet, I was almost invariably thrown from side to side with each swerve.

I was squashed between the wall and the cumbersome, diesel-stained grumbling engine-block of the vehicle, which divided the rear troop-carrying area from the front command area. The engine was so loud that it was almost impossible to hear anything through my mobile phone or radio. I was forced to yell into the receiver. I broke down the information into short sentences, hoping that the guys in the OGL headquarters could hear enough of what I was saying to piece together our location during each report. I couldn't help but be frustrated at the inadequate UN communications equipment and the consequences of this oversight for us during our hazardous transit.

As we entered the town of El Khiam, I could see that it had sustained significant damage from Israeli bombing. Many houses were completely destroyed and I tried to stop myself from thinking about the loss of life that had undoubtedly occurred. A lot of the roads had been destroyed by aerial bombs, leaving enormous craters that made them utterly impassable. On several occasions, we needed to backtrack and find an alternative route, but this was easier said than done in our large APCs, which were slow and difficult to turn around. It became a priority for me to ensure that the UN was informed about each and every road we encountered that was blocked or destroyed, to prevent further UN convoys being sent down them. Every second that was spent on these roads was another second in which lives were on the line. In the back of my mind I felt like I was gathering this information to ensure Big Mack, Du, Wolf and Hans-Peter had a safe passage in the coming days when they too were replaced at PB Khiam.

We were making reasonable progress, given the number of times we had to find alternative routes. An hour into the drive, near the town of Al Qusayr, we began descending a steep hill known affectionately to UN observers as Pinky Hill, because civilians walking up its sharp incline would usually have bright pink faces.

I was checking the area for any signs of danger, when I suddenly noticed two Hezbollah soldiers on the road some 400 metres in front of our convoy. They positioned themselves, and then, without warning, fired a Katyusha rocket from a base plate in our direction. I watched, my mouth agape in disbelief, as it hurtled directly towards us. The rocket was spiralling through the air, straight towards the windscreen of our vehicle. The Indian corporal, who was observing from the roof through the turret beside me, scrambled back inside the vehicle, slamming the hatch in one motion behind him. *Oh my God, this is it!* I closed my eyes and, as I braced for the impact, I caught myself whispering, 'Goodbye Clent.'

A moment that felt like an eternity passed. Nothing. Whether intentionally or not, the rocket cleared our vehicle by mere metres and sailed on into Israel.

The corporal, who, aside from Pat and me, held the next highest rank in the convoy, peered at me in sheer bewilderment. His tanned complexion, weathered through the recent summer, had now turned very pale and pasty in colour as the incident started to register in his mind. He went into shock. I gave him a reassuring smile and wondered how long these near misses and our phenomenal run of luck could continue. Long enough to get us to Tyre unscathed, I hoped.

The driver planted his foot hard on the accelerator and we headed at top speed down the hill towards the two Hezbollah fighters. As we approached, they scurried off into the thick foliage that surrounded the creek beside the road, discarding the Katyusha launching frame, which was still positioned in the middle of the road. Was Hezbollah now actively targeting UN vehicles?

It was an anxious moment as we waited to see what Hezbollah's intentions were, but thankfully we did not see their fighters again. This episode gave further urgency to our objective to get out of the area as quickly as possible.

A short distance further on, we reached the junction of two roads simply identified by the UN as the northern and the southern roads. My first instinct was to anticipate retaliatory fire from Israel to the Hezbollah provocation that narrowly missed us, so I directed the convoy to divert from our planned route and head to the nearby UNIFIL position 9–1, where Hans-Peter had taken shelter earlier that afternoon. Coincidently, and just shortly after this, the UNIFIL force passed a radio message for us to take shelter at the compound.

I elected to take the southern road because it followed the terrain of the steep *wadi* with high cliffs on both sides of the road. These cliffs would provide good protection from shrapnel if we needed it; only a hit from directly overhead could take us out. The decision to divert to 9–1 proved to be a good one, as an artillery bombardment commenced all the way along the border including our planned route to Tyre, shortly afterwards.

After that type of provocation from Hezbollah, the Israelis would employ their pre-emptive artillery fire plan, which involved hitting designated targets randomly; then jets would swoop in and bomb the area where the rocket signature had registered.

Intermittent periods of fire from Israel continued well into the evening and, as a result, our convoy had to remain at 9–1 overnight. I was relieved to be within the relative safety of a UN base, and thankful we were not still out on the road attempting to get to Tyre in the dark. But at the same time, I had a pang of disappointment. We had only made half of the high-risk journey and I had wanted to keep the convoy moving while we had momentum, to get the dangerous drive over and done with. I dreaded the phone call to Clent to tell him that, although I had left PB Khiam, I would not be in Tyre that night, as we were stranded halfway.

On the positive side, there was plenty of food and water at 9–1. Between barrages of fire, I took one of the most appreciated showers I've ever had and even washed my long hair, which had become matted with sweat, dust and smoke. With the need to conserve water on PB Khiam, it was the first time I had showered since the war started, a week ago. The water ran black with dirt as the olive oil soap lifted a week's worth of perspiration and grime that had seeped deep into the pores of my skin. It was absolute bliss to feel the cool water wash over my body—a simple pleasure I don't take for granted any more.

Since running out of clean uniforms on day one, I had been rotating my dirty uniforms. This was an attempt to boost my morale—I was at least putting on a different desert camouflage uniform each day, even if it was already filthy. As I again pulled my sweat-drenched, grimy uniform back on, it seemed to smell so much worse now because I was clean.

Clent called during the evening to tell me that the UN families had been ordered to move into the rear-duty headquarters, and he had been asked to go with all the off-duty UNMOs and their families to The Rest House Resort on the southern side of town. Israel had notified the UN of its intention to heavily bomb Tyre the next day, so UN headquarters had directed all UN personnel and their families in Tyre to gather at the resort, ready for evacuation. Israel was then told that all UN personnel and families were assembled there, so it could hit Hezbollah targets throughout the town without inadvertently killing UN personnel.

Soon after, my headquarters phoned and directed that we would complete the last hour of the transit to Tyre very early the following morning, in an attempt to get into town before the bombing started. It was just my luck that Israel was preparing to bombard Tyre on the very day that I would be trying to reach it. Exhausted, I drifted off to sleep, praying to any god that was listening to give me the strength and courage to bring my convoy safely into Tyre in the morning.

Several near misses from Israeli bombs broke another night of desperately needed sleep. The UNIFIL bunker was quite a distance from where I was actually accommodated and I wished I was back at PB Khiam with my team-mates. Beyond the close bond that had formed between us, we were a slick team, with unqualified confidence in each other and always having each other's back. Here, despite the well-intentioned and wonderful hospitality of my Indian hosts, I felt alone.

As morning broke, I nervously waited for the go-ahead to move to Tyre. We were ready to roll when the local UNIFIL commander informed us to 'stand down'. Israel was about to bomb a section of the route we planned to take. The UN would not approve any movement on the roads in the absence of Israel's assurance that they would not bomb the designated route during our transit.

Then the Israeli Defence Force, via UN liaison officers, gave the UN another window of opportunity for our convoy to move to Tyre, agreeing to hold fire during the time we were scheduled to be on nominated roads. I should have been reassured by this; however, from my experience during the first week of the war, I knew that Israel did not always keep their end of such deals and that in the past our convoys had narrowly survived near misses despite having these approved windows of opportunity to move. I would have liked to think Israel had had their reasons for doing this, but I found it hard to rationalise, having only just survived so many near misses myself.

During the war, communications between the two UN forces, the armed UNIFIL and my unarmed UNTSO, appeared to be intermittent at best. UNIFIL was now in charge of my convoy's 'go or no go' decision. After several frustrating hours of getting in and out of the vehicles—each time mentally and physically preparing ourselves for the journey ahead, then to be stood down because Israel had recommenced bombing the area—we finally got the green light from headquarters and were back on the road. One hour to go, and we should be in Tyre.

Pat was again travelling in the rear of the second vehicle while a lieutenant from India replaced the corporal crew commander from the previous day. The lieutenant showed no interest in taking charge of navigation, leaving me to decide which road networks to try during our final dash. He was riding in the lead vehicle with me, observing from the vehicle's turret. I could only assume that UNIFIL's decision to replace the corporal with a higher ranked soldier in the vehicle was due to the higher level of risk associated with the day's drive to Tyre. I wasn't filled with confidence and my anxiety had reached a peak, more than at any previous time in my life; I needed to push these feelings aside and appear calm and confident in front of the soldiers. A panicked officer is definitely not good for morale. To cap it off, the well-meaning UNIFIL commander at 9–1 left me in no doubt that it was going to be a perilous journey by repeatedly wishing us a safe transit.

The drive was even more precarious than I had imagined. There was so much destruction and blast damage in virtually every town and village we passed through. It was one horrific scene after another. Smouldering shells of buildings, wrenched open as if they were coconut husks; mangled bodies—some old, some young and some indistinguishable. The devastation was widespread all along the border.

One particular village had sustained such heavy bombing that it appeared that every single building was damaged or destroyed. The power lines had been knocked down and were dangling across the road, preventing our passage. Our convoy screeched to a halt. We did not know if the lines were still 'live', and the Indian lieutenant ordered several of his soldiers out of our vehicle to hold them up, to allow our two APCs to pass underneath.

These courageous soldiers searched through the rubble of bombed houses for pieces of debris to use to hold up the power lines. It was a surreal image to see soldiers standing on tippy-toes, holding pieces of ruptured plastic water piping and raising the power lines as best they could. Despite their efforts, the metal lines scraped along the length of the roof of the vehicles, which was a little unnerving!

The Lebanese people who had survived in these destroyed towns were incredibly shaken and desperate. As we travelled through their towns, some would wave their arms frantically and motion to us, in what appeared to me as a plea for us to stop and help them. I imagined they were hoping we would take them with us to safety. I truly wanted to help them all, but I couldn't. UN policy

UN armoured personnel carriers delayed by downed power lines and blast debris, Lebanon War 2006.
http://www.youtube.com/matinajewell

forbade the transport of civilians without prior approval and, more importantly, it was just impossible to do so as we did not have any room in the vehicles for extra passengers.

I was consumed by emotion, and an overwhelming sense of guilt and helplessness at leaving them all behind. Never before had I felt so inadequate. The despair, pain and anguish in the eyes of the Lebanese people were etched into my memory. They will stay with me forever.

Israeli aerial bombs had targeted the road networks and created huge craters, often more than 2 metres deep and about 10 metres wide, rendering the roads in most cases impassible. That made it incredibly hard to find a viable road that would get us to Tyre. I spent an hour or more redirecting the convoy, checking every single road north and south of the main road, which was identified by the UN as the 'echo southern road', in a futile attempt to find a way through. This echo southern road was the agreed road I was to use, but it had been bombed and destroyed.

The roads we were now travelling hadn't been used by the UN before and some weren't even marked on the map, making it extremely difficult to navigate. Reluctantly, we were forced to turn around and backtrack to an area we had passed at least 50 minutes earlier and try a much more northerly approach to Tyre. I had never travelled on these northern roads before, and I was navigating by consulting a map that lacked significant detail and by comparing it to the terrain I could see around me. Given the inaccuracy of the map, I gravely feared getting lost.

The window of allocated time for our transit had already closed and pressure mounted with each passing minute. I knew I had to find a viable road and find it fast, though the nervous energy coursing through my veins was not helping. I did not hold much hope that Israel would delay their bombardment of Tyre and the roads surrounding the town just because two UN vehicles were still en route through the area. I was thankful for the military training and skills the Australian Army had equipped me with, which helped me channel the adrenaline and focus rather than panic.

I was now on the very last road marked on my map, our last chance to get through to Tyre using this northern approach. I felt completely gutted when I saw that it too was blocked—an Israeli bomb had gouged a huge crater through the centre of it. We were now in a dire predicament.

I punched my fist into my map and exclaimed, 'Geez, you've got to be fucking kidding me—not this road too!' I was frightened by the realisation that we had been on the road far longer than planned and were outside our agreed window for travel with Israel. It was tormenting—we were so close to our destination and I could even see some of Tyre's buildings, but I just could not find a way to get there.

Reassessing my options, I struggled to suppress my anxiety. I expected bombs to start exploding around us at any moment. But, just as I started to give up hope of getting into Tyre and was preparing to go all the way back to the UN position 9–1, two Lebanese police officers approached our convoy. They had come from the gendarmerie barracks that was adjacent to the bomb crater. One of them headed towards the Indian lieutenant, who had alighted from our vehicle to take a closer look at the crater, in the hope that we might somehow be able to negotiate it. The other police officer came up to my vehicle door. He spoke with me and, between my poor Arabic and his broken English, I explained our situation and he in turn gave me directions to a dirt road not marked on my UN map. I was again thankful for my training—it seemed that those few tough months learning to speak a bit of Arabic might just have saved us, by providing me with another option into Tyre. *Al humduliah wa Yasser!* ('Thank God and Yasser'—my Arabic language teacher!)

The policeman explained the dirt road cut through a banana plantation and eventually joined another dirt road that ran parallel to the southern bank of the Litani River. Neither of these roads were marked on my UN map, so I would never have known about them; and, even if they had been marked, I would not normally have considered taking them, due to the landmine threat in southern Lebanon. Going off road was forbidden. But with the assurance from the policeman that they were safe and the imminence of the Israeli bombardment, scheduled to commence at any moment, we didn't have many options. The Indian lieutenant returned to our vehicle; while investigating the bomb crater, he had received the same advice about the dirt road from the second policeman and he too was keen to try it. The lieutenant then radioed his UNIFIL headquarters and, with their approval, we decided to risk taking the road.

We made quick progress through the banana plantation and were soon on the narrow single-lane dirt road that ran along the Litani River. The size of our bulky armoured vehicles and the narrowness of the road made for slow going as the land dropped sharply away from the edge of the road, down to the river 10 metres below. On the other side of the road was a steep embankment, so we were forced to drive with our wheels ever so close to the edge of the drop into the river. We inched our way closer towards the Mediterranean Sea, where I hoped we would reunite with the main highway that would take us to Tyre.

Suddenly, we came to a grinding halt. Four civilian vehicles were approaching from the opposite direction and it was impossible for them to pass us on this narrow piece of road. Their front vehicle stopped nose to nose with our convoy. Although this created a new problem, I was actually relieved because the sight of oncoming vehicles gave me a sense of confidence that the remainder of this road must still be open and would hopefully allow us to get into Tyre. I had not seen many vehicles on the road since the war started and these were the first we had encountered since leaving PB Khiam. The occupants were agitated and clearly distressed. They had white 'surrender' flags displayed from each overloaded car.

Just as I was preparing to get out of my vehicle to speak with the driver of the first car, I received a phone call from my OGL headquarters, notifying me that Israel was commencing aerial bombardment and we were in the target area. The radio operator passed on the order for me to turn my convoy around and return to the UNIFIL position 9–1—the position that we had left several hours earlier. I tried to explain that it was physically impossible to execute a U-turn to do this, due to the size of our APCs and the narrowness of the road, not to mention that we had just become stuck in a traffic jam! The headquarters operator was not a native English speaker, so I was having great difficulty trying to explain our predicament—the geographical impediment and the fact that we were on a road not marked on the UN map. Clearly frustrated at his end too, the operator passed the phone over to someone else. Unexpectedly, a familiar Australian accent came on the line—it was Amanda. She had moved from Tyre down to Naqoura and was now in the headquarters. I was flooded with relief to hear her voice.

Amanda was an outstanding army officer—competent, thorough and decisive. I knew that, in conjunction with the chief of OGL, she would be taking charge and making things happen. I explained the situation to her: that we simply could not turn around and it was too dangerous to attempt reversing backwards several kilometres along the meandering road, dangerously close to the drop into the river. Once we overcame the problem with the civilian vehicles blocking the route, I felt I had no option other than to continue driving forward along the road to where I envisaged it would join the highway adjacent to the Mediterranean Sea. Only when we reached this junction, several kilometres away, would we have enough room to do a U-turn.

Amanda understood the situation and agreed I had no alternative. She assured me that she would contact UNIFIL command to determine what actions I should take once we reached the road junction—whether to turn around or to make a dash for Tyre. She also explained that the UN could not hold off the Israeli aerial attack any longer and that we were in grave danger. Worse still, the very road we were travelling on was a designated target.

Amanda was professional, but I could hear the concern in her voice. She said: 'Matti, you have to do something and get yourself out of there.' I later found out that she was so alarmed about our situation that she called our Australian commander in Jerusalem and apprised him of my predicament and her concern for my safety.

While I had been talking to Amanda, the Indian lieutenant had dismounted from the vehicle and successfully managed to convince the terrified Lebanese civilians that they needed to reverse back several hundred metres to an area where we might be able to pass them. This was an incredible feat in itself, as they were not interested in backtracking over one inch of the ground they had already covered. They simply wanted to continue their dangerous journey to the relative safety of the north as quickly as they could.

It was an anxious few minutes as we tried to squeeze the armoured vehicles past them. At times we had half a wheel off the road, hanging precariously over the sheer drop to the river below. I couldn't bear to watch but, at the same time, I couldn't bear to close my eyes and not see what was happening. Thankfully, I was distracted by my mobile phone vibrating in my pocket.

It was Clent. Through extremely broken reception, I told him that my convoy was held up and having difficulty proceeding. I was unsure if he could hear my explanation over the engine noise, the static radio transmission and the dodgy phone reception, but I tried to simplify the situation and strobe the information by shouting, 'CONVOY BOXED IN! DIFFICULT TO MOVE BACK OR FORWARD!' Then the phone dropped out.

I tried to call him back repeatedly over the next few minutes, but with no result. Israel had started jamming the phone system—bombing was about to recommence in earnest.

Negative thoughts washed over me like a tidal wave and into every corner of my mind, making me feel sick to my stomach. It seemed that this was the moment I had dreaded since my premonition in the bunker at PB Khiam. I wished I had the opportunity to tell Clent that I loved him, just one more time. But my phone was dead.

14 A Life-changing Moment

Every moment felt like an eternity. Finally we managed to edge past the civilian vehicles and we were on our way again. Word came through via radio confirming that UNIFIL had overruled the order from UNTSO headquarters that we should return to 9–1; instead, we were given convoy clearance to make a high-speed sprint to Tyre despite the imminent Israeli aerial raid. Since it was impossible for us to reach the safety of UNIFIL position 9–1 before the inbound air strikes began, I agreed that our best chance of survival was to make this last-minute dash.

We were on the main road approaching Tyre from the north, travelling as fast as we could. I could see the Mediterranean Sea glistening through the window of the right-hand side of my vehicle—it was a reassuring sign that we were heading in the right direction. There were copious amounts of blast damage and debris strewn across the road and we had to dodge them and weave our way through. Several civilian cars were also using this main road and frustratingly they would dart and turn in front of us without warning. These drivers were panicked and just wanted to get to their destination as fast as possible, without consideration for what else was on the road. Their driving was even more erratic than usual.

I estimated now that, by the most direct route, we should be only fifteen minutes from our destination, The Rest House Resort. However, given the amount of bombing Tyre had sustained over the past week, it was likely that many roads were cut and I had planned several back-up routes to get the convoy successfully through the city. I predicted that it would actually take us far longer than fifteen minutes to get there. We were so close, surely it would be unfair to have reached this point only to be hit by an aerial bomb now? I prayed that Israel would hold off its attack just a few more minutes—the time I needed to get my convoy to the other side of town in one piece.

Then, on the outskirts of Tyre, my life was turned upside down. A civilian vehicle, while attempting to avoid a crater and debris from an Israeli aerial bomb, cut in front of our convoy. At that time I was briefing headquarters on my mobile phone and I did not anticipate the evasive manoeuvring we were about to undertake. The driver hit the brakes hard, to avoid crashing into the car. I didn't have time to brace myself and, since there were no grip handles or seat-belt restraints, I was catapulted forward into the right-hand side of the bullet-proof windscreen.

I smashed into the windscreen with brutal force. On impact, I winced and cried out 'Aarrrggggh!' There was a sickening thud as my limp body hit the hard surface. Predictably, I came off second best.

The pain was instant and intense. I had hit the junction of the windscreen and the vehicle door with the right side of my body. My neck and right shoulder had taken the full brunt of the impact and my back had whiplashed around the solid Kevlar plates in my flak jacket body armour. I thought I was going to vomit from the acute pain that shot down my spine.

I struggled to pick myself up off the floor of the vehicle and repositioned myself tenderly back on the wooden bench seat. My entire body seemed to be hurting. I collected my mobile phone, which had flown out of my hand during the incident—surprisingly,

Matti being thrown into the bullet-proof windscreen of the armoured vehicle, Lebanon War 2006.
http://www.youtube.com/matinajewell

it was still working and the UN headquarters staffer was holding on the line. I hastily explained that I had just been thrown into the windscreen but was okay, and that my bigger concern was that the UN had personnel at the gates of the Rest House ready to receive us, because I did not want to spend any time waiting outside if the aerial bombardment had started.

The Ghanaian driver and Indian lieutenant looked at me with concern and asked if I was okay. Despite my excruciating pain, we needed to keep moving. We were so close now. As with any of the knocks I had received previously on the sporting field, I expected I would be sore for a while, but I hoped the pain of the initial impact would ease to a badly bruised throb over time. The adrenaline from the impact took care of the pain for the moment and I was able to remain focused on getting the convoy through the last few kilometres to the southern side of Tyre.

We continued at speed towards the Rest House in Tyre and, surprisingly, the road network I had selected was still passable, so we made good time. The UN had cordoned off the area surrounding the resort with armed UNIFIL soldiers, in an attempt to prevent Hezbollah forces from firing their rockets from close proximity. A wave of emotion swept over me at the mere sight of the resort: I was so relieved to see the UN compound. Our convoy had been through a lot together over the past two days but we had made it.

Despite my back pain, and spurred on by the knowledge that fighter jets would be bombing the area at any moment, I got out of the armoured vehicle without assistance. I had to push through a bank of journalists, some of whom were snapping photos. It seemed absurd that they were there and wanting an interview, when all I wanted was to get to safety. I declined to give a comment and struggled down the path to the UN rear-duty room on the beach side of the Rest House building, wearing my Kevlar body armour and carrying my equipment sack.

When I turned the corner of the building, which was located right on the sandy beachfront, I saw Clent. He was staring at me in complete and utter disbelief. He rushed over to embrace me as the realisation began to sink in that we were both alive and back together. I'll never forget seeing his face and falling into his arms that first time after being separated. Clent's eyes welled with tears of joy. We both choked back the intense emotions that we were feeling; we hugged each other tightly, not wanting to let go.

From the roof top of the resort Clent had witnessed Israeli jets bombing in the direction I had just come from and he had become convinced I wouldn't make it to the Rest House alive. Now that I was standing before him, he simply could not believe his eyes and became immobilised by shock, not comprehending that I had somehow survived the aerial assault.

His trance-like state was overtaken by positive emotions, mixed in with confusion, relief and exhaustion. I snapped him back to reality, and asked, 'Any chance of a hand with my gear? It's really heavy and I've hurt my back.' He grabbed two armloads of gear while I immediately set about briefing the UN command chain on the situation in Tyre, the countryside of southern Lebanon and the roads we had travelled on over the last two days.

I was desperate to ensure we didn't risk the lives of any more UNMOs during future team rotations and resupply runs, by sending them down roads that I could confirm were destroyed and impassable. Every second spent on the road in Lebanon substantially increased the risk of being injured or killed. I explained to the UNMOs still waiting to relieve team-mates on patrol bases along the border that it was a bumpy and hazardous ride to and from the posts; they diligently marked on their maps the roads that I knew had been destroyed by bombs. I also suggested that helicopters might need to be considered for future rotations of personnel, rather than vehicles, due to the ongoing destruction of the road networks by Israel.

I had copied the video clips of the truce violations that I had taken on my camera from PB Khiam onto the computer system at the base prior to my transit to Tyre. I now made sure a copy of the footage I had recorded en route to Tyre was given to the UN as evidence of the road conditions in southern Lebanon and violations of the peace agreement. The Indian lieutenant had also filmed the transit from 9–1 to Tyre for UNIFIL. I was utterly exhausted, but still managing to find energy from somewhere. I planned to do my duty and then I was determined to make sure Clent got out of Tyre and out of this mess.

Needless to say, there was absolute chaos all around us in the Rest House. The UN was simply not prepared for this type of crisis and was trying to organise an evacuation of the displaced and worried families. There was no bedding or food, and limited water for about 100 UN personnel and their families taking shelter at the resort. The UNMOs had done the best job they could to accommodate people, but they simply did not have the resources required.

•

There was sporadic bombing in Tyre throughout that afternoon, including near misses to the resort from Israeli 1000-pound aerial bombs. The windows shook and debris fell within the resort complex. I was on such an adrenaline high that I ignored the sounds of carnage outside. Now that Clent and I were reunited, I didn't care what happened as I had a bizarre sense of reassurance and relief. I knew he would soon be evacuated and I would continue my duties with the UN in Lebanon until this crisis was over. By the time a ceasefire was achieved—essentially bringing this war to an end—I envisaged my year-long posting with the UN would be complete and we would return home to Australia.

Before I knew it, the day turned to night. My first evening back in Tyre was actually quite surreal. Clent had brought with him to the Rest House a bottle of Moët champagne—he had planned for the two of us to enjoy it while celebrating the end of my time in Lebanon. Although the scene was not quite as he had imagined it, later that night we shared the Moët with some of the off-duty UNMOs and their families.

We didn't have any glasses, so we were taking swigs straight out of the bottle. We passed it around and the mood lightened, if only for a moment, as we savoured the bizarre irony of toasting friendship and good health with French champagne in the middle of a war zone. It was the nicest champagne I had ever tasted, and even better after the hectic week I had endured on PB Khiam and on the road. As memorable and as welcome as the champagne was, however, the entire scene seemed too crazy to be real.

The champagne did little to ease my back pain, which was getting worse by the minute. The intense pain seemed only to ease if I hunched and crumpled forward. It felt like I had very bad bruising deep into the tissue the entire way down the right side of my neck, shoulders and back. I could feel the muscles tightening and stiffening around the vertebrae in my back, going into taut knots. I had learnt, from previous sports injuries, that it was beneficial to keep my body moving and to get the blood flowing to these areas so they didn't cramp up. With help, I gingerly got to my feet to move around.

I took a quick cold shower in the resort's outdoor beach change-room before putting back on my sweaty uniform, as I still had no clean clothes to change into. I knew that my clothes smelt dreadful—with an odd mixture of sweat, diesel, smoke and gunpowder—but there was little I could do about it. Thankfully, everyone else was also a little dirty and personal hygiene was not high on the list of priorities by that point.

I went over and thanked the Ghanaian and Indian soldiers who had made the dangerous trip with me to Tyre. At their request, we posed for a photograph in front of the armoured vehicles that had protected us during the journey; judging from their beaming white smiles, they were delighted to have this memento. I tried to straighten up, but I couldn't and had to remain hunched over for the photo; I wished and hoped that my back pain would ease soon. I needed to soldier on, but the effort to move around seemed to be causing me more harm than good and my condition was clearly deteriorating. I could no longer stand up straight and I felt embarrassed about having to stoop forward to relieve the pain, so I lay down to see if that helped.

We settled down for the night on the tiled floor of the Rest House along with all the other off-duty UNMOs and their wives, kids and visiting friends. Clent and a couple of team-mates created a makeshift bed on the tiled floor, fashioned from a couple of flimsy cushions scavenged from the resort's beach chairs. We positioned ourselves as best we could away from the glass windows, in case they shattered in a bomb blast, and hunkered down behind a couple of small chairs.

It was a disturbing scene, with bombs exploding, children screaming, people crying, limited food and water, no beds or sleeping gear, and the UN caught short under pressure. We waited for news about the evacuation of the UN families and friends. As I shut my eyes, I prayed that Clent and these good families would soon be safe and out of this bedlam.

In the early hours of the following morning, 19 July, I woke after a fitful sleep in absolute agony; I had numb, tingling sensations in my arms and legs, and excruciating pain in my back. It was now clear to me that I had sustained a much more serious injury than I had first thought. I would later learn that I had damaged five vertebrae (three fractured and two 'wedged' vertebrae, meaning they had been crushed on one side) as well as serious nerve and muscle damage.

I was very concerned as I knew that apart from the small hospital at Naqoura—which was staffed by civilian UN workers, most of whom were preparing to evaucate—the UN relied on medical facilities from the host country it was serving in. This meant that the only option for me to obtain medical treatment in Lebanon would be from a local hospital. After a week of intense battle, I had no doubt that the hospitals in southern Lebanon would be crowded with injured and dying people. They would be overwhelmed already, treating their own casualties.

Clent was very worried. Despite the brave face I was trying to put on and my downplaying of my injury, he intuitively knew that I was suffering immensely. I was extremely worried about the numb, tingling sensations I was experiencing down my legs and right arm in particular. I reported my injury to Commandant Rossa Mulcahy, an Irish UNMO who had voluntarily assumed command in the absence of the deputy chief and operations officer. Rossa, a brilliant army officer, who was doing his absolute best in an incredibly bleak and desolate situation, told me that the chief UNIFIL doctor had moved to Tyre and was at the Rest House. He pointed her out to me and said he would arrange for her to assess me.

An hour or more passed by, and I still had not been examined by the doctor. We could see her at the other end of the room—she seemed quite content to chat with her friends rather than examine me to assess and manage my increasing pain. She just didn't seem to comprehend the extent of my injuries or the pain I was experiencing.

As far as I was aware, I was the only UN person at the Rest House who had sustained a severe injury, so it wasn't as if there was a long queue of people vying for her time. Now, I'm not a qualified medical practitioner, but I would have assumed an injured soldier complaining of numb, tingling sensations and severe back pain—after being involved in a vehicle accident—would register as cause for concern for the head UN doctor responsible for UN personnel in that area. Or, at the very least, arouse enough concern to pay a visit to make an assessment. Not so. After Clent had made several gentle approaches, he now pleaded with the doctor to get her attention. Shortly afterwards she sent an assistant medic over to assess me.

By this time I really needed some pain relief. I was still lying on a couple of dilapidated cushions on the hard, tiled floor, now alternating between my left and right side as the pain was intolerable. Surely the UN could do better than this?

Clent was perplexed and again voiced his strong concern for my welfare to the UN doctor, who, somewhat begrudgingly, came over and prescribed some pain relief tablets. However, these seemed more suitable for a slight headache than for serious back pain with tingly nerve sensations. I asked her if I could use the ambulance stretcher that was positioned near the glass doors a few metres away. The stretcher was on wheels, was able to be adjusted into various sitting and lying positions and had a bright orange padded mattress held between two side rails. I thought that this might provide a way of helping me lie flat and straight, rather than on the cushions that continually slipped and moved underneath me on the floor.

The doctor denied my request, saying, 'We might need that stretcher later for other people who might be injured and have to be moved by ambulance.'

'Surely if an emergency situation occurs, we can just move me back onto the floor,' I suggested. 'But, for now, while the stretcher isn't being used, couldn't I lie on it?'

My logic fell on deaf ears and I remained on the cold tiled floor. All I wanted was some good, solid medical support so I could continue doing my job.

I spoke with Brad Smith about my injury, which had rapidly deteriorated overnight, and he passed this information on to Amanda as our national senior in Lebanon, who reported my condition to the Australian commander in Jerusalem. Brad even spoon-fed me a tin of beans from a Hindu ration pack while I lay flat on my back, because it was now too painful for me to sit up. I needed Clent and Brad to help me to the bathroom, as I could no longer stand or walk on my own. Worried about my worsening condition, they worked together to help me as much as they could. Brad was a godsend and his calm reassurance was invaluable.

We reported my deteriorating condition to Commandant Mulcahy. He was very concerned about me, particularly since I could no longer stand or walk without assistance. He was considering moving me to a Lebanese hospital, but reports that Israeli bombs had damaged the hospitals at Saida, just north of Tyre and the UN facility of Naqoura, made us all anxious.

Clent was apprehensive, even though I tried to reassure him that I was not his responsibility. I knew my words were doing little to ease the sense of burden he was feeling. He was remarkably strong—or just a sucker for punishment! I wouldn't have blamed him for running as far away from me as possible after the test he had endured. Ironically, though, this adverse situation was making our relationship closer and stronger than ever.

The media agencies from around the world that were renting rooms at The Rest House Resort had made a continuing story of the UN families 'holed up' there. Included in the group of journalists was an Australian reporter from the *Sydney Morning Herald* who was very persistent in trying to create an Aussie angle from my circumstances. I politely declined his requests and alerted the Australian commander in Jerusalem to the situation via Amanda, who was stationed in the OGL headquarters in Naqoura.

In the Australian Defence Force, soldiers are not permitted to make public comment without higher approval. Operational security, and in particular media comment during military activities, is taken very seriously and tightly controlled; but this was not the case with the UN. Having seen UNMOs conducting media interviews by phone with journalists in their home countries, I was astounded by the lack of media control. It appeared the UN had no procedures established to prevent UNMOs from conducting media interviews and releasing sensitive information during a time of crisis. I assumed this leaking of information by UN staff would not have been received well by the Israeli government either.

Israel informed the UN that its aircraft would be heavily bombing Tyre again the next day. As a result of this news, the UN not only stepped up its intended evacuation of all civilian UN staff and UN families from Lebanon to Cyprus by ferry but also planned to evacuate all UNMOs from Tyre, moving them down to the headquarters in Naqoura. The plan was to completely withdraw all UN personnel from Tyre prior to the Israeli bombing. The evacuation of the UN families to Cyprus was scheduled to take place that evening, but the crew of the civilian ship assigned the task baulked at coming to Tyre while a war was still raging. Apparently, the crew were not initially informed of their destination and were horrified when they ultimately found out that they were heading into a war zone. After securing a guarantee from Israel of safe passage through their naval blockade and no bombing during the transfer of passengers to the ship, the UN rescheduled the ferry evacuation for the following morning.

I told Clent that he must go with the others, but he was adamant that he would not leave me, especially when I was in such a dependent medical state. I was the UN's responsibility, not his, I told him, but he insisted that we were in this together and he wouldn't leave until my medical situation was resolved. I loved him for his bravery and commitment, but I also wanted him out of there, to be safe; his best option was to leave for Cyprus with the UN families and approved refugees in the morning.

I could hear a ruckus outside but, since I was unable to move from the floor without assistance, I couldn't see what was happening. I was later told that local Lebanese people had begun flooding into the Rest House, because they deduced that Israel might avoid bombing near the UN. They were trying to gain the relative safety of the compound and were sheltering along the fence line. These were desperate people in fear for their lives.

My intense back pain was now compounded by a numbness that was radiating not only down my legs but to my hands, particularly my right hand. The tingling sensation down my legs and the excruciating pain in my back were still cause for concern and I began to fear that these injuries might be permanent. I tried to stop my mind from exploring the thought that I might never be able to walk again. I knew that this could no longer be simply deep bruising. The impact on the windscreen had caused some kind of substantial damage and I was now in the frightening situation of being completely and totally reliant on the UN.

At Brad and Clent's insistence, the UN doctor examined me again. This time she was more thorough and suggested I might have fractured one or more vertebrae, but she could not be sure without an X-ray. She reported to the UNIFIL headquarters and also the UN in New York that I needed to be evacuated. This same information was also passed by Commandant Mulcahy to the UNTSO headquarters in Jerusalem. The UN had helicopters in Lebanon, some of which were equipped for medically evauating injured personnel, but I was told that they could not be used for my evacuation due to the danger from aerial bombardment. So it was planned that the following morning I would be moved by road to a local Lebanese hospital.

It was an extremely chaotic situation in Tyre as the UN personnel attempted to protect everyone taking refuge at the Rest House while sorting out a multitude of other problems, my injury being just one of many issues. My condition would have been confusing for the staff in the UN headquarters in Jerusalem, since my vehicle convoy had arrived unscathed in Tyre the day before and I had attempted to push through the pain to continue working. I had experienced a gradual onset of symptoms as the adrenaline wore off during the afternoon and evening. Had I been screaming in pain and debilitated at the time of injury, things would probably have been different. Now that I was incapacitated, there were several people trying to help me, but there did not seem to be one single person or point of contact who was responsible for my welfare, taking charge of the situation and organising proper evacuation arrangements in light of my serious injuries.

As day turned to night on 19 July, I had a strange and over-whelming feeling. It was a sensation that endured—I no longer feared dying. That may sound terribly melodramatic, but it was exactly how I felt. How anyone could feel completely comfortable and at ease with the concept of dying was bizarre to me, but the feeling of enduring love and togetherness that I now felt with Clent was all-consuming. Knowing that he would do absolutely anything for me helped me to convince him that the best thing for me was for him to evacuate and reach safety. I explained that he needed to leave so I could receive medical treatment and then hopefully continue doing my duty as an UNMO during this crisis. Reluctantly, Clent understood and agreed to evacuate to Cyprus.

The UN in Lebanon was making every effort to see that everyone visiting UN personnel—including all friends and family visiting UNMOs who were stuck in Tyre, whether they held a UN identification card or not—were placed on the UN evacuation list. Clent was simply one of a handful of people in this situation and had been put on the list by UN officials organising the evacuation.

Clent was the responsibility of the Australian Embassy—not the UN—so he phoned the Australian ambassador to Lebanon, Lyndall Sachs, for assistance. She summed up the situation quickly and suggested she would call Major General Clive Lilley, the head of UNTSO in Jerusalem.

The ambassador informed Clent that the ferry was actually commandeered by the Australian Embassy, to evacuate Australian foreign nationals, and that he would definitely be permitted to board it in the morning as an approved Australian evacuee. She explained to him that she had agreed to evacuate the UN civilians and families as a favour to the UN, because there would be room on the ship. Clent was still on the Australian list of evacuees. Relieved in the knowledge Clent would reach safety in the morning, I settled down to get some sleep.

15 Nightmare Evacuation

After a night of little sleep, I awoke the following morning in even more pain than the day before, so I was thankful that the plan was for me to be moved to a Lebanese hospital. In the meantime, Clent would be evacuating to Cyprus.

But there'd been a new development. Commandant Mulcahy told me that overnight the UN had decided that the only way for me to receive medical attention safely was to be evacuated with the families to Cyprus. At literally the last moment, I was being added to the list of evacuees authorised to board the MV *Serenade*, which was due to arrive shortly in Tyre harbour. This was a welcome change of plan.

Clent was completely exhausted, not having slept much over the past week. His weariness was alleviated slightly by the news that I would be evacuating with him. Although my wellbeing was not technically his responsibility, I knew he felt like it was up to him to get me out of this chaotic situation. Clent's burden of responsibility was eased somewhat when we were informed that the UN doctor herself was evacuating from Tyre with her two teenaged children. The UN had directed her to escort me to Cyprus, and provide medical care during the transit and at the other end.

An hour later, the time at last came for us to travel to the port. After lying on a couple of cushions on a cold floor for two days, I was now beyond pain—I had tingly sensations in several parts of my body, and all my muscles were cramped and in spasm. The doctor had given me an injection of pethidine, but it had done little to ease the pain. She talked of the need for an X-ray, to confirm her diagnosis of a spinal injury and to guide subsequent treatment, but this could not be done until we got to Cyprus, which was a twenty-hour boat ride away.

The Australian Defence Force has a 'Golden Hour Rule'. This stipulates that any battlefield activity must be supported by a medical evacuation plan that ensures any injured soldiers can be transferred to a hospital with surgical capability within the first critical hour after injury. Research has shown that the chance of survival is dramatically increased if treatment is obtained within the first 60 minutes post-injury. Unfortunately for me, the UN does not operate with this same system; I knew that a rough voyage across the open ocean was a less than ideal means of medical evacuation, so I was incredibly grateful that Clent and the UN doctor would be accompanying me during the move to Cyprus.

The doctor now requested that I move onto the ambulance stretcher. I thought this was a little strange, because she had not fitted me with a neck collar or spinal brace, but I simply assumed that the UN had not supplied this form of medical equipment to its staff. I was keen to get going so, with assistance, I struggled onto the ambulance stretcher. Even slight movement brought on awful stabs of pain. However, I managed a wry smile at the irony that I was now finally using the stretcher that had remained vacant for the past two days.

By this stage I was gravely concerned that I had sustained a permanent injury and was worried about further aggravation from the movements I would undoubtedly experience getting onto the ship and then during the bumpy sea voyage. Hopefully, I was going to a hospital in Cyprus where they could deal with this pain effectively, because it was unlike anything I had ever experienced before.

The UNIFIL sergeant medic secured me on the stretcher with a couple of straps across my chest and legs, pinning my arms down and holding me firmly in place. The sergeant was in charge of taking me by ambulance to the wharf, so he took control of the stretcher and pushed me out to the waiting ambulance. He then made three attempts to shove the stretcher into the back of the vehicle—on each attempt using more and more force as he tried to make its collapsible legs fold and the stretcher glide into the tray of the ambulance. But they wouldn't.

The stretcher was being smashed hard into the back of the ambulance. Each attempt came to a jarring and abrupt halt. The force reverberated through the stretcher and caused me to scream in increasing pain with each blow. I was now crying from the pain; as tears ran down my face, I pleaded to Clent and my UN team-mates nearby to please stop the sergeant. There was obviously some problem, and he was causing me excruciating pain, which was shooting down my spine with every repeated attempt.

Clent was horrified to see me once again in more pain than necessary and appealed to the doctor to intervene. The sergeant was directed to lower the stretcher to ground level by manually folding its legs; with the help of Clent and four men, I was then lifted into the ambulance tray.

Shaking from this ordeal, I was finally secured in the back of the ambulance. Clent was aghast to see that the sergeant's actions had hurt me and apologised, even though none of it was his fault. Clent was then told by the doctor that he was not permitted to travel to the ship in the ambulance with me; he would need to go in another UN vehicle. It gave me comfort to have Clent by my side and I hated the idea of being separated from him during what could be a short but high-risk journey on the roads, through a town that continued to receive shelling; but I was tired and in too much pain to fight the decision. We would reunite at the port in ten minutes.

As the ambulance drove out of the Rest House compound, it suddenly became obvious to me that the stretcher was in back to front. There was an electric fan doing a futile job of cooling my feet in my army boots—where I assumed my head should have been. I now realised that this was probably the reason why the sergeant had been unable to get the legs to fold automatically—they couldn't because the stretcher was around the wrong way. It was also not locked securely into place and so, as we turned each corner, it slid from one side of the tray to the other.

The UN doctor, travelling in the back of the ambulance on a bench seat beside me, tried to steady the stretcher, but she was not strong enough to stop it from slamming from side to side. Through gritted teeth, I pointed out to her that the problem seemed to be that the stretcher was in back to front—I indicated the position of the fan. She agreed, and cursed the incompetence of the sergeant. For the rest of the drive I continued to bash into the wall each time we cornered, causing me to wince in pain.

Mercifully, it was a relatively short trip and we soon arrived at the assembly area for Tyre port, which the Lebanese gendarmerie and UNIFIL infantry soldiers had cordoned off for the evacuation. I thanked God that this ambulance trip was relatively short, because I was already bruised and battered from it and I was not sure I would have survived a longer journey with this ambulance crew.

Having worked out en route that the stretcher was in the ambulance back to front, it dawned on me that the legs would not simply fold down automatically when it was pulled out of the ambulance. Several people would need to lift me out and safely lower me to the ground—the same technique that had been used to get me into the ambulance back at the resort, but in reverse. To my horror, instead of ensuring that the sergeant understood his mistake with the stretcher and did not compound it further by attempting to single-handedly extract me from the vehicle, the UN doctor darted out of the ambulance and headed across to the transit area.

Seconds later, my worst fears were realised as the sergeant medic started to pull the stretcher out of the back of the ambulance on his own. *Surely he's not going to try to do this by himself?* I was looking up into his face, pleading for him to stop because I knew what was going to happen; but I was powerless—strapped to the stretcher and unable to move. My cries of 'STOP! STOP! STOP!' were either not understood or ignored. The stretcher legs did not unfold, and the stretcher and I crashed down from the full height of the ambulance onto the bitumen road.

The pain was unbearable. I was overcome by a wave of nausea and cold sweat; I could taste the bile rising in my throat. I felt like I was going to pass out. Some of my fellow UNMOs, who were busy with other tasks and had just arrived at the port in separate UN vehicles, heard my screams; so too did Clent, who witnessed the entire episode from the other side of the port. They were all now running to my aid.

But the disastrous series of events did not end there. The sergeant medic then, in what I can only assume was an attempt to rectify his mistake, tried to elevate the stretcher to waist height, as it should have been if it had exited from the ambulance correctly and its legs had folded down automatically. But, instead of pressing the button that allowed the stretcher to be raised, he fumbled and pushed the wrong button, which caused the stretcher to bend in the middle and fold forward.

This forced me to be seated in an upright position, while I was still strapped in to the stretcher. The top strap, which had been secured across my chest, had slipped up so it was across my throat and restricting my breathing. When Clent arrived on the scene, I was gasping for air. This folding forward movement was exceptionally painful, as it put pressure on the fractured vertebrae in my lower back.

The UN doctor must have returned by now, because I could hear her telling Clent not to raise his voice at the sergeant. Clent demanded that she take charge of her team. I'm not sure I would have been able to show the same composure and self-restraint as Clent had if our roles had been reversed.

While this exchange of words was taking place, I was choking and sitting crumpled forward in the stretcher. The medical staff appeared to be more concerned about saving face than helping me back into a supine position. Eventually the sergeant removed the strap, allowing me to breathe freely again.

With the stretcher returned to a flat position, the pain in my back was so intense that I wished I had taken my chances with the Lebanese hospitals. I requested that the sergeant remain a safe distance away from me, so that no more 'accidents' could occur to my detriment. Clent was beside himself, apologising for letting me travel on my own. I reassured him that none of this was his fault, but I knew he continued to feel dreadful. I was in very bad shape now; I feared that I would become a paraplegic as a result of the fall from the ambulance. I had a loss of feeling in my arms and legs, while getting an alarming tingling feeling all over my body.

It was a hot summer's day and the sun was fairly blasting off the black bitumen and concrete. I was lying face up on the stretcher baking in the heat, waiting for the ship to arrive which would, hopefully, finally, take us to safety. Time seemed to drag, as if I was on a long-haul flight from England. After I had been in the sun for quite a while, with no sign of the evacuation ship in sight, Clent suggested to the UN doctor that perhaps they should find me some shade or put me back into the ambulance, so I wouldn't get burnt. This time, without the 'assistance' of the sergeant medic, I was loaded back into the ambulance.

Three hours passed before we heard the ship was finally in sight and that preparations were being made to load the evacuees. We were informed that I was to be the first to board the ship and there was a British military medical team awaiting my arrival on board.

Words cannot adequately describe the relief that consumed me when I heard about the British medicos. I then caught my first glimpse of the aging Greek cruise ship that had been contracted by the Australian Embassy and the UN to take us away from Lebanon—it was like a gift from the gods. Despite being a little broken physically, I had somehow survived the most surreal week of my life. I was hoping this nightmare would now finally come to an end. We were off to safety and medical expertise in Cyprus.

The ship was surprisingly large, much bigger than I had imagined. Due to the unknown depth of the Tyre port and the large draught of the ship's hull, the captain of the *Serenade* elected not to come alongside the wharf in the harbour, for fear of running aground. Instead, the ship remained offshore and lowered its anchor. The plan was that evacuees were to be ferried from the wharf to the ship on smaller lifeboats.

Each round trip would take an hour, but the UN had only been given two hours to load the evacuation ship and leave Tyre before the Israeli ceasefire would end. When the UN departed, bombing would recommence at Tyre in earnest. The window of opportunity for the evacuation had virtually expired before the *Serenade* even arrived, because the ship was hours late into harbour.

Compounding this time pressure, loading evacuees 20 to 30 at a time using two small watercraft would take hours to complete, given that we were told there were nearly 1000 evacuees, including 140 UN personnel and family members, waiting at the wharf. There was no way we could possibly load all the evacuees before the ceasefire ended. This realisation was causing great concern among everybody waiting to evacuate—people were anxious to ensure they were in the first few boatloads in case not all would make it on board if hostilities erupted.

As I was passed over the gap between the wharf and the lifeboat, I caught a glimpse of my apartment and felt a sudden pang of sadness that I would never see it again. I remembered that I still had all of my personal effects there and wouldn't be able to go back and collect them. I also realised I'd never have the chance to say goodbye to the staff at La Phoenician restaurant and many of the other wonderful locals who had treated me with such kindness during my stay.

Once on the lifeboat, we then began a very rough ride out to the ship. I was lying on my stretcher on the deck of the boat, surrounded by UN wives and children. This was the first time I had really been exposed to the grief of the UN families, who had just said their teary farewells to their husbands and fathers—my UNMO colleagues, who were staying behind to continue reporting on the war. The children around me struggled to understand why their fathers could not go with them and had to remain behind.

The wives were amazing—displaying incredible strength and courage in what was such a terrifying and difficult situation. I couldn't even begin to imagine how a mother might try to explain to a five-year-old child that their father had to remain behind in this war-torn country.

Once I was on board the *Serenade*, a British military doctor who headed up the UN medical team in Cyprus, Major Jo Halford, greeted me. She was on the ship to provide medical aid during the voyage to Cyprus. Much of the UN support that came from Cyprus was provided by UN staff who had volunteered on their days off work. Some of these UN volunteers were working around the clock by doing a normal day's work in Cyprus and then helping with evacuations from Lebanon during the night. What made this effort even more impressive was that many hadn't been 'ordered' by their higher headquarters and weren't part of a UN contingency plan. They were doing this out of the goodness of their hearts, a fact that made me even more grateful for their assistance. It was heartening to see people working so hard and pulling together in the war effort.

Matti on stretcher, evacuating by life boat, Tyre Harbour, Lebanon War 2006.
http://www.youtube.com/matinajewell

The medics in particular were of great benefit and, along with the ship's doctor, they treated hundreds of evacuees for minor injuries during the transit to Cyprus. Although my accompanying UN doctor had travelled on the tender craft with me to the ship, I wasn't sure where she was at this time.

Dr Halford instantly became my guardian angel. She was astounded that I had been transported by road and then by boat to the ship without even a neck collar or spinal board—standard procedure. She immediately insisted that the people carrying my stretcher lower me to the deck and that I not be moved another inch without the fitting of appropriate stabilising restraints. I was then transferred onto a new stretcher from the ship's medical centre so the ambulance stretcher could be returned to the wharf on the next lifeboat.

On hearing that there was a patient with suspected spinal injuries about to be transferred to the ship, Dr Halford had had the foresight to send two of her medical staff, armed with a standard two-person empty stretcher, to work out a suitable route for carrying me through the ship's labyrinthine and narrow passageways. The two medics ensured that they had devised the best route for moving me on a stretcher safely from the place where I would first arrive on board to the medical facility. This involved going up three decks and then back down two. Their preparatory work not only saved time, but made sure that I was not further injured by bending me around impossible corners and tilting me in tight passageways.

Dr Halford and her medics were meticulous professionals. Once they had carried me incident-free in just a few minutes to the medical centre, they quickly stabilised me and cut off my uniform to complete a thorough physical examination. They were working from a small room that had a large examination light positioned over a stainless steel bench, which was in the centre of the room. This bench had a thin mattress on top of it to make an examination bed for patients. If this was the only area for medical treatment, then it did not appear that the ship would be able to handle many patients at the same time, so I was fortunate to be the only major injury among the 1000 or so evacuees. The medical facilities were basic but sufficient to keep me stabilised for the journey to Cyprus.

Dr Halford administered a healthy dose of much-needed pain relief in the form of morphine. I could feel the icy cold drug slide through my vein and up my arm; I then caught my breath as it engulfed my chest cavity. It was like a semi-adrenaline rush and it left my body in an amazing state of relaxation and comfort. I was instantly soothed and in a wonderful calm state after so many days of acute tension. For the first time in over a week, I felt safe. Relaxed. I could faintly hear Clent thanking Dr Halford profusely for her care—she was a brilliant doctor. Through my haze I could sense his relief that I was finally in good hands.

My mind was dreamy now and the relief was truly sublime. Suddenly I remembered that it would be Clent's 30th birthday when the clock struck midnight, in just a few hours. Before all the hostilities began, I had planned to have a marvellous surprise birthday party for him in a swanky five-star hotel in Beirut with our Australian and UN friends. Israeli bombs had destroyed my plans, and possibly the swanky hotel as well.

Impulsively, I grabbed Clent's hand and jokingly said, 'See, babe, I didn't forget your 30th birthday. Look at this—I've teed up a Mediterranean cruise to Cyprus . . . And I've arranged some fighter jets to fly over with fireworks . . . You're never going to forget your 30th!' In my drug-induced stupor I thought I was hilarious, but Clent was sick with concern for me and simply wanted the nightmare to end. It was the only time I have ever seen him devoid of humour. I couldn't blame him—he had endured the biggest test of his life, having lived through a war with a front-row seat. It had been a tough ten days in the life of a marketing executive, that was for sure!

In the end, it took nine hours to load the evacuees. All 1000 personnel were evacuated, thanks to the bravery of all involved, not least the skipper of the *Serenade*, who, despite Israel's pressure on him to withdraw his ship from the port with less than half of the evacuees loaded, stood his ground. We later heard that the skipper told the Israelis he wouldn't leave evacuees stranded on the wharf and, if they bombed a ship carrying refugees and flying UN and Australian flags, then they had better prepare to explain to the world their actions. It was a gutsy decision and I have no doubt the skipper's courage saved lives.

Israel resumed its bombardment of Tyre and the areas surrounding the port, despite our evacuation still being in progress. Thankfully, the ship and its cargo were spared from any direct fire. When at last the ship slowly pulled away from the war zone, smoke billowed from a burning fuel station on the retreating shore-line. It was another nerve-racking day in Lebanon.

Several hours after I was loaded onto the ship, my accompanying UN doctor arrived at the medical centre. She asked if Dr Halford could take responsibility for me during the passage to Cyprus so she could remain with her children and get some sleep. I was very happy to remain under the care of Dr Halford, and she was also comfortable to continue providing medical treatment for me during the sea passage. It was agreed that the UN doctor would resume care for me once we arrived at Larnaca in Cyprus, because the ship was under instructions to return to Beirut immediately to evacuate another load of refugees and Dr Halford needed to remain on board.

During the rough sea passage from Lebanon to Cyprus, my angel of pain relief, Dr Halford, administered another three doses of morphine to help me get through the transit. In my semi-tranquillised state, I was finally able to sleep, a need I'd suppressed for over a week.

Clent refused to leave my side. He simply would not let me out of his sight now, not after witnessing me being dropped out of the ambulance. But thankfully he managed to drift off to sleep in his chair next to my bed, aided by a couple of beers smuggled into the ship's medical centre by the crew to help celebrate his 30th birthday. We both slept peacefully, heading for the safety of Cyprus.

16 Mayhem in Cyprus

In the early hours of 21 July the *Serenade* docked at Larnaca port, marking our safe arrival in Cyprus. It was time to leave the professional care of Dr Halford, who ensured I was gently moved onto a spinal board with a neck brace and head blocks prior to disembarking. As an additional precaution, my head was taped down to the stretcher to ensure absolutely no movement of my neck during transit to the hospital. Quite different from how I had been delivered into Dr Halford's care in Lebanon.

The other evacuees disembarked first, then I was carried with great care by the medics, retracing the same passageways used to board the ship before going down the gangplank. We were greeted on the wharf by the UN's Hungarian ambulance team. The UN had established a peacekeeping force in Cyprus in 1964, after repeated attempts failed to end hostilities between Turkey and Greece, and around 900 military and police personnel have remained there ever since. Dr Halford and her team of medics were peacekeepers with this contingent.

I was keen to be loaded into the ambulance and moved to the hospital, because the spinal board I was lying on was quite uncomfortable. But there was a hold-up—my accompanying UN doctor was nowhere to be found. Because she had previously agreed to reclaim responsibility for my care from Dr Halford upon my arrival in Cyprus, she was now required to escort me to the hospital. Despite frantic attempts to locate or contact her via the ship's paging system and her mobile phone, we were unsuccessful. There was no response and no sign of her.

The *Serenade* was due to depart for another evacuation run, this time to Beirut, and Dr Halford, who had taken such good care of me overnight, was needed back on board, so it was impossible for her to accompany us to the hospital. After waiting a while, the ambulance crew became concerned about the possibility of other urgent tasks, so the decision was made to proceed to the hospital without the missing doctor.

Once I'd been safely loaded into the back, the ambulance crew asked Clent: 'Where to?' Having just arrived in a foreign country, we hadn't been told which hospital I was supposed to be taken to—the UN medical practitioner responsible for my care was expected to have this information. We didn't even know which town I should be taken to, let alone which hospital. After a brisk debate among the ambulance team, they decided to take me to the Larnaca General Hospital, the closest hospital to the wharf.

A short drive later and I was safely in the emergency department. Things seemed to be running smoothly until the UN ambulance team, with other duties to attend to, left us at the hospital. Their departure meant we were now on our own in a strange country without any support or contact with the UN.

By this time I had been on the spinal board for over an hour and I was starting to feel very uncomfortable—my muscles were twitching and protesting about being restrained on the hard surface. It was difficult to gain the attention of anyone in the emergency department as they didn't speak English and we did not know Greek (the language spoken in this part of Cyprus). Clent desperately tried to get someone to help me as he knew that my pain was rapidly returning and my condition was going downhill fast. We needed that UN doctor, but where the hell was she?

The emergency waiting room saw a steady stream of people with various injuries. We assumed some of them were refugees from Lebanon, because of the nature of their injuries, their appearance and the fact they were speaking Arabic. The atmosphere was tense and anxious. The faces of the patients told the story of the pain and anguish they had suffered—everyone needed assistance, but these were unusual times and the hospital staff were overwhelmed by the number of casualties.

I was soon in a state of severe distress. I had not had any pain relief since receiving morphine on the ship the night before and, despite repeated requests for assistance, hours passed in the emergency department without any medical attention. My entire body went into spasm and I was terribly frightened because I was losing my vision and speech, and the pain was intolerable. I was slurring my words and was incoherent, unable to speak properly. I had started wriggling around on the stretcher, attempting to remove the strapping myself so I could get off the spinal board. We later discovered that the advisable time on a spinal board should be 45 minutes or so—beyond this, muscles are likely to spasm severely, creating further complications. I had by this time been on the spinal board for over three hours and was suffering symptoms similar to those of a stroke! Clent was frantic and once again fighting to get me medical support in a foreign country.

Eventually, medical staff noticed me writhing in pain and came to my aid. I was thrashing about uncontrollably as an emergency staff member stabbed my thigh with an auto-injector syringe, delivering an unknown drug into my body. The sedation was immediate—the next few hours were a blur while I remained in a semi-conscious state—and I was taken away for an X-ray and then moved to a ward. Once in the ward, we were again left on our own. Clent's concern for me was clear from the worry lines etched on his face. We had been in Cyprus for nearly ten hours, but, apart from a cursory glance by a team of doctors on their ward rounds while I was still sedated, I had not been properly examined by a doctor.

Having just survived a war zone, we were perplexed that our problems still persisted. Clent was contemplative and considered all of our options. Neither our Lebanese nor our Australian mobile phones worked in Cyprus and, even if they had, we didn't have contact numbers to call local UN personnel. Clent was anxious to get me out of this situation. It was now four days post-injury: I needed proper medical attention, a diagnosis and a treatment plan. I was worried that irreparable damage was being done to my spine as a result of this delay in receiving appropriate treatment.

After Clent had once more asked for help from the medical staff and while we were still working through our options, a muscled security guard strutted into the ward and announced that visiting hours were over. 'All visitors have to leave the hospital immediately,' he declared in a thick cockney accent. Clent was relieved to hear that he spoke English, and tried to explain that we had just evacuated from Lebanon and that he could not leave me on my own again. Unmoved, the security guard sternly insisted that Clent leave immediately. The large man then moved his face to within inches of Clent's, taking an unnecessarily threatening stance in his attempt to exert his authority. Clent is quite the diplomat and would normally have taken this in his stride, but I sensed that this stand-off might be the final straw for him—he had been to hell and back in the past week. So I declared: 'If he has to leave then I am going too!' After all, I had not been seen by a doctor anyway.

In my drug-affected state, I tried to fling my sheets aside, remove the cannula from my arm and stand up. All of my attempts were utterly unsuccessful. Clent reiterated that he was not prepared to leave me and that the security guard would need to get his boss to discuss this matter further and come to an agreement. Mercifully, it was the last we saw or heard of the guard or the visiting hour issue.

Later in the afternoon, Clent left the hospital in search of a shop where he could buy a Cypriot sim card for his mobile phone. We really needed communications and the public phone at the hospital had a long queue of evacuees waiting to use it. It felt like Clent was gone for an eternity and it took a concerted effort on my part to remain patient. When he returned, he explained that he had managed to buy a sim card and had successfully contacted Dr Halford, who was still on the ship. Through a stroke of genius, he had managed to get the satellite phone number for the *Serenade*, now heading to Beirut, by first calling directory assistance in Cyprus and using a passerby to translate the Greek phone number of the head office of the cruise ship company and then the satellite number for the skipper, who paged the medical centre. Dr Halford promised to contact the UN in Cyprus immediately to get us some assistance. We should never have been taken to the public hospital in Larnaca, she said, but rather to the UN-contracted Apollonion Private Hospital, over an hour away in Nicosia.

For me, this indicated there was no formal UN command link between UNTSO and the Cyprus UN mission. This coordination of my care should have come from UN New York, which is the higher headquarters for both missions. Without that formal command authority in place, it seemed that the UN staff in Cyprus were providing support as best they could to issues they were made aware of, rather than acting on higher directives. As there seemed to be no formal link between the UN missions in Lebanon and Cyprus, it wasn't surprising the ambulance crew were never briefed on which hospital to take me to.

Dr Halford's calls back to Cyprus soon brought a response. Clent received a call offering support from the Australian Federal Police (AFP) contingent, which was working within the UN mission in Cyprus. While we had been on board the *Serenade*, travelling to Cyprus, a wonderful AFP officer named Donna Rech had come to check on me in the medical facility. When Donna heard of our current situation in Larnaca Hospital, she immediately notified the commander of the AFP contingent in Cyprus. By chance, the AFP commander was Superintendent Col Speedie, whom I had actually worked with on a previous deployment in the Solomon Islands a few years earlier. I knew Col was a good operator and it was reassuring to know he was on the job. I slapped Clent a high-five for his creative thinking under pressure.

We now had the vital UN contacts in Cyprus that we needed. But our problems were not over yet. The UN doctor from Lebanon, still missing, had been named on my admission paperwork and Larnaca Hospital insisted that she sign the release forms before I could be discharged. Without her approval and signature I was going nowhere.

Clent phoned the AFP headquarters again and asked for their help in locating her. A few hours later, they finally found her at a hotel in Larnaca. She came to the ward and agreed we needed to transfer hospitals. She apologised for not escorting me from the wharf to the hospital and explained that she had dropped her mobile phone overboard, which was why she could not be contacted. She signed the discharge papers and left—we were once again on our own, waiting to transfer to Nicosia.

Later that evening, the same Hungarian ambulance team once again loaded me into the back of their ambulance to transfer me to the Apollonion Hospital. But, just as we were driving out the front entrance of the Larnaca Hospital, an order came over the UN radio to cease all movement immediately. A terrorist threat had been received on UN assets in Cyprus.

Come on—you have got to be kidding me! I couldn't believe that after all we had endured in Lebanon, we were once again under attack—this time in a different country. This bloody nightmare just seemed to continue.

The ambulance team requested special permission from the UN to move to the Apollonion, despite the code red status on UN movement. Twenty minutes later, approval was granted and we were once again making an anxious journey in a UN vehicle. I took heart from the fact that at least Clent was with me this time and, although I was still nervous about ambulance stretchers and being dropped again, I reasoned that surely it couldn't happen twice in 48 hours.

The hour-long trip in the ambulance was relatively uneventful and we arrived safely at the Apollonion Private Hospital, where I was seen immediately by orthopaedic surgeon Dr Christodoulou. After a thorough spinal examination, the surgeon agreed with the initial assessment that I had sustained a spinal injury, and he was concerned about the numbness I was experiencing in my extremities. I was settled with pain relief medication and drifted off to sleep while Clent once more took up his observation post in a chair by my bedside.

•

The following morning I was still in substantial pain, but I felt a sense of relief to at least be in the right hospital. Clent had informed the Aussies in Lebanon of our new contact phone number in Cyprus. Not long afterwards we received a text message from Brad, who was still on the front-line of the war in Lebanon, requesting that I contact the Australian Embassy in Beirut. Brad asked if I could request that the ambassador's office obtain some more phonecards so that the three Australian UNMOs could continue to communicate with UN staff in southern Lebanon. I was concerned, but not surprised, that communications within the UN mission continued to be a problem. Although my injuries had forced me to leave the mission area, I was so glad to still be able to help my Aussie team-mates—even just in this small way.

I phoned Brad to tell him that the embassy were happy to action the request for phonecards. Brad was appreciative and told me that PB Ras, one of the four UNTSO patrol bases, had received three direct hits from Israeli shells on 19 July, severely damaging the operations room. The base had taken in 31 civilian Lebanese refugees who were seeking shelter from the Israeli artillery strikes—thankfully, its bunker was separate to the main building and there had been no casualties. Despite these direct hits to a UNTSO patrol base, the decision had been made to maintain the unarmed UN peacekeeper presence. Brad was part of the team that manned PB Ras and I shared his concerns for the safety of all involved. I wondered again why the UN had decided not to withdraw the unarmed peacekeepers.

The next couple of days passed in a blur. Clent continued to maintain contact with the UN in Cyprus and with our friends and family in Australia, while I struggled with my pain, which persisted despite the strong pain relief I was receiving. I was still experiencing numb, tingling sensations in my arms and legs, and particularly down my neck and along my right arm into my right hand. This lack of sensation in my extremities weighed heavily on my mind. Despite my best attempts to stop my mind going down this path, I couldn't help worrying about how bad the long-term impact might be.

In between her evacuation runs to Beirut, Dr Halford visited daily to monitor my progress. She had written and submitted to her commanding officer a detailed report which was quite damning of the poor standard of care I had received from the UN after the injury and during the evacuation. Recently transferred from her civilian medical practice into the British Defence Force, Dr Halford was the sort of person who made you feel good about humanity—she wanted to make a positive difference. Not only did she feel morally bound as a doctor to help me; she was also driven to try to rectify the wider coordination problems between the UN forces operating in different countries, as a result of her first-hand experience evacuating refugees from Lebanon.

Dr Halford insisted on an MRI of my spine. We could hear her in the corridor saying, 'I don't care that it's Sunday—find someone on this island to run the MRI machine that I can see is located in the building next door.' The MRI was duly arranged, but unfortunately it was inconclusive. The low quality of the scan, I was told, meant that it wasn't possible to determine the exact extent of my injuries. Dr Halford and the orthopaedic surgeon, Dr Christodoulou, were convinced I had sustained damage to one or more vertebrae, and they were strongly advising the UN that I should be medically evacuated to Australia for further investigation.

I was informed by the medical staff that they had received phone calls from my Australian commander in Jerusalem. They had difficulty convincing him I needed to be evacuated for specialist spinal care in Australia or Europe. I was surprised by this as I knew Amanda had emailed him several days ago (during my transit to Cyprus) to inform him that the doctors suspected I had fractured two or more vertebrae; therefore their assessment shouldn't have come as a surprise to him.

It was explained that my commander had requested that I be returned to Lebanon as soon as possible. I was later told by my new army careers advisor, Major Phillip Hills, that my commander had also extended my posting on this mission by three months. This extension had also been approved by higher headquarters in Australia and a posting order had been issued to reflect the extension of my deployment. I understood that the MRI of my spine was inconclusive, but I was confused as to why my commander would extend my posting to the UN in spite of medical advice that I needed to be evacuated to specialist care.

I was disappointed that my commander had contacted the hospital directly, but hadn't wanted to speak with me. After all, he had the new number to my hospital room and my Cypriot mobile phone number. In fact, I had not received a single phone call from him since the war started nearly two weeks ago. I did not expect a long conversation with him, but a confirmation that he understood the extent of my injuries and a quick offer of support would have given me a huge psychological boost.

My entire world had been turned upside down; beyond the physical pain, his silence further exacerbated my feelings of isolation. I understood the UN needed every able-bodied person at work in Lebanon during this hectic period, which was exactly why I had attempted to soldier on when I was first injured in Tyre and continued doing my duty despite the significant pain. I too wished I was not injured and off the battlefield, since I felt my skills and experience were needed on the ground.

I wanted to be there with my team-mates but I could no longer function in a war zone; as a result of my injuries, I would now be a burden, not an asset, to my team. The doubt expressed about the severity of my injuries, and the request to have me returned to duty in Lebanon, left me in no doubt that he and UN headquarters in Jerusalem were out of touch with my medical circumstances. This disturbed me, as I was dependent on them to coordinate my evacuation home to Australia. Years later I would reflect on this situation and suffer intense feelings of disillusionment.

Late in the afternoon on 23 July, my spirits received a much-needed boost: Superintendent Col Speedie came to the hospital to visit. An Australian accent and a familiar face, albeit from a few years ago, was just what I needed. He reassured me that he was doing everything he could to help me get home in one piece. We spent much of the afternoon chatting; he and I reminisced about our time serving in the Solomons. Clent and I thanked him for having allowed his wonderful AFP staff to visit us on several occasions. They had brought snacks, warm support, and had even taken Clent out for a beer and a meal. Donna Rech visited us often, as did Patricia Murphy, who was the wife of one of the UN staff—we really appreciated their support and generosity.

We had been isolated from news outside our own predicament, but we now learnt from Superintendent Speedie that Cyprus had been inundated by a mass evacuation of refugees from Lebanon. There was a shortage of accommodation, and flights out of the country were now fully booked for many months. This meant it might take some time for the UN to be able to organise my medical evacuation. While this was a concern, I was in much better care now and I had been fitted with a spinal brace, so, if we had to be patient, then so be it.

Things really took a turn for the better on 24 July, six days after injuring my back and three days after arriving in Cyprus. Early in the morning, I was woken by Clent's arrival from the nearby budget hotel he had found for himself. He was very excited. You can always tell with Clent—his entire face beams with boyish enthusiasm when he has good news that he is busting to divulge.

He had just received a phone call from my former commanding officer, Colonel Andrew Condon.

I had worked very closely with Colonel Condon as his adjutant in Sydney, a year prior to being awarded the UN position in the Middle East. He was professional, highly respected and an accomplished commander; I felt privileged to have worked with him and to have received his sound guidance and mentoring as a junior officer. So I instantly shared Clent's exuberance at this news. Clent went on to say that Colonel Condon was actually in Cyprus and was on his way to the hospital to see me. Tears of joy welled in my eyes because I knew that, with Colonel Condon involved, good things were bound to happen—I was going to get home; he would make sure of it. At long last, this nightmare would be over.

An hour later, when Colonel Condon walked through the door of my hospital room, I struggled to control my emotions, given my predicament and the mere sight of this man I regarded so highly. Colonel Condon was out of uniform and looked like he had been working long hours.

At first, I thought it a remarkable coincidence that he was in Cyprus and that perhaps he was on holidays. I soon learnt he was there on business: the Australian government had sent a special task force of 120 Defence people, code-named Operation Ramp, to assist our embassy in Beirut evacuate Aussie nationals from the war in Lebanon. Colonel Condon had been appointed the commander, leaving his wife and young family in Sydney with only a few hours' notice for a deployment with an undefined timeframe. He was coordinating the evacuation of over 6500 Australian and approved foreign nationals through both Cyprus and Turkey, and the onward evacuation to Australia, operating from his headquarters in Larnaca. This was an incredible task for such a small force to achieve.

In another small-world coincidence, Colonel Condon explained that Superintendent Speedie, whom he had also met during preparations for the mission in the Solomon Islands in 2003, had been at the Larnaca wharf in the early hours of that morning overseeing evacuation operations and they had bumped into each other by chance. Superintendant Speedie told him that I had been injured in Lebanon and was now at the Apollonion Hospital.

At first Colonel Condon had doubted this information because I had emailed him a brief message confirming my safety only a week before from PB Khiam in Lebanon. Colonel Condon had replied to my email, saying that, based on the news footage reaching Australia, things didn't look great in Lebanon. His advice had been to ensure that I was keeping in regular contact with my parents as they would be concerned and distressed by the images in the news coverage, and to make sure that I trusted my own judgement if I got into difficult circumstances. His supportive email had given me a great boost.

Colonel Condon went on to explain that the previous day he had been notified that an Australian UNTSO officer had been injured in Lebanon and had been evacuated to Cyprus. He had sought confirmation of the name and was concerned when he was told it was me. Together with the doctor from his contingent, he had gone to find me but he had been given the wrong hospital and I was not there. This had caused him to doubt the accuracy of the information he had received. The following morning, at Larnaca Port, with help from Col Speedie, he had got Clent's mobile phone number and tracked me down.

It was quite a surreal situation briefing Colonel Condon, and later his staff, about my experiences during the war. I shared with them footage that I had recorded and photographs of Tyre harbour that showed large cargo ships entering the port. These pictures could be used to demonstrate that it was safe for ships with a large draught to berth alongside the wharf in Tyre, rather than anchoring offshore, if future evacuation runs were required.

Even though I had lived through the ordeal, I felt completely removed and emotionally detached from it all—as though I was explaining someone else's experience. It was a far cry from our relatively benign time working together planning and coordinating logistics support from Sydney.

I took Colonel Condon through pictures of the Tyre harbour and surrounding regions that later proved useful in getting his Australian evacuation teams in and out safely. I shared information on aspects of the war and specifically about Tyre, in the event that he needed to send Australian troops into the city to help refugees. I relished the opportunity to be useful again by contributing indirectly to operational activity, even though I was now off the battlefield.

I privately shared with Colonel Condon my concern for the three Australians still operating in southern Lebanon and the lack of support they were receiving. It was a discussion in confidence that I only felt comfortable having with him, as we had worked closely together for many years and he knew me well. He knew that I would not raise these issues without the strongest of reasons for doing so—for the sake of my team-mates still on the ground. I felt extremely awkward, but I hoped that, by informing a senior Australian officer in this way, I might ensure that every possible action could be taken to enhance the safety of those still serving in Lebanon. Colonel Condon listened intently and assured me that these issues would be addressed. He said he would also discuss my situation with my Australian commander in Jerusalem, to ensure he understood the severity and extent of my injuries.

Later that evening, Major Clare Swiderski, the Australian contingent second-in-command, who was also located in Jerusalem, rang Clent's number. She asked to speak with me, so Clent handed over the phone. She was a classmate from ADFA and Duntroon, as well as an old friend for over a decade; she had even shared time off work with me when we stayed at my parents' house near Byron Bay. So I was eager to speak with her about my injuries and because I hoped she might also have some news of how my team-mates were faring at Khiam.

But when I took the phone, it was not Clare—it was my Australian commander's voice on the other end of the line. It seemed that he had asked Clare to call Clent's mobile number on his behalf. I was pleased to hear from him, as I thought I could finally let him know directly about my circumstances and injuries. But there wasn't time—the conversation was short and abrupt. He apologised for not being in contact sooner, explaining that he just hadn't had the time to do so, and assured me that he would call each day from then on to get an update on my situation.

I was delighted to hear he would now be in closer contact as I would need his involvement to coordinate the evacuation to Australia. He was not only my Australian national commander but also the UNTSO chief of operations. But sadly, that was the last phone call I ever received from him.

Colonel Condon took charge of my welfare. Given the UN's operations focus dedicated to the war in Lebanon, he set about ensuring I was released by the UN, so I could be under his direct responsibility and that of the Australian Defence Force, which would coordinate my medical evacuation back to Australia.

I was finally going home.

17 An Unthinkable Tragedy

By 25 July I was beginning to feel optimistic again. I knew that Colonel Condon was coordinating my evacuation back to Australia and things were finally starting to look up—I was relieved beyond belief that the roller-coaster nightmare was finally coming to an end. This day had started out no differently from what had become the usual routine: a procession of medical treatments and painkillers. But it ended terribly.

It was almost midnight. Clent had just said goodnight and was about to return to his hotel, a twenty-minute walk from the hospital. As he moved to the door, his mobile phone beeped. There was a text message from Brad Smith, still in Lebanon. Clent looked puzzled and handed me the phone so I could read the message and make sense of it. The text message was brief, but it would change our lives forever. It simply stated: 'PB Khiam is down, one dead and three unaccounted for.' Military people use the term 'down' to communicate that a person or place has been compromised or destroyed.

My mind raced as I tried to absorb the news. Was this message really saying that Khiam was destroyed, and that one of my team-mates—my brothers—was dead? I could still picture Wolf's charismatic grin, Du's gentle and considerate nature, Big Mack giving me a massive farewell hug and Hans-Peter's confidence in my ability to get the convoy safely to Tyre. This couldn't be true! I had been with them only a few days ago. We had all promised each other to go for a drink soon—once the war was over—to laugh, cry and chat about what we had all lived through and the strong bond we shared as a result of the most testing days we had ever experienced.

That one of them was dead and the others unaccounted for was absurd. It just wouldn't sink in. This was ridiculous, utterly unbelievable. I simply could not accept it. It had to be wrong.

Clent leant over my bed and gently hugged me close to his chest in an attempt to console me, but I wasn't crying. There were no tears, just a horrific sense of disbelief and a sickening feeling in the pit of my stomach. This news didn't seem real, and I needed to clarify what had happened. I needed more information. I questioned what exactly this text message was telling me. My mind, in a medically induced state of drowsiness, fumbled through various scenarios and kicked into a panicky, yet clumsy, overdrive. My thoughts were flooded with questions—endless questions. How could this have happened, and why? A direct hit would have killed everyone at the base, yet there was only one reported fatality. I started playing out possible scenarios: maybe Hezbollah had forced entry into the patrol base and attempted to take the team hostage. Wolf must have put up a fight, so the Hezbollah fighters would have killed him and then taken the other three guys hostage.

This seemed like a possible scenario. It could explain 'One dead and three unaccounted for.' Was this what had happened? Surely this couldn't be, but it could give hope that the other three were still alive somewhere. At least that was something to cling to. But why would Hezbollah take UN personnel as hostages? There was no benefit in doing that—they would only bring world condemnation down upon themselves. I needed answers, and I needed them immediately.

We tried to call Brad back, but the phone lines were down and we couldn't get through. 'Bloody hell.' I tried to think. Who else could I call? I contemplated phoning Colonel Condon, but I thought he was probably asleep and I didn't want to wake him up—I was conscious of his other operational commitments in Cyprus.

My thoughts then grasped for some kind of reassurance and hope. Perhaps there was a mistake? After all, I had only received a text—surely, if one of my team-mates were dead and the other three missing, I would have been informed formally by the UN or at least by my Australian commander in Jerusalem? But deep down I knew this was perhaps a little unrealistic as the UN's first priority would be to secure the situation on the ground and attempt to recover my missing team-mates, and then notify the next of kin.

But, as unrealistic as it may have been for me to expect a phone call this early on, at the time I was tortured by a feeling of further isolation.

I reluctantly called my brother, Mark, in London, even though I knew it was the early hours of the morning there and I would be waking him up. I asked him to look at the late television news and search the internet to see if there was any information about PB Khiam. I hung on the line, anxiously waiting for an explanation of what I hoped must have been a mistake. However, Mark soon returned with grim news—BBC television had a breaking story that an Israeli fighter jet had made a devastating direct hit on the bunker of PB Khiam with an aerial bomb.

It got worse. Mark then read directly from the website. It was unlikely that any of the UN personnel manning the position would have survived such a deadly strike and it was suspected that they had all been killed.

His words did not register immediately in my mind. I was numb, incapable of showing any emotion. My hospital room suddenly felt cold and silent, as though I was in a void and time was standing still. The voice of my mother, who was visiting Mark from Australia, broke the silence—her shock, condolence and sheer grief clearly evident just from her tone. It did little to help my mind absorb the tragic news. I then spoke with my father, but there is little to say at such a time—words were inadequate.

Although my parents didn't say it, I knew they were immeasurably grateful that I had been spared the tragic fate of my team-mates;

but I was unable to share this feeling. The entire situation seemed surreal and I ended the call wishing I had some words to comfort my family, but I hadn't.

Normally, in this type of situation in the military, you would expect to be surrounded by an entire force of people. Armies fight together, and we grieve together. But, apart from Clent, I was on my own, an entire country away. I actually wished I was back in Lebanon. I wanted to be with my other team-mates and talk to them about this; perhaps then it would feel real.

Clent and I sat through the night, holding hands in silence while my mind continued to scroll through various scenarios and possibilities. I did not know what to do, who to call, what to think, or even how to feel. I wanted to scream.

Suddenly an overwhelming sense of guilt and anguish washed over me. I felt ashamed to be alive. Why had I been spared after so many close calls and near misses, yet my team-mates had been taken? Three of the guys had children—it seemed so cruel that those children would have to grow up without their fathers. In some ways, since I did not have any dependants, I felt it would have been easier and had less impact on other people if I had been killed instead. My heart ached for the wives and families.

As the reality sank in about how close I had come to death, my grief turned to anger. How could Israel have hit our patrol base? The Israeli military had the coordinates of all the UN positions and there was no excuse for them to fire on a UN position—especially the bunker of the patrol base. How could this happen with state-of-the-art precision weapons systems that struck with pinpoint accuracy? There did not seem to be a reasonable explanation, no matter how much I racked my brain in search of answers.

I questioned too why the UN had decided to leave the unarmed peacekeepers manning the bases, after so many near misses and even direct hits from Israel's powerful military. No doubt this decision was weighing heavily on the headquarters staff, now that my team-mates had paid the ultimate price.

I tried desperately to stop myself thinking about those last few minutes on the patrol base and wondering whether my team-mates had known, even for a moment, of their impending fate; but I couldn't stop exploring those thoughts. Had they been afraid? Even if they had, I couldn't imagine them sharing their concern with each other. They were all too professional and courageous. I knew they would have continued doing their job as best they could—desperately trying to ensure the UN stopped Israel's barrage of fire around them. I wondered again if they had known what was coming—I prayed that they hadn't and that their passing had been swift and pain free.

Clent stayed with me throughout the night. I was so thankful he was with me, as I could not imagine how I would have coped on my own. The emotional roller-coaster ride that we were enduring just would not end—it was relentless, and had now suddenly taken another dive for the worst just at the very moment when I thought it was over. I was dejected and knew I was heading down a spiral of empty despair that seemed well beyond my control. It was the longest, coldest, most empty night of my life.

It seemed to take forever for the sun to rise the next morning. We found a news channel and I watched the images of what was left of PB Khiam being shown repeatedly, as the world reacted in shock and disbelief at Israel's actions. Because the commentary was in a foreign language, we couldn't understand the audio, but the images of destruction were enough to tell the story.

The devastation was difficult to fathom—to the extent that I could barely recognise PB Khiam. The two-storey building was completely flattened and ripped to bits. There was nothing left but a pile of rubble. One thing was for sure, after seeing the images—no one could have survived.

18 Life's Tough Lessons

I was struggling to accept the horrific fate that had befallen my team-mates at PB Khiam. My mind kept trying to convince me that there had been an awful miscommunication, and that the boys were still alive. I had a persistent feeling that I would wake up one morning to discover that the terrible events of the past two weeks had simply been a bad dream—that the war had not happened, that I was not injured and that my team-mates were still alive.

The second I woke every morning, the heaviness and the grief would overwhelm me as I remembered what I was waking up to. I struggled to come to grips with the reality of the events in Lebanon, and felt ill-equipped to handle the situation and the multitude of turbulent emotions that came with it.

The only time in my life that I had ever felt remotely like this was when I was an eighteen-year-old army cadet at ADFA in Canberra. My best friend at ADFA was Nicki DeWit, who came from the Victorian country town of Horsham. We were the only two army girls in the first year in our 50-strong cadet division and we had become great mates, through the many demanding times we had spent together in the field on army training exercises. The day before the Easter holiday break in 1995, cadets from my division mustered together for an impromptu meeting. On the way to the hall and while still speculating on the reason for the call-up, I noticed an ambulance parked beside the northern edge of our building block, where police tape had been strung up and a tarpaulin was on the ground, like a crime scene. We sat around in the hall waiting. In my mind, I congratulated Nicki for her absence. She had probably gone for a run or was at the gym and, by default, missing out on this interruption to the day.

But something was definitely wrong. The commandant and senior staff officers of ADFA gathered outside the doors. They were huddled in discussion and, oddly, the chaplain was in the group. What was going on? Maybe a cadet was in trouble and we were all going to get a 'rocket' to warn us to behave. Perhaps the entire division was going to be punished for something one of us had done. Whatever the reason, we knew it was big and we sensed things were about to be very unpleasant.

Eventually, the commandant and an entourage of staff members entered the room. Our squadron leader quietly and formally announced that Nicki had fallen from the window ledge of her room and was dead. I don't remember what else was said that morning in the hall. I wanted to burst into tears, but was just too stunned to do so.

My frame of mind then was the same as it was now: I could not accept the horrible, incomprehensible news. Others howled with grief. Crying people hugged me. I questioned the reality—perhaps there had been a terrible mistake. Maybe it was another cadet, not Nicki, who had died. I simply couldn't absorb the thought that such an unfair and freakish accident could possibly have happened to my friend. Nicki had everything to live for—she succeeded at whatever she put her hand to, she was popular, intelligent and talented. What was the sense in a productive and shining life like hers being cut short at such a young age?

For the remainder of the day we were all required to give statements to an investigating officer on our whereabouts the night before. A group of psychologists came in and began grief counselling. Nicki had been in town drinking and partying that night, before returning to her room. It was said that when her body was found the next morning, she was clutching a few mini Easter eggs in her hand. From this, many of us deduced that she had been trying to surprise the first year cadets in her section for Easter—a plan which had ended in tragedy.

Nicki's room was on the top floor, three storeys up, and outside each window was a sizable window ledge. When cadets accidentally locked their keys in their room, sometimes they would perform a 'ledgie', which meant climbing outside the window of the room next to yours and edging your body around the building and onto your own window ledge, giving you access to your room. Although strictly against academy rules for safety reasons, ledgies were frequently performed as part of pranks or to avoid asking the duty officer to unlock your room (which could result in punishment).

It appeared that Nicki had decided to play the role of the Easter Bunny for her first years and perform a ledgie to deposit little Easter eggs on their window sills. Somehow she had lost her balance and fallen to her death. It was a freakish accident.

Though everyone was shocked, we appreciated that the commandant and staff had understood how hard the news would be for those who knew Nicki and were her mates. They had considered the impact this would have on us, and had taken the time to speak with us directly and offer counselling and immediate emotional support. That leadership and compassion was what I might have hoped to receive in the terrible days after my team-mates were killed. Other than the text message from Brad, I never heard from the UN or my Australian commander about the fatal bombing of the base—which seemed to compound my sense of disbelief about the entire situation and my lack of acceptance of their deaths.

Lying in my hospital bed in Cyprus, I found myself exploring the many decisions in my life that had led me to this point. How had a girl from the beautiful beaches of Byron Bay ended up wounded in Cyprus, having narrowly escaped the horrors of war-torn Lebanon? I had too much time for reflection and I was starting to question everything in my life, every decision I had made on my journey.

I had experienced the most magical childhood any kid could ever dream of. I was born and raised on a small farm on the outskirts of Alstonville, a village in the hinterland 30 minutes' drive from the now-famous beaches of Byron Bay. I was part of a tight-knit family of four with my parents, Roger and Helen, and my brother, Mark, who was two years older than me.

My father, a schoolteacher for some 37 years, was not only an exceptional educator but also an enthusiastic hobby farmer. Dad was truly gifted—with two green thumbs; he had a passion and natural instinct for growing and nurturing tropical fruit. After school and on weekends, we ran a successful subtropical fruit orchard—mangoes, bananas and avocados, as well as macadamia and pecan nuts, just to name a few. But the main produce was pawpaws—we had 3000 pawpaw trees and we would scour the orchard for ripe fruit every day, in order to pre-empt flying foxes having a nightly feast. On the weekends we packed green pawpaws and sent them to the fruit markets in Sydney, to be eaten raw or cooked as an Asian delicacy.

We were typical Aussie battlers; my parents were constantly toiling, working two or three jobs to make ends meet. They prided themselves on earning enough money to give my brother and me opportunities well beyond what they had experienced.

The beach culture had a large impact on my life. Weekends were spent surfing, swimming or sometimes riding our horses through the waves and up the long sandy beach at Lennox Head, one of my favourite places in the entire world. Mum had ridden horses on her family's farm as a child and, when I asked for a pony, it was a done deal. We ended up with a total of eight horses, and we even bred foals and broke in the horses ourselves. The fact that I grew up in this idyllic world usually produces interesting questions about how I ended up joining the army.

Sport was another passion in our family. Mum and Dad introduced us to competition in the local pony club, where Mum became the chief riding instructor. Dad encouraged my brother and me to join a number of sporting teams, for which he often ended up as either the coach or the manager. The active involvement of my parents in our sporting careers strengthened our family's close bond, which is something I became more and more appreciative of as I got older.

Growing up, I was forever grateful that I had been blessed with my brother, Mark, who was a wonderful role model and best friend. We were very close. He even allowed me, his kid sister, to hang out with him and his mates. Fortunately, his mates accepted me and became pseudo 'big brothers' too, which I thought was great. That was, until I became interested in dating boys—it was virtually impossible to meet guys when ten older 'brothers' were looking out for me. So, from an early age, I had boys as friends and enjoyed being part of a team based on mutual respect.

Mark was my hero. He was an all-rounder, a champion sportsman and a gifted student with a talent for art and music. I idolised him and constantly wanted to emulate him. My somewhat ambitious attitude was, 'Anything Mark can do, I can do . . . And perhaps even better!' I'm sure this 'me too' attitude irritated him, but he took the time to encourage me and showed pride in my efforts. His achievements kindled my own ambitions and competitiveness. He taught me that anything was possible with hard work, courage and determination. My inherent genetic disposition for stubbornness sometimes played a part too.

Sport came easily to me and nothing made me happier than playing team sports. I had inherited good hand-eye-foot coordination, which seemed to enable me to succeed relatively quickly at most sports I dabbled in. My tomboy upbringing also helped as I was willing to have a go and play anything Mark played, including running on in his Under-8 boys' soccer team when players failed to show. However, I ended up focusing my efforts on volleyball. Mark played volleyball for New South Wales and captained the state's Under-17 boys' team. At the age of twelve, I joined the Under-17 girls' team and played in my first national titles when I was thirteen.

I played for four years in the New South Wales Under-17 team, playing as captain for the final two years. I went on to tour China with the state Under-19 team when I was sixteen years old, after the Under-17 team folded due to lack of funds. The journey that I began when I was twelve with the New South Wales team culminated in my selection in the Australian junior volleyball team and shaped my character enormously. Travelling to a culturally different country like China at the age of sixteen really changed the way I viewed the world. My parents sacrificed so much to give my brother and me these amazing experiences that would shape our lives, and they always encouraged us to strive to achieve our greatest ambitions and not to be afraid of how far our dreams might take us. I returned from China not only a better volleyball player, but a far more appreciative and focused teenager. I wanted to leave home and pursue a career that would take me overseas, so I could experience different cultures and learn more about the world.

My school years weren't all smooth sailing as my sporting ability exposed me to another type of character building experience. I had been part of a group of girls who had been friends since preschool—we had been terrific mates virtually all of my life. Shortly after I returned from China they invited me to a party where they publically announced my eviction from the group because they were 'sick of competing with me'. I had been blindsided by this as I felt our friendship had never been based on competition, but rather mutual support and pride in each other's achievements.

At the time I couldn't understand what I'd done wrong, but I knew this event was going to shape my personality. The following week I spent a few days at school on my own, hiding in the library and not wanting to be seen in isolation. News of what had happened travelled around the school like wildfire—Matti, the girl who had gone away to China, had been humiliated. This made for juicy gossip but, remarkably, another group of girls took a different attitude and rescued me from the library by inviting me to hang out with them. I enjoyed my new friends and we are still close to this day.

I took several months to recover from what I thought at the time was definitely the worst experience I would ever have to endure in my life. But from it I learnt more about true friendship, human behaviour and myself. Until the incident with my former friends, my life had been easy and positive. I had always been liked and I enjoyed others' approval; I was a bit of a softy and naïve, wearing my heart on my sleeve. This experience toughened me up in many ways, and helped prepare me for what my future career and the world would throw at me in years to come.

As a teenager, right through until almost leaving school, I had my heart set on being a physiotherapist, so I could travel the world with Australian sports teams. My representative sporting career took me away from school for weeks on end, to the point where Mum and Dad clamped down on the level of my sports activity in my final year at high school, to try to get me to focus on my studies.

In the end, my dedicated studies were rewarded and I scored much higher than I had expected in my final year. Even so, I just missed out on my first preference, physiotherapy. Earlier in the year, I had applied for ADFA, where I could complete a degree through the University of New South Wales while at the same time undergoing officer training. The selection process had been challenging, but the army had sent me a letter of acceptance, inviting me to begin the course in Canberra in 1994.

Why ADFA? Well, I loved the idea of working in a team; fitness and sport were high on the agenda; the military paid for my university degree, so I would not be a financial burden on my parents; and most importantly I would get to serve my country at home and abroad. With so many positives, I decided to check out what military life had to offer and joined the army as an officer cadet.

My parents supported my career choice as they felt it was unlikely that I would see active duty; like me, they focused on the skills and unique opportunities I would experience in the army, rather than the possibility of my going to war. My brother and grandmother, by contrast, vocally protested against my enlistment. My grandmother had lost two of her five brothers during World War II and then nursed my grandfather, who suffered from recurrent attacks of malaria as a result of his service in the jungles of New Guinea. She could not understand why I would choose such a career when I had so many alternative options to consider. She had witnessed the horrors and aftermath of war and was dismayed that her youngest grandchild—a girl, no less—would choose this path in life.

But my mind was made up and there was no turning back. I had decided to join the Australian Defence Force.

19 Challenges on the High Seas

After I had completed my first year of a science degree at ADFA, I received offers during the Christmas break from a few universities inviting me to study physiotherapy; the entrance score for that degree had dropped substantially that year. With twelve months of science under my belt, as well as my Year 12 high school score, I was now eligible to complete a degree in physiotherapy. But a lot had changed in my life in that year.

At ADFA, I was now part of a military family. My parents had noticed how I no longer spoke in terms of 'I' or 'me', but instead described events in my life in terms of 'we' and 'us'. I felt I would be letting the team down if I changed career, and I didn't want to leave my mates. So, during a brief trip home to visit my family and with careful consideration I declined these offers. I then returned to Canberra with a much stronger sense of commitment to my army career.

After Nicki's death in my second year, ADFA became a different place for me and I'm not sure I ever fully healed after losing my best friend. She was so vibrant; she was starting out in life and her loss left a big hole in my heart. It just seemed so unfair. Over the years that followed I often found myself wondering what achievements Nicki would have accomplished if she had still been with us: Where would her postings have taken her? What achievements could we have shared together? Would she have met the man of her dreams? Would she have ever become a mum? In many ways I drew on her memory to give me strength during some of the more challenging periods of my career, and she inspired me to grit my teeth and get through.

The remainder of my four years as a cadet undergoing officer training passed relatively uneventfully. After three years, I graduated from the tri-service academy with a Bachelor of Science degree from UNSW, and then joined my army colleagues at the Royal Military College (RMC) Duntroon, for twelve months of specific army officer training. I was offered a further year of study at ADFA under the honours degree program after Duntroon, but I declined this opportunity. By this time I felt like I'd spent my entire life studying and was keen to put my military training into practice with 'the real army', commanding soldiers.

Looking back, my years at ADFA and RMC were definitely a challenge both mentally and physically. At times we were pushed to our limits and beyond, and there was never an easy day in the life of a military cadet. But they were some of the best years—we worked hard but also created our own fun. No one graduated as an individual, because it was impossible to get through the system on your own; you needed to rely on your mates, work as a team, and know each other's strengths and weaknesses. The friendships, often forged through adversity during ADFA and RMC, remain strong as the years roll by.

During my officer training I learnt many skills that prepared me for my career in the army. But, as a woman in a male-dominated environment, I found I needed to walk a fine line between being respected by the guys as a professional, competent and capable operator, and maintaining my femininity. Women made up less than 10 per cent of the army when I joined and, although this percentage is slowly increasing, I imagine today's servicewomen still face a daily balancing act and similar issues to those I encountered. I am deeply appreciative of the women who served in the army decades before me—they were the trailblazers, enduring hardships and creating opportunities for the girls who followed in their footsteps. As a result of their determined efforts I truly had a blessed career.

I graduated from Duntroon as a lieutenant and was allocated to the Royal Australian Corps of Transport. My first posting was to the Perth Logistics Battalion. During this three-year posting I chose to learn to speak Indonesian after work hours at the Edith Cowan University. Having completed the first semester, I had the great opportunity to study Bahasa Indonesian with the Special Air Service Regiment, a privilege normally restricted to Special Forces soldiers only. I was thrilled to work with some of the best trained soldiers in the world, and found that I had an aptitude for languages and enjoyed the course immensely.

In late 1999 and early 2000, trouble arose in East Timor and I was moved to Darwin to work with the 9th Force Support Battalion during the International Force East Timor (InterFET) campaign. From there I specialised in amphibious operations and water transport, which saw me join HMAS *Kanimbla*, one of the Australian Navy's two amphibious ships, as the second-in-command of the ship's army department.

Amphibious warfare is the use of naval ships, helicopters and landing craft to deliver troops, vehicles and military assets ashore to areas potentially held by the enemy. Amphibious ships are specialised to carry army vehicles on their lower decks and have the capacity to carry extra soldiers, who can be transferred ashore into battle using the ship's helicopters and watercraft. As the amphibious operations officer, I would be responsible for offloading 450 soldiers, their vehicles and equipment to the beach, using at times up to ten watercraft and six helicopters. There were a lot of moving parts to coordinate simultaneously, but I thrived in this complex challenge.

Only a few weeks after being promoted to captain, I took command of the army department as an acting major after my boss fell ill and had to leave the ship. Thankfully, my experienced senior soldiers rallied behind me, making the task less daunting; they overlooked my inexperience and, through mutual respect, supported me in my unexpected appointment, the resulting demands of a major multinational exercise and two operational missions overseas.

The *Kanimbla* sailed for the South Pacific in June 2001. Australia had sent a small International Peace Monitoring Team to the Solomon Islands to monitor a ceasefire between warring ethnic militia gangs and to encourage disarmament. Our ship was a backup, in case there was a need to evacuate the monitoring team or to provide a venue for meetings. As it happened, the team did not have a contest on its hands and that gave me the time I needed to rehearse amphibious operations with my army department as we patrolled the islands of the Solomon archipelago.

My two-year posting to a navy ship provided me with a number of unique opportunities that I would not have had serving in an army unit. The navy was having trouble recruiting officers for the physically demanding navy divers' course, and when I was asked whether I was interested, I jumped at the chance. As it turned out, I was the first army woman to do this course and I went on to command *Kanimbla*'s dive team after I completed the training. It involved a month of the most physically torturous exercise I had ever endured, such as finning across Sydney Harbour and back again in heavy overalls, long hours, little sleep and scuba-diving by day and night; but I loved every second of it.

I then couldn't believe my luck when I was asked by the skipper of the *Kanimbla* to also qualify in the skill of fast-roping from helicopters. Fast-roping is a special technique using a rope without a safety harness to get to the ground from a helicopter in ultra-quick time. We would use fast-roping during operations when assaulting a hostile wharf or boarding another ship. The army has an operational need for this specialist skill in hostage rescue or counterinsurgency operations, and therefore only allows Special Forces soldiers and commandos to conduct it. Women are not allowed to serve in Special Forces, so I would never have imagined, in my wildest dreams, being trained in this technique.

The first time my army team and I practised fast-roping from helicopters was during an offshore patrol in the Solomons. As well as being an exciting moment, it proved to be a reunion of sorts with three of my ADFA navy classmates, Natalee Johnston, Karly Pidgeon and Toni Wilson. I remember the experience vividly.

I could hear myself breathing heavily inside my helmet, which had a dark sliding visor that covered the top of my face. The noise of the Sea King helicopter was muffled by my ear plugs and by the thick helmet that pressed my ears against my head. My body was tense and braced against the buffeting of the windy down-draught from the rotor's blades that pushed air through the open side door of the chopper. A rope, attached to the hoist connected to the roof, lay in a coil on the floor. Further inside the aircraft cabin, members of my team were also ready and waiting with their visors down, ready to plummet from the aircraft.

Next to me was Karly. As she shouted out the warning call, 'Thirty seconds!' above the swirling wind, the chopper moved over the stern of the ship and began to hover 30 metres from the flight deck. Below lay the white dot of the bull's eye circle, which denoted the centre. Karly then muscled out the rope, which uncoiled under its own hefty weight as it fell to the deck.

The pilot flying the helicopter was Natalee. Toni—who had been in the class a year behind Karly, Nat and me—was in charge on the ship's bridge, manoeuvring the vessel to face into the wind for our fast-roping practice. Quite by chance, it was an all-girl show commanding this exercise—something our instructors at ADFA would never have predicted!

Leaning out of the helicopter door, Karly gave directions to Natalee, who in turn adjusted the hover position above the moving deck of the ship, while Toni steadied the ship to the northwest, a course chosen for optimal sea swell, and to reduce the wind over the deck—critical safety factors in helicopter operations. I had completed all my previous static training with ease, but this was my first time roping onto a rolling ship's deck—in front of a bunch of sailors, who watched curiously to see how the army girl went.

As I sat perched on the edge of my canvas seat, gazing out of the chopper door to the blue ocean and the heaving deck of the *Kanimbla* below, I questioned the wisdom of my decision to volunteer for this in the first place. Unbeknown to my army team behind me, I was actually terrified of heights. In a brief moment of insanity, I had thought I would conquer my fear by learning to fast-rope. What was I thinking? My first roping experience had been at ADFA, abseiling off the tallest buildings in Canberra—a terrifying yet thrilling experience that I had at that time, many years ago, made a mental note never to repeat. I wished I had reminded myself of that before now.

As my mind grappled with the notion of how high we were above the deck, my stomach started to churn and I suddenly felt the urge to be sick. My eyes frantically searched the cabin of the chopper, hoping to find some reassurance. I focused on my corporal, who was sitting opposite me, beaming with enthusiasm and excitement; he gave me the thumbs up signal, but it didn't inspire me with confidence.

At least I didn't have the extra weight of an army backpack, body armour or rifle slung across my shoulder, as I would if on operations. I wondered if one day I would lead my men on an actual mission—little did I know that, only a few months later, I would be doing this for real on operations in the Middle East.

Suddenly the rope was fully unfurled, with a good metre lying on the deck. Karly barked, 'Go!' I glanced at my soldiers, who were all looking at me and waiting for me to lead them out the chopper door and drop safely down the rope to the ship's deck. There was no time to change my mind now.

I swung out, my knees and feet clamped onto the rope, using the technique we had practised repeatedly. My gloved hands gripped the rope hard, attempting to slow my rapid descent. With no safety harness or mechanism to stop my fall, I did not want to give a moment's thought to the fact that I was 30 metres up in the air.

The trick was to use my feet and inner thighs to take my weight, rather than my arms; I used my hands to squeeze or release pressure on the rope, to control my speed. In a split second it was all over. I reached the deck and turned my face upward, giving the thumbs up for the others to follow. Suddenly brimming with confidence, I couldn't wait to do it again!

•

Just days after HMAS *Kanimbla*'s return to Sydney from the Solomons, the world was stunned by the terrorist attack on the World Trade Center in New York, on 11 September 2001. The crew's leave was cancelled and we immediately set sail for the North Arabian Gulf, to participate in Operation Enduring Freedom.

We served as part of the UN-sanctioned Maritime Interception Force alongside Spanish, Dutch, German, French, British and American vessels. The focus was on observing, interrogating and, where necessary, boarding suspicious vessels carrying Iraqi oil and other commodities in contravention of UN sanctions.

The commanding officer of the *Kanimbla*, Commander David McCourt, decided en route to the Gulf that we could be required to enter hostile harbours with a very real terrorist threat. He was mindful of the attack that had killed seventeen crew members of the USS *Cole* a year earlier, in October 2000, when the American destroyer was alongside the wharf in the Yemeni port of Aden.

The Australian Navy doesn't practise close protection of its ships in port, unlike the American Navy. We also do not have Marines (soldiers who specialise in amphibious operations) or troops assigned to Australian Navy vessels to provide protection while alongside a hostile wharf. In the absence of close protection capabilities, Commander McCourt appointed the navy operations officer, Lieutenant Commander Iain Jarvie, and me as the ship's force protection officers. Although we weren't Marines, we were required to design a security plan to protect the ship while alongside the wharf and to train the crew to fulfil these roles while we were sailing to the Gulf.

This was no small task. Writing standard operating procedures, preparing a defence squad and training the crew to protect the ship in an insecure port, on top of our other duties, would normally take months of careful preparation. We had two weeks before we would be in the Gulf, doing it for real.

During the fourteen-day voyage from Sydney to Bahrain, we gave the crew a refresher course in weapons handling and conducted shooting practice off the stern of the ship, using large sea buoys thrown overboard and dragged behind the ship as targets. The echo of gunfire reminded the ship's company that they were sailing into a combat zone, where things could quickly turn nasty. Once alongside a wharf in the Middle East, members of the ship's crew would need to stand guard around the clock; we would have four 50-calibre machine guns mounted on the upper decks and rifles at observation posts around the ship. Soldiers and sailors would need to patrol the wharf area and operate checkpoints on the approaches to the ship, searching for explosives hidden in vehicles or on suicide bombers.

The *Kanimbla* is a multipurpose ship, so we sailed to the Middle East prepared to fulfil one of six different roles ranging from amphibious operations to being a hospital ship. It was up to the Maritime Interception Force, once we arrived in Bahrain, to determine which tasks we would be allocated.

Soon after our arrival at the wharf in Bahrain, we learnt that the *Kanimbla* would be a platform for Special Forces operations, launching American Navy sea, air and land personnel (SEALs). SEALs are the US Navy's elite fighting forces, employed as storm troopers to conduct counterterrorism raids and for the more delicate business of covert reconnaissance and surveillance, as well as hostage rescue.

To my knowledge, Australian naval ships had never worked with the SEALs previously. Certainly our team hadn't. The senior hierarchy from the SEAL team came aboard for meetings with the commanding officer and the department commanders (I was one of the four heads of department) to discuss what lay ahead. Discussions were concise and businesslike, allowing us to cover a lot of ground in a relatively short time.

While the Americans mouthed their enthusiasm about working together, I knew that they were being polite—we would need to prove our worth and earn their respect. When the commanding officer introduced me as one of his ship's force protection officers, there was a look of surprise on their faces. They then learnt I was also the officer responsible for loading and unloading their watercraft. Getting specialised, fully-loaded SEAL speedboats on and off the ship as quickly as possible by day and night was going to be a challenge. They knew it and I knew it, but I was looking forward to proving to all in the room that my team and I could get the job done.

As the rest of the crew went into town on leave, my army team remained on board to help the SEALs load their stores and equipment onto the ship. A few hours later, two SEAL speedboats were alongside and we started training over four intense days and nights, including hoisting the watercraft on and off the ship. These were impressive high-performance boats that could reach incredible speeds on the water, despite being weighed down with heavy machine guns and a team of SEALs. They were a formidable sight in action.

I was extremely proud of my soldiers when our Aussie ingenuity, preparedness and hard work paid off. Within a few weeks we were able to launch a SEAL team in under twenty minutes at night—without lights or radios, so they could go undetected by the enemy. The SEALs genuinely liked working with us and we were chuffed when a group of American admirals visited the *Kanimbla* to observe our techniques. We were launching and retrieving SEAL teams and their boats in less than half the time that US Navy ships took to achieve the same result—and we hadn't sustained any injuries during the many training runs required to perfect our technique and cohesion between the teams. The *Kanimbla* soon had the record for boarding smuggler ships—sixteen in one day. My soldiers and I relished the opportunity to work with and learn from the SEALs; they were such capable and professional operators.

Now that the *Kanimbla* was conducting operations with the SEALs, we had to vacate the forward deck to make space for their speedboats. This required offloading into the sea the two Army Landing Craft (LCM8s) we had brought from Australia for amphibious roles. However, the LCM8 vessels were designed for beach landings and sailing short coastal passages, not for keeping up with a mother ship on the high seas. After two sleepless nights in a severe storm that generated rough seas, with waves crashing onto the decks, the LCM8 crews became exhausted. It was getting extremely dangerous and admittedly there was a degree of army pride at play, trying to keep up with the navy; however, this situation was starting to take its toll.

I implored Commander McCourt to allow the LCM8 boats to go to shore as soon as possible, to take refuge from the continuing storm. I was convinced that to fail to do so would run the risk of an accident. Not only was there a potentially serious safety problem, I urged, but there would also be an erosion of morale if we didn't find a more suitable role for the LCM8 crews. I suggested that perhaps the Americans would have alternative work for them to undertake, closer to shore.

Commander McCourt agreed and directed me to take charge of the lead boat and head for the Kuwait naval port, where the American SEALs were already using the harbour facilities. He said he would obtain diplomatic clearance for us to enter the port while we were en route. He suggested that I take whatever weapons I needed and, once I got ashore in Kuwait, I should find a Kuwaiti military official and 'do your diplomatic thing'. I wondered, as I climbed down the rope ladder at the side of the *Kanimbla* and found myself on the heaving deck of the LCM8 ready to set out, what exactly that meant.

In my mind, I questioned whether there would be sufficient time for the captain to get an emergency diplomatic clearance to enter the port. I really didn't want to sail into a port in an Islamic country as an armed woman in charge of two uninvited military landing craft without clearance. To the Kuwaiti Navy, we could have anything or anyone onboard. I was hoping they would give us time to speak with a representative and not act in haste. At best I faced a diplomatic incident; at worst an accidental fire fight.

As soon as I got onto the LCM8, I could see that the crew were delirious with exhaustion. The Kuwait naval port was eight hours away at the boat's top speed of 8 knots. I offered to steer and look after the navigation while the crew got some rest, as it was far more important for them to be on the ball when we arrived. The guys gratefully fell asleep immediately.

The sea conditions were horrendous. As I looked out of the windows of the wheelhouse, the view of the skyline would disappear, completely blocked by a wall of angry grey-green water, which would then curl and crash onto the well deck of the boat. I wondered how much more pressure the windows of the wheelhouse could take as each wave smashed into the glass beside and in front of me. The bow of the LCM8 would ride up over the lip of the wave, and then the entire craft would roll and plunge into the trough between incessant oncoming walls of water.

The pounding swell was relentless. The shallow and flat design of the LCM8's hull meant that we slid off each wave and slapped, rather than pierced through, the oncoming water. I held my breath each time as the force of water crashed and then vibrated through the steel hull of the 70-tonne boat. I had to grip the wheel hard with both hands, and it was a constant struggle to maintain our course. The ocean was in a terrifying mood and we were like a bobbing cork being thrown around inside a washing machine. I could not even see the coastline, so I had to trust in the compass, hoping we would remain on course and eventually reach our destination. Through the long and bumpy ride, I thought, *I'm probably now qualified to drive one of these watercraft.* Talk about a baptism of fire.

After six long hours of wrestling the boat through the awesome swell, with the spray crashing over us, a crew member finally relieved me. I had been wondering how they could sleep through such a ferocious storm. I immediately jumped onto the radio, hoping to gauge the reception that awaited us in Kuwait.

I could finally see the port on the horizon, but the only messages I received in response to my radioed request for permission to enter and come alongside at a berth were in Arabic. They could have been telling me to 'piss off', for all I knew. I spoke with Commander McCourt, who advised that we still did not have official diplomatic clearance to enter the harbour, but that we were to proceed despite this. He reassured me that, if there was any problem, I was to state that we were conforming with international maritime law—as ships seeking shelter in harbour from adverse conditions. Commander McCourt also mentioned that the Australian Army brigadier in Kuwait, who had been frantically trying to gain the short-notice diplomatic clearance, was not impressed with me or the navy for putting him in a politically compromising position with his Kuwaiti counterparts.

Exhausted but without clearance, I was left with no option but to take my convoy of two watercraft and enter the port as directed. I hoped I would successfully be able to 'do my diplomatic thing'—whatever that was! We came alongside what appeared to be an empty area of the wharf. My crew were decked out in their protective gear, nervously manning the 50-calibre machine guns on the upper deck of each LCM8. Trying to look as friendly and as non-threatening as one possibly can with a flak jacket, holstered pistol and Steyr rifle slung over my shoulder, I headed off to find a Kuwaiti official.

As I approached the end of the wharf, a Kuwaiti naval officer advanced and, as we drew closer, he said, 'Welcome to Kuwait' in perfect English. This was my lucky day! I explained the reason for our unannounced arrival with profuse apologies. He welcomed us as guests to his country, and even invited me and my crew out to dinner.

I learnt that he was a Western-educated man. This was fortunate for me, as I would later discover that many Muslim and Kuwaiti men would not accept a woman serving in the army, let alone her being in command of an all-male crew. During my deployment, many despised me and showed it in some uncomfortable ways, such as spitting at the ground in front of me, or refusing to speak with me simply because of my gender. Others, it turned out, wanted to marry me! Some middle ground would have been nice.

The six-month deployment to the Arabian Gulf saw the *Kanimbla*'s crew survive a number of close calls at sea and alongside in port, many of which went unreported in the media at the time, possibly in an attempt to allay fears among the family and friends of the crew. The force protection measures we had developed en route proved to be vital. While we were alongside in the Oman port of Muscat, a speedboat full of men wearing balaclavas approached the ship at high speed; this daring attack was averted, and I am sure this was in no small part due to the protection measures we had established.

During my hectic two-year posting on HMAS *Kanimbla*, I was involved in back-to-back overseas deployments, all of which presented me with amazing learning opportunities and enabled me to consolidate and build on all of my skills and training. Although army by service, I loved the navy life and had become a diehard enthusiast of all things amphibious. I now had a first-hand appreciation of how the navy operated and I respected and admired their service. But it was time to head ashore, taking my new-found skills back to the army.

20 Adventures in Paradise

In January 2003, I was posted to the 9th Force Support Battalion in Sydney as the adjutant for the commanding officer, Lieutenant Colonel Andy Condon (later my saviour in Cyprus). But shortly after I arrived at the unit, Lieutenant Colonel Condon and I were summoned to Canberra to participate in planning for another Australian-led intervention in the troubled Solomon Islands. It was during these planning sessions that I first met Federal Police officer Col Speedie (later to be the commander of the AFP in Cyprus), who had conducted a reconnaissance of Honiara, the capital of the Solomon Islands. Together we came up with a plan for military logistical support to the Federal Police in the Solomons.

It was my fourth military operation in the five years since I had graduated from Duntroon. Although I was tired, I didn't want to miss this next gig. I had grown fond of these overseas missions—the excitement, the 24/7 lifestyle, putting years of training into play, and, invariably, the highs and lows that go with all military operations.

On 24 July 2003, Australia deployed a 2000-strong Australian-led Regional Assistance Mission to the Solomon Islands. The task force was led by an Australian diplomat, Nick Warner, and consisted of Federal Police officers supported by armed military troops from Australia, New Zealand, Fiji, Tonga and Papua New Guinea. Called Operation Helpem Fren (literally 'Helping a Friend' in the local language, Tok Pisin English), the intervention aimed to restore law and order to the Solomon Islands, and to create a secure environment in which to deliver development assistance.

Since 1999, armed ethnic militia gangs had been intimidating the population and occasionally fighting with each other. There had been a coup in June 2000 and the economy had collapsed. The Solomon Islands had become a failed state that could be a sanctuary for terrorists or criminals. Australia had decided to act after receiving a request from the Solomon Islands' prime minister, who feared another coup.

For the first week on the ground in Honiara it rained. And rained. And then it rained some more. Mother Nature was not on our side and I longed for my dry cabin back on the *Kanimbla*. We deployed to Henderson Field (now the site of the Honiara International Airport), where US Marines had fought the Japanese in the Pacific campaign in 1942. Our equipment and tents were totally saturated after three days of non-stop torrential rain and, combined with the exhausting humidity, it made for a most unpleasant stay.

The rain was like nothing I had ever seen before—it fell in continuous sheets of water. The tents were awash with thick, sticky mud and there was no chance of drying out our clothing or equipment. The humidity was oppressive and the air was thick with mosquitoes, which struck at will on unsuspecting targets. The makeshift field toilets began to flood with the rising water table and I feared an outbreak of dysentery could halt our entire operation. Thankfully, this didn't eventuate and the troops remained professional and focused despite the difficult conditions. In fact, the soldiers toughed it out and actually thrived on the challenge as we continued to be unlucky with the weather.

In contrast to the military's living conditions, during this time our AFP compatriots were housed in an air-conditioned beach resort hotel; they were permitted to have a beer after work and ate from crockery laid out on white tablecloths, rather than army ration packs. This was simply the conditions the Federal Police were entitled to, but, together with their generous pay and allowances, the contrast led to some resentment among our troops.

Despite these challenges, a couple of months into the operation the intervention was going well. By August, troops and police had arrested and imprisoned scores of corrupt Solomon Islands officials and members of armed militia gangs, while at the same time impounding hundreds of weapons. The leader of the Guadalcanal Liberation Force, Harold Keke, had been arrested in the first couple of weeks, although Jimmy 'Rasta' Lusibaea, the leader of the other militia gang, the Malaita Eagle Force, remained at large. He was reputed to have murdered or maimed scores of people with a group of vicious young louts, whose lawless behaviour was infamous.

The force commander sent out several infantry platoons to various targeted islands to locate Jimmy Rasta and members of his militia. Still carrying weapons, the militia continued to cause unrest in the local community. Female liaison officers were sent to patrol with the infantry platoons, in the hope that they might be able to glean information from the local women. The women and their children were the main losers in this ethnic war as they had lost their husbands and sons during the violence, and they seemed pleased with the disarmament process. It was hoped they might reveal where weapons were hidden and the locations of armed militiamen.

I was assigned to fulfil one of these female liaison officer roles—to be flown by helicopter to Malu'u, known to be the home island of Jimmy Rasta. As we took off, I sat opposite Sergeant Simaima Lavemai, a female member of the Tongan Defence Force. Beneath us, as we gained altitude, the typically crystal-clear blue sea around this island paradise revealed itself. We banked hard to the left and, if it were not for the seat belt and centrifugal forces, I would have been thrown straight out of the chopper door and down with a splash.

After a flight of an hour or so, we descended onto a soccer field, seemingly in the middle of nowhere, where a large crowd of locals, who had seen and heard the helicopter approaching, gathered in eager anticipation of our arrival. They were absolutely fascinated by our helicopter, pointing at it and yelling in bewilderment, 'Mix master belongum Jesus' which roughly translates to 'flying egg-beater that belongs to Jesus'. Some of the islanders had never seen white-skinned people before, let alone helicopters, so I can well understand how these strange flying machines must have seemed to have come from the gods.

Also waiting to meet us were members of a Papua New Guinea (PNG) infantry platoon that we were assigned to patrol with. They seemed pleased to see us and were quite welcoming; however, awkwardly, the lieutenant platoon commander misinterpreted the significance of my arrival. Due to my rank as a captain, I was more senior than him and, as a result, he assumed I had been sent to command the operation on Malu'u. He and his soldiers looked to me for decisions and guidance; although I was happy to assist where appropriate, my repeated explanations that I was just an attached liaison officer, not the appointed commander, continued to be misunderstood.

At the first village we visited, the chief herded all the women away from the gaze of the armed PNG soldiers. Simaima and I were permitted to follow them into a grass hut and we began to chat as best we could. The Solomon Islands were previously a British colony so English, or a form of easy-to-learn Tok Pisin, was shared. I soon learnt that the most exciting thing in my backpack that I had to offer them were Wet Ones wipes, complete with a vanilla-scented fragrance. The women were amazed at how the disposable cloth cleaned children's faces, and how it felt to touch and smell. I imagine that the cloths were kept for well beyond their one-use intention. This ice-breaker was crucial in encouraging the women to talk to us, but unfortunately they couldn't provide any valuable information.

Over the following weeks we conducted patrols to a number of communities. It was an amazing cultural experience and I thoroughly enjoyed spending time learning the customs of the island women. But we were having no success in finding armed militamen, or gaining useful information about the location of Jimmy Rasta.

Life at our small base on Malu'u was pleasant. The PNG soldiers were master chefs and provided a feast of exotic gourmet food experiences, accompanied by perfect harmony and kinship. Succulent local lobsters, cooked 'hangi-style' in an underground oven, were a welcome change after weeks eating exclusively preservative-riddled army ration packs that for me induced heartburn. My taste buds relished the delights my PNG and Tongan colleagues served up to us each evening. With a full belly, I slept soundly under the tropical stars; I often drifted off wondering how my colleagues at headquarters in Honiara were coping with the mud.

I loved patrolling to new villages, despite an often arduous hike in full patrol gear (weapon, ammunition, pack and 10 litres of water) through thick jungle. Up and down the mountainous terrain we climbed to reach the remote villages. The local people were always friendly, more than inquisitive and truly delighted when we kicked a soccer ball with the kids or simply sat and chatted. To see a white woman in military camouflage uniform with a rifle was intriguing and caused much curiosity. Many just wanted to touch my hair and skin, because they were so different from their own. Children sometimes rubbed the top of my hand to see if my skin was black underneath—they would giggle with surprise when they found it was truly white in colour. This made me laugh too as the children were adorable—so innocent, curious and accepting of my different skin, eye and hair colour. A couple of the little ones snuggled into my arms. I wished they could remain naïve to the modern world and in doing so retain the wonderful aspects of their isolated culture.

After several weeks hiking around Malu'u, we found ourselves at a beach where a local produce market was set up. We were bartering for food and chatting happily with the stall owners when suddenly those around us fell silent. All stared ominously towards the beach. A large speedboat was heading our way and, as it drew closer, I made out a group of men. They appeared to be armed with rifles and shotguns.

By the time the boat nudged into the beach to let them off, I could see the elusive, yet unmistakable, Jimmy Rasta, adorned with his trademark bandana and dark sunglasses. He stood at the bow confidently, an air of arrogance enveloping him. He and his entourage jumped out of the boat and menacingly sauntered through the market crowd. As they headed up the beach towards us, a stab of fear went through my entire body. I instinctively drew my rifle to my side.

I was surprised at their boldness. There were twenty or so of us, and we were all well armed, with our rifles slung over our shoulders and in clear view. With seeming indifference, Rasta and his crew meandered through the market and calmly asked the PNG soldiers who was in command. To my horror, the soldiers pointed to me.

Rasta approached with a beaming smile and in well spoken English said, 'Welcome.' He shook my hand, before doing the same with each of the PNG soldiers. Like the cheery naval officer I had encountered in Kuwait, he was keen to please and make us feel welcome. I was in too much shock to be nervous about being face to face with the notorious militia leader, and was relieved to be accompanied by the platoon of PNG soldiers and an Australian Intelligence Corps sergeant nicknamed JP. Rasta explained that he was having a party the following night and asked us to join him as his special guests.

After several months of unsuccessful tracking, I knew that my headquarters would not believe that we had been brazenly approached by Rasta and his crew, unless I could provide evidence. So I asked if he would mind having his photograph taken with us. He obliged and posed for the photo. It was a bizarre, but cordial, encounter with the Solomon Islands' Most Wanted.

We were not permitted to arrest Rasta and his men as this was a task for the police. So, after Rasta and his men left the markets, we rushed back to base to contact our headquarters in Honiara to report the incident; JP and I emailed through the photo of our new friend, confirming that it was indeed Jimmy Rasta. The mood at headquarters changed quickly and the force commander called a meeting with the AFP. Soon after, I was informed that approval had been granted for us to attend the party and gather further information.

The following evening, I was extremely anxious at the prospect of going to a party as the special guests of the Pacific's version of Osama bin Laden—after all, he was suspected of murder, rape and torture. I put on a fresh uniform that was soon drenched with sweat in the tropical humidity. I warned all the soldiers to have their rifles loaded and ready, and to be on high alert. Complacency in the party atmosphere could be dangerous.

We arrived to find Rasta sitting cross-legged on the ground, front and centre of a big gathering, looking at a performance area where men clad in grass skirts were dancing and singing to traditional music. Rasta jumped up with a welcoming gesture and insisted that JP and I sit next to him, while ushering the rest of the platoon into a position of honour. Dancing, singing and music continued as women brought out food on banana-leaf platters. A bamboo band struck up, and young men started hitting the ends of plastic pipes with rubber thongs, creating a loud and rhythmic *bounk, bounk, bounk* sound. It was not possible to talk over the music, so I sat in silence next to Rasta. This appeared to be the way—no chit-chat; just eat, watch and listen.

Rasta appeared to be more comfortable in the presence of my male sergeant so, during the entertainment, I left JP with him while I moved away from the music to speak with the local women. They told me stories of murder and violent assaults committed by the Malaita Eagles against them. They were glad to have us there to protect them, fearing that any 'after party' could turned nasty. However, at the end of the night, we all left without incident.

The following morning we compiled a report of our attendance at the party for the Federal Police, who then interviewed people from the community and finalised eyewitness accounts. The police soon tracked Rasta by various means, before arresting him in a raid on his family home several weeks later.

With the successful arrest of both leaders of the warring ethnic gangs, the unrest in the Solomon Islands settled and the remainder of our six-month deployment ran relatively smoothly. Before I knew it, I had returned to Sydney, working again with Lieutenant Colonel Andy Condon, and a year later preparing for the deployment to the Middle East with the UN.

•

Looking back, my entire career had been a hectic period of back-to-back operations and exotic postings—it all seemed like a blur. However, these musings over better days suddenly made my current situation seem even more poignant. Just how serious was this spinal injury and would I be able to walk and run again? I'd led a successful and rewarding career in the army so far, but I knew very well that, if I couldn't recover and return to the high level of fitness and athleticism required for an army officer, I could lose my military career.

These worries compounded the deep grief I was feeling over losing my team-mates from PB Khiam. My career meant the world to me, and I didn't want to lose my military family and not be able to serve with my mates. My career was my purpose in life—I couldn't lose that too. Although there are risks of injury or death associated with military service, nothing prepares you for the reality when it happens.

As I lay injured in a hospital bed in Cyprus with Colonel Andy Condon coming to my aid, I tried to process all of this and what my future might hold.

21 Broken in Mind and Body

It was the responsibility of the UN to provide medical treatment and to organise my evacuation back to Australia. But, with the war continuing in Lebanon, it was clear to Colonel Condon that it would be preferable for me to be transferred into the hands of the Australian Defence Force as quickly as possible. Sometimes this kind of transfer can drag on for quite a while, but all parties recognised the urgency of moving me to specialist spinal care. Even so, it took almost a week for all the administrative processes to be completed.

In the meantime, Colonel Condon ensured that I was reviewed by Squadron Leader David Mitchell, the Australian Air Force doctor with Operation Ramp in Cyprus. Squadron Leader Mitchell agreed with the diagnosis of one or more fractured vertebrae and the need to evacuate me to Australia as soon as possible. Colonel Condon also recognised that the management of my psychological state was just as important as the treatment of my physical injuries. He organised for Captain David Said, an Australian Army psychologist serving in Iraq, to fly in and see me in the hospital in Cyprus.

Although it was for only one session, I really appreciated the extraordinary efforts the ADF and Colonel Condon made to get me some much-needed support, even though at the time I was technically not Condon's responsibility. During his brief visit to Cyprus, Captain Said even drove Clent to a nearby shopping centre to buy some clothes, because we had evacuated Lebanon with a 5-kilogram limit on personal belongings. Clent's laptop, passport and travel documents had made up a big part of his weight allowance, so some fresh clothes were much needed and appreciated.

Colonel Condon also recognised that Clent needed a break from the hospital, where he had spent many days and nights by my bedside; he invited him to attend a function at the house of the Australian ambassador to Cyprus. Dressed in his best evacuation clothes, Clent relished the opportunity to enjoy some Aussie hospitality, support, and time away from the hospital.

As soon as the approval had been processed, I was back under the command of the ADF, and Colonel Condon coordinated my medical evacuation to Australia. The first leg of the journey was via a medical SOS Lear jet from Nicosia to Frankfurt.

The Lear jet was a tiny aircraft that had only enough room for one patient on a stretcher and three medical team members. A doctor and a paramedic were attending me, and they would escort me for the entire trip back to Australia. Fortunately, this left one seat spare, which allowed Clent to travel with me. This was extremely fortuitous because, due to the overwhelming demand for flights from evacuees from Lebanon, it would have been many weeks' wait for Clent to have secured a seat on a commercial flight out of Cyprus. The Lear jet was permitted to fly at 45,000 feet—higher than most commercial aircraft—an altitude that provides a much quieter and smoother ride for injured patients. Once we were on board, feeling safe and secure in the hands of the highly trained German medical team and sedated with sufficient pain relief, I drifted into a deep, tranquil sleep.

In Germany, I was transferred to a Qantas 747 aircraft for the flight back to Australia, with a short stopover in Singapore. This flight brought an unexpected challenge. The medical crew had been advised that nine seats in the economy section of the plane had been removed so that my stretcher could be secured to the floor. We were the last to board the flight; all 400 or so passengers were seated and eager to depart when I was transferred into the rear of the plane using the hoist that brings the catering carts on board.

We now discovered that the seats had not been removed at all. After some deliberation, I was positioned on top of the headrests of nine vacant seats, next to the fuselage and parallel with the aisle; the seats were in their customary upright position and the stretcher was strapped to the top of them. But these straps did little to stop me and the stretcher moving incessantly with the constant vibration of the plane during the 22-hour trip. An additional harness, made from the same strong material used in car seat belts, was also used to secure me during takeoff and landing.

I lightheartedly suggested that it was like a first-class flight gone wrong: while I was able to lie completely flat, as my doctors had instructed, being perched on top of the headrests of the seats meant that my face was only 30 centimetres or so beneath the overhead lockers. My fellow passengers must have been wondering what was going on, because my two intravenous drips—of morphine and fluids—were hanging off the outside of the lockers. It was not an ideal situation, as a number of the cabin crew were needed to help lift me whenever an intravenous-induced bathroom break was required, since I had not been fitted with a catheter.

I was unwittingly a unique form of in-flight entertainment for several children, who stared at me with mouths agape. But I didn't really mind. The Aussie accent of the cabin service manager over the announcing system reassured me that I was heading home—and that was all that mattered.

Clent was able to travel on the same Qantas flight with me. However, the only seat left on the plane was in first class, at the very opposite end of the aircraft to where I was located. I joked that the first-class luxury was all part of his 30th birthday present, which he had well and truly earnt, and he teased that I should feel privileged to see him during the flight since it was at least a two-beer trip back to check on me.

I flew from Germany to Sydney in a semi-sedated state in the excellent care of the medical team, dressed only in a polka-dot hospital gown, since my army camouflage uniform had been cut off me during Dr Halford's examination on the ship. The rest of my clothing remained in Lebanon. The Qantas crew were outstanding; even though they didn't know any of the story of my trauma, they sensed that I had been through quite an ordeal and were wonderfully caring and hospitable—they even bought me an enormous bunch of Singaporean orchids during the stopover there.

When we eventually touched down in Sydney, in the very early hours of the following morning, we were met by a concerned Brigadier Mick Kehoe, the head of the Transport Corps and also Colonel Condon's direct boss. Eighteen years earlier, Brigadier Kehoe had lost one of his best mates, Captain Peter 'Bags' McCarthy, who, like me, had been a military observer with the UN in Lebanon. 'Bags' was tragically killed on his very last day in Lebanon, when his UN patrol vehicle ran over an anti-tank landmine, killing him and wounding his Canadian team-mate. Brigadier Kehoe had feared that I might have become not only the second Australian killed on this mission but also the second Transport Corps officer killed in Lebanon, since 'Bags' had also been from this corps.

It was an emotional homecoming for me. Brigadier Kehoe's welcome was greatly appreciated. Yet the whole scene did not feel real.

It had now been fourteen days since I had sustained my injury in Lebanon. On arrival in Sydney, I was immediately transferred to the army hospital at Holsworthy Barracks, which is about an hour southwest of the city centre. The MRI that had been taken in Cyprus had travelled back with me and was sent to be reviewed by a specialist in nearby Liverpool. Previously, the MRI had been reported as inconclusive; however, this time the report was that one vertebra was wedged (meaning crushed on one side) and two more vertebrae were fractured.

The following morning a CT scan finally revealed the full extent of my injuries: three fractured and two wedged vertebrae, plus associated nerve and tissue damage. It was a shock to hear confirmation of the extent of my injury for the first time. But it was also an enormous relief when the doctor explained that the fractures were deemed 'stable', and he reassured me that I should be able to walk again in time, with hard work and intensive treatment. I was so thankful to be under the care of Australian doctors and for the exceptional effort Colonel Condon and the Australian Defence Force had put into getting me home in the best shape possible. It seemed ironic that I had survived all the bombings in Lebanon but had been severely injured inside an armoured vehicle in a road accident.

An army psychologist conducted a counselling session with me at the Holsworthy army hospital. But soon afterwards she was diverted to what I was told was a 'higher priority' case in Iraq, where a rocket-propelled grenade had exploded in an Australian camp. A well-meaning chaplain was assigned to me instead, and this required explaining and reliving the ordeal with someone new for the third time.

Now that I was home in Australia with medical resources available, I thought I would be assigned a regular counsellor or therapist to help me decompress and begin to process some of the trauma and grief of the war. I knew it would take me a number of sessions and continuity with a therapist was paramount. Each time I had to introduce myself to a new therapist, and divulge my grief and trauma, it required trust and a considerable emotional investment; it was a step backwards to have to start all over again. I wanted some guarantee that there would be more than one session involved and continuity with the professional treating me.

The UN media management of my case was a source of bemusement for me. The only media statement released was by Major General Clive Lilley, chief of staff at UNTSO; in an Australian ABC radio interview, he said that an Australian male officer had been slightly injured in a vehicle accident in Lebanon, but he was perfectly fine. An explanation as to why my circumstances necessitated this change of gender and the downplaying of my injuries was never given.

My parents, who were visiting my brother in London, changed their return flight and flew to Sydney to be with me as soon as they could. I know that the kilometres of distance that separated us exacerbated their feelings of not being able to protect me during my ordeal. This isolation from me was difficult for them to endure and has subsequently had a profound effect on them both. It was such a relief for them to actually see me in one piece and to know that I was safely home.

While in hospital at Holsworthy I very much appreciated the phone calls, visits and well wishes from my family and many of my friends—some of whom travelled great distances to see me. Clare, my second-in-command in Jerusalem, called to check on my progress after hearing the extent of my injuries; it was great to receive her call and also to gain an update on the war as I continued to be concerned for the safety of my team-mates remaining in Lebanon. Many army personnel visited me, including Major General Mark Kelly and Brigadier Mick Kehoe, and their supportive words gave me enormous encouragement. Two of my team-mates, Tore and Jarno, who were still working in Lebanon and Israel, managed to track down my hospital number in Sydney. Simply to hear their voices and encouragement was beyond what any words could explain.

Meanwhile, my back muscles were a complete ball of spasm. They were constantly in 'protective mode', locking down as part of their natural defence mechanism to guard my spinal cord. These tight muscles needed to be released, so I undertook two agonising physiotherapy sessions a day. I dreaded the arrival of the smiling physios each morning. They would take me away in a wheelchair to 'torture' me with their exercises and treatment regime. It was hard to comprehend that something so painful could possibly be good for you.

I ended up spending about two weeks in Holsworthy military hospital. Towards the end of my stay I gradually started to weight-bear and could walk short distances.

The commanding officer of the hospital, Lieutenant Colonel Georgeina Whelan, was good enough to let Clent stay in the hospital with me for a few days, until he found a temporary place to camp in Sydney. Lieutenant Colonel Whelan was a highly regarded and no-nonsense sort of woman, whom I admired greatly. A few days into my stay in hospital my positive facade came crashing down, which the doctors told me was inevitable, but I felt terrible and just wanted to be left on my own. After I spent a day feeling sorry for myself, Lieutenant Colonel Whelan blasted me—at the time this was a shock, but it was exactly what I needed to get back on track and I will be forever grateful for her tough love. I was then transferred for a further week's hospitalisation at the army hospital at my new posting location of Bandiana, at Albury-Wodonga, before being discharged to rest at home, while receiving daily outpatient treatment by the army medical staff.

It was essential to have family support, but unfortunately there weren't any army bases in the Byron Bay region, and so it was not an option to be posted close to my parents. But the posting to Bandiana turned out to be a stroke of luck, because Clent's family now lived in the area, having moved into town after selling the family farm. Once I had been released from hospital, we actually moved in with Clent's parents for a couple of months; an influx of contractors into the Albury region, while the new freeway was being constructed, had resulted in a shortage of rental properties there.

During those initial months after hospitalisation, I was quite despondent and at times downright unbearable to be around, but they doused me with their love and support, despite myself and even when I didn't deserve it. While we were still looking for somewhere to live, I continued my intensive medical treatment. Clent's entire family was a godsend. His brothers, Brent and Kelv, who lived in Melbourne, were always on hand whenever my medical appointments took me there. On several occasions when I suffered abdominal attacks, they even accompanied me to the emergency department and spent the night beside my bed waiting for me to recover enough to be discharged.

My parents still lived in Alstonville and my brother was in London; despite the geographical distance, making it difficult for face-to-face contact, they provided me with crucial and constant support throughout my rehabilitation. I am blessed that both Clent's and my family are such incredible, selfless and supportive people. Without them, I am not sure we could have coped.

The chief of the army, Lieutenant General Peter Leahy, visited me a couple of days after I was released from hospital at Bandiana. It was a tremendous gesture of support. General Leahy expressed his desire to have my story told on the ABC program *Australian Story* or on Andrew Denton's *Enough Rope*, and to use me to promote army recruiting. However, shortly after the general's visit, a number of factors conspired against that plan. Although I was never officially informed why, I suspected that a more careful consideration of the political sensitivities—including the Israeli strike on PB Khiam and my less-than-ideal medical evacuation from Lebanon—made my story somewhat of a risk for Defence.

After I was told by an army PR officer that there was no interest by *Australian Story*, Andrew Denton or any other media in my story, I asked to be allowed to focus on my medical rehabilitation and the responsibilities associated with my new job—dealing with strategic level planning for the Transport Corps. My debilitating injuries and likely medical discharge from the army probably further soured the story for Defence and—unsurprisingly for a PR machine famous for its reputation management—the idea of using me as a role model for recruiting was also abandoned.

Months into my treatment, I started to comprehend that I was in for a long and exhausting rehabilitation process. I was physically, emotionally and spiritually broken and it would require all my determination and courage to get through. Despite the amazingly selfless support from Clent, my family and friends, I felt like life's goalposts had suddenly moved, halfway through the game, leaving me stranded and disoriented. I had so many unanswered questions. What would happen to my military career, my health and my future physical capabilities? Being extremely fit and athletic was part of my identity, and I could not imagine a life without this. Would I get over the feelings of despondency and numbness? Would I always have survivor guilt? What would happen to my relationship with Clent? I felt my injuries made me a burden, so marrying me wasn't an attractive prospect and he deserved better. As time dragged on, I wasn't even sure if I wanted to continue playing the game of life any more, now that so much had been taken from me.

Every week was an unending procession of medical appointments—chiropractic, physiotherapy, acupuncture, hydrotherapy and massage—it was almost a full-time job. I also began counselling with Captain Rob Sneesby, a likable and highly regarded army psychologist based at Bandiana who had given me his word he would complete more than one session with me. Rob quickly assessed that I needed concurrent treatment with a psychiatrist due to the frequency of flashbacks I was experiencing from my time in Lebanon, and the poor sleep patterns resulting from severe back and sciatic nerve pain. I was referred to Dr John Cronin in Melbourne on a once-a-month treatment basis. My nerves were shot. Any sudden noise caused me to hit the deck, aggravating my back injuries. While watching the movie *The Patriot* at Clent's uncle's house one rainy Sunday afternoon, the battlefield noises sent me diving for cover; in the process, I accidentally threw my full glass of red wine all over their white fabric lounge, their light carpet and my favourite white jumper. It was an unnerving and costly experience, from which I learnt that I was now affected by action films—I was so jumpy and on edge that I just could not watch them.

It was embarrassing and humiliating when flashbacks or sudden noises affected me in public—many people reacted with smirks. I imagine they probably thought I was a drug addict, or just plain mad—perhaps they were right. I felt that I had no friends to talk things over with: my UN team-mates were dead or posted back to their homelands, and my ADFA mates were scattered around the country and the world. I was fortunate to have Clent. Although I wished he had not experienced the war, the fact that he had, and so understood first-hand some of what I was feeling, was invaluable to me.

For many members of the Defence Force, admitting you need psych support is viewed as being weak. Therefore, there is a stigma associated with psych support and a fear that it will have a detrimental effect on your career. Even now, mandatory debriefing after returning from operations is often only undertaken begrudgingly by soldiers. Because of this deeply ingrained belief, I found myself quite reluctant to admit that I needed assistance. I knew I needed help in understanding why events in Lebanon continued to flash through my mind and why I couldn't sleep. But at the same time, I worried that admitting this would hinder my career prospects—the generally held perception was that psychological issues and command responsibility are mutually exclusive in an officer.

Despite this internal struggle, my support network convinced me that receiving intense counselling might help me adjust. After some monthly sessions, I agreed to daily treatments with Dr Cronin for a week, which we hoped would be more effective. Clent said he would drive me to Melbourne and then catch a flight home so I could have the car there. But it was only when we arrived that we discovered I would need to be admitted into a civilian psych hospital to receive the daily treatment—a very different scenario from what I had envisaged. The only room available in the hospital required me to share with a seriously ill woman who was struggling with a mental disorder as well as drug and alcohol dependency. I was immediately uncomfortable. Clent was concerned for my safety and that this arrangement would compromise my mental state; he insisted that the situation was not acceptable.

I discussed the situation with Captain Sneesby, who agreed that staying in a hotel close by would be the best option for that evening and that he would speak with Dr Cronin the next day to organise a more suitable accommodation arrangement. Clent was happy with this outcome and settled me at the hotel before catching his flight home to Albury. The next day, Dr Cronin agreed that these arrangements were not suitable and that he would speak with the civilian medical staff back at Bandiana, who were responsible for my welfare and would need to approve the changes. Unfortunately, this change created an issue for the staff at Bandiana, because they would be legally liable if something happened to me while undergoing intense psychotherapy. To stay with relatives or in a motel, as I had during previous monthly visits to Dr Cronin, was no longer an option.

I then spent a frustrating four hours, from eleven in the morning until three in the afternoon, waiting in my car outside the psychiatric hospital for a decision about what to do. By this stage, alone and now distraught, I just wanted to go home. It had been a voluntary decision to go to Melbourne, but I was now told that I no longer had a choice in the matter and I was not permitted to drive home.

Eventually, I was ordered to drive myself to RAAF Laverton hospital, on the other side of the city, where I was placed under 'watch' by nursing staff. I could be treated by Dr Cronin each day, but would need to stay at the hospital under supervision. Although I understood the legal issues the staff at Bandiana were bound by, I felt embarrassed, and the handling of the entire incident was a devastating blow for me as I headed to rock bottom.

I really struggled against the notion of losing my independence and came to despise my need for assistance. In the early stages of my recovery, I had even needed help to dress, bathe and simply move around. I resented dependency. I was 30 years old, and yet I had to be treated like a three-year-old. I felt like a burden on everyone I loved, especially Clent, who remained by my side even though I had urged him to just forget about me and get on with his life. I didn't want to hold him back any more.

We had only known each other for a little over a year by this stage and boy, had I put him through the wringer! Talk about one hell of a getting-to-know-you process. I thought back to PB Khiam and Wolf, who had jokingly asked whether I put all my boyfriends through a war before considering a more serious relationship. If only he had known how much that process would entail and how much Clent had endured as a result. I certainly wouldn't have blamed him if he had decided to end our relationship, as I was no longer a happy person to be around. At times I wished he would leave, so I could just be miserable on my own.

My back and psych injuries were not my biggest medical concern—the undiagnosed abdominal attacks, which had started in the Solomon Islands and continued into my tour in Syria, returned now with a vengeance despite the medication. This time they were more frequent and far more intense. Emergency trips to hospital every week, and sometimes more often, became the norm. This, along with my other medical treatments, became my new way of life.

The abdominal attacks led the doctors to start testing for terminal illnesses and I spent months worrying that at any moment I might be told more bad news. The anxiety and stress took their toll. It must have been even worse for Clent—the helplessness he felt while watching someone he loved endure such chronic pain was a form of torture. After endless months of medical tests and no answers, I reached the stage where I would almost have preferred to hear bad news, in the absence of no news at all.

All I could do was wait for the next series of tests or for an impromptu ambulance ride to the hospital's emergency department in excruciating pain. During such crises, my muscles would be convulsing in spasm and this would invariably set me back weeks with the physio. Unable to diagnose the cause of these incapacitating abdominal attacks, the doctors in emergency would treat the symptoms, ultimately administering the strongest pain relief and anti-nausea medication available. Wiped out by these drugs, I would take days to get some strength back after each episode. And through all of this, we were still not addressing the root cause of the problem, despite canvassing the best specialists around the country. No one seemed to have a clue about what was making me so very ill.

Around this time I turned 31. Clent's birthday present gave me an opportunity to start turning things around—it was the world's most adorable kitten. He was a tiny ball of thick, black, fluffy fur with bright green eyes and an enormous bushy tail that seemed to be out of proportion to the rest of his body; like a skunk, he proudly carried his tail bolt upright when he walked. Clent had rescued him from the local veterinary clinic, which had a program for taking in stray litters of kittens. As everyone with a cat knows, cats choose their owners, rather than the other way around. Thankfully, he dashed straight into my arms and I instantly fell in love with him and set about thinking of a suitable name.

During the war on PB Khiam, I had shared with Wolf my plan to get a dog when I returned to Australia and that I would name it 'Khiam'. Wolf liked the name so much that he asked if he got another puppy would I mind if he named it Khiam as well. Although the word 'Khiam' now held so many sad feelings for me, I thought perhaps by naming my kitten Khiam this might remind me of the good times rather than just the sad ones. Pets are amazing therapy and Khiam the cat remained with me each time I was confined to bed—sometimes for days on end—and he seemed inherently to know when I was unwell.

The army had promoted me to the rank of major following my return from Lebanon, and appointed me to a staff position responsible for a dozen senior soldiers dealing with strategic-level planning for the Transport Corps. But, as much as I wanted to get back into work, the continued attacks of abdominal pain, which inevitably took me to hospital and then required time for recovery, made it impossible for me to do justice to my role and the people who relied on me.

After about six months, the army removed me from this policy management position and replaced me with another major; I was put into a pool for unassigned officers. Although I understood the army had no option than to stand me down due to my ill-health, I felt like a failure. This became another source of loss and grieving. I felt I had let down not only myself but, more importantly, my team and my new commanding officer. Instead of being an asset to his unit, I was constantly in hospital—a passenger and a liability to the group. My self-esteem and confidence plunged to all-time lows. Because of my physical injuries, I was not able to exercise, which meant I had gained considerable weight, further exacerbating my feelings of inferiority and my lack of self-worth.

I spiralled downhill and felt out of control. As the fog of depression descended on me, I asked myself: *Why bother even getting out of bed?* I no longer had a job, a role or a purpose. What was the point of even getting dressed? Clent had resumed his corporate career in a challenging marketing role with a multinational company while I spent my days in my pyjamas, counting down the hours until he returned home from work. While his job demanded long hours and frequent travel, I considered it a special effort just to get out of bed and move to the lounge, rather than sleeping through as much of the day as I could. There was something comforting about hugging my doona and pillow as I waited for the wave of sleep to engulf me and take me away from the world. I didn't even want to be awake; sleep was an escape from the harsh reality of what my life had become.

I knew I was heading in a dangerous direction—into the darkness of depression—but I didn't have the strength or desire to fight it. Thank God for Clent's strength of character and loyalty—he was my rock. I would surely have given in to those dreadful thoughts of self harm if he had left me during this period.

In an attempt to cure my abdominal illness, the doctors removed my gall bladder, believing it was responsible for my severe pain attacks. But it turned out to be perfectly healthy, and the attacks continued. However, a procedure using X-ray guidance of an anaesthetic injection to alleviate nerve damage in my neck was successful; the doctors blocked the nerve and this relieved some of my spinal pain, rectifying the daily migraine headaches and constant numbness and tingling in my right hand, which had given me grief for ten months, ever since the accident. I was appreciative of any small improvement in my condition; to stop the headaches and regain some normal sensations in my right hand was a great step forward.

Meanwhile, military colleagues told me to 'just forget about Lebanon and get on with things'. But, as much as I tried, that was more easily said than done. I was experiencing flashbacks and horrific nightmares about the war. Although I craved the escape provided by sleep, each night I was afraid to fall asleep because the same nightmare would replay over and over of what I imagined it would have been like during the final hours on PB Khiam, before the fatal bombing. No matter what I did consciously in an attempt to think of something else, my subconscious was consumed by these thoughts.

I could no longer sleep without prescribed pills and painkillers; but even then, I would wake more tired than the day before. At night I would lie awake in bed, with the sciatic nerve pains down my legs throbbing continuously. I was becoming more and more drug dependent, which scared me in itself. Night-time was now my enemy—I feared the dark and was even unable to remain in the house on my own, forcing me to stay with Clent's parents whenever he was away with work.

I didn't want anyone to see me in my poor state, so I retreated from the world, my family and friends. Pain was the only constant, and a daily reminder of the nightmare that had started with the Lebanon War. I was eventually diagnosed with post-traumatic stress disorder, which the Defence Force regards as an irreparable condition, and so, to my mind, on top of my physical injuries, signalled an end to my career in the army.

Standing as a further obstacle to moving forward was my fear that Clent, quite reasonably, might decide to move on with his life and leave me. I felt as though I didn't have much to offer any more.

22 Battles on the Home Front

Twelve months after being injured in Lebanon, there was mounting pressure on me to leave Defence altogether. Due to my injuries, my case was raised at the army medical board, where I was deemed no longer medically fit to continue serving in the army; I was to be medically retired. I was informed of this determination in writing and the discharge date was set to occur three months later.

However, this raised the question as to whose care I fell under. Defence had determined that I was unfit for duty and that my injuries were permanent and unlikely to improve; therefore, in their view, I should be discharged and become the responsibility of the Department of Veterans' Affairs (DVA). However, DVA did not want to know about my case until there was an absolute diagnosis of my abdominal complaint; they also wanted to wait another eighteen months or more before they would look at deeming my spinal injuries permanent and stable.

This meant I would be discharged from the army without the appropriate level of medical cover under DVA. I didn't even have the option of paying for private medical insurance, because I had a significant pre-existing medical condition that providers would not be obliged to cover.

I was severely sleep deprived, my self-esteem was nonexistent and my morale had hit rock bottom. I knew I was slipping into depression but I really didn't care about anything much any more. From the moment I opened my eyes in the morning to the time

I went to bed at night, I beat myself up about the cruel twist of fate that had resulted in my team-mates being dead and me having survived. Every now and then, fleetingly, I felt a desire to do something substantial with my life, to make Wolf and the guys proud. But invariably, I would take one step forward only to have my health bring me crashing back down.

My confidence left me altogether and, as a result, I clung to Clent, praying that he would not leave me too. I was no longer the woman he had fallen in love with; instead, I was a distant, irrational, unresponsive shell of my former self, submerged in a world of negativity, self-pity and pain. I was drugged up and beaten down by my own vicious thoughts.

•

Shortly after the 2006 Lebanon War ended, the Lebanese government awarded me two Republic of Lebanon war medals. But I knew nothing about them for two years—the Australian government, it turned out, withheld them from me.

The medals were finally delivered on 22 December 2008. I had just returned home with Clent's mother, Christine, from another fruitless medical procedure, four hours away at the Royal Melbourne Hospital. Shoved under the doormat was a mysterious-looking yellow envelope bearing the army's rising sun insignia. When I opened it, I was overjoyed to discover its contents. Along with the medals was a letter emblazoned with a Lebanese flag and three impressive certificates written in Arabic.

Tears of happiness streamed down my face as I explained to Christine that the Lebanese government had awarded me the medals in appreciation of my service and sacrifice during the 2006 war. One medal was the Republic of Lebanon War Decoration, 'awarded for acts of bravery in war or in the cause of national security', and the other was the Republic of Lebanon Wounded in Combat Decoration. Never in my wildest dreams had I envisaged that I would receive a foreign country's war medals. I was immediately roused by the prospect that this might be the positive boost I needed to get my life back on track and pull me out of my state of depression.

But then a further item fell out of the envelope—it was a hard copy of an email exchange involving the Honours and Awards section of the Australian Defence Force, between a defence civilian and a navy lieutenant commander. The officer had contacted Honours and Awards on my behalf, requesting approval for me to be permitted to wear the medals on my army uniform. The email explained that the Australian government had received the medals more than eighteen months prior. The delay in advising me of the awards and issuing the medals to me had been the result of discussions at senior levels of Defence about whether or not I should be allowed to receive the medals and wear them on my uniform.

My elation turned to shock. And then anger. I was horrified that my own government could have withheld these medals. My medals, which were of such significance to me. My hands were trembling and I collapsed on the lounge sobbing in a frenzy of emotions. 'How could they have done such a cruel, callous thing?' I blurted out. Adding insult to injury, the email went on to say that I was permitted to keep the medals as a 'memento' of my time in Lebanon. I felt this to be a terribly poor choice of wording, and I found it insulting and insensitive. I felt it insinuated that my medals were some sort of souvenir from a holiday, not an acknowledgment of service in a war zone where my team-mates had been killed.

I frightened myself by my reaction to all this—I was completely out of control. I felt a dangerous combination of depression mixed with wild, raging emotions of anger and despair. Thankfully, Christine was with me and she is a trained volunteer counsellor with the state emergency services. I was in such a vulnerable state that day that I hate to think what I might have done if I had been on my own; I might have even given up entirely and tried to take my own life. Looking back at the situation now, I know that the contents of the email triggered a deep, dark anger that I had been bottling up; this incident became a further major blow to my mental health.

The following day I thought more about the odd way in which the medals had been presented to me. Instead of a ceremony and formal occasion to mark the award of foreign medals, which was military protocol, they had simply been delivered anonymously—left under the front doormat of my home. It appeared that the envelope had been hand-delivered by Defence staff as it was an internal Defence envelope and did not have any postage stamps or marks to indicate that it had been sent through the ordinary mail. The fact that I did not have to sign for receipt of the envelope seemed to me that it had not been delivered by a commercial courier. With no requirement to acknowledge receipt of the medals, I wondered what would have happened if the envelope had been stolen from my doorstep. I informed my commanding officer about the strange delivery and presentation of the medals and he was as stunned as I was—not only had the medals not been delivered by my unit, but he had no idea that I had been awarded them in the first place.

•

For some time I had been worrying about my future and the bureaucratic gap that I was falling into between the Defence Force and Veterans' Affairs. I seemed to be living in a grey area. Not only was there the question of when I would become the responsibility of DVA, but there was also the question of how my injuries were classified and what health cover I would receive. DVA only provides health cover for injuries that have a diagnosis and are proven to be related to service in the military. I was lucky to have been serving on a UN mission that encouraged us to take evidence of violations; as a result, I actually had video footage of the accident in which I broke my back. This was very beneficial in proving that my injuries were service related. However, because there was no diagnosis of my abdominal condition, it could not be confirmed as having been caused by my army service—I was concerned that this illness was not going to be covered by DVA. This would result in me being medically discharged from the army without adequate health cover. How was I going to pay the medical bills when the likelihood of me being able to work was not high, given my health condition, ongoing illness and frequent emergency hospitalisations?

I sought advice and assistance from the advocates at my local Hume Veterans' Centre—wonderful volunteers, most of whom are former soldiers who were themselves injured during their military service. These advocates volunteer their time and knowledge to assist current service personnel in the difficult task of navigating through all of the legislation and administration that is required to gain health cover under DVA. My case was particularly complex—I had multiple injuries, there was still no diagnosis of my abdominal condition and I had been injured on a peacekeeping mission that had been classified as a non-warlike operation. Under DVA's rules, entitlements for exactly the same injury will differ, depending on whether the soldier is injured on duty in Australia or overseas, or whether an operation is declared 'peacetime', 'non-warlike' or 'warlike'. Because entitlements under DVA are linked to how an operation is classified by the Defence Department, which in turn is linked to which Australian war medal is awarded with a particular mission, I was told by the advocates that it was crucial to get my service in Lebanon upgraded to warlike service, which they felt was justified since the UN had deemed it a war.

Faced with having to fight two government departments for war service recognition and health cover entitlements, I felt an overwhelming sense of abandonment. I was deeply traumatised and the constant struggle was taking its toll. Every phone call to DVA was like going into battle yet again because each time I seemed to be shuffled from one DVA representative to the next; no case manager provided a single point of contact and continuity.

After a difficult phone conversation with one particularly insensitive DVA representative, I retreated into the shower and collapsed into a foetal position on the floor, crying uncontrollably as the water splashed over my face and body, washing my tears of anguish down the drain. My sobbing became louder and louder until I was howling uncontrollably. My body was shaking with each wave of emotion that poured out of me in a desperate plea for answers and help. But no one heard my cries—I was at home on my own.

After purging my grief and anguish in the shower, I was emotionally exhausted. I dragged my soaked body back to bed, not even bothering to dry myself. I wondered how many more days like this I could endure—if there was a light at the end of this tunnel, it was nowhere in sight.

Thankfully, the advocates were there to help and they advised me that I needed to consult a lawyer who specialised in military issues. After exhausting all other avenues—I felt the system should work without this intervention—I employed Greg Isolani, the lawyer recommended by the advocates, to argue my case with DVA for health cover and with Defence for war service recognition. My injuries would require medical treatment for the rest of my life and I wanted to ensure I would not be bankrupted by medical fees in the process. This was important to me because there was a high likelihood of future complications and an expectation by my treating doctors that my medical condition would further deteriorate over time. Greg Isolani also advised me not to take legal action against the UN for the mismanagement of my injuries, because by doing so I would forego any entitlements from the Australian government.

My primary focus was to obtain adequate health cover under DVA; but I also felt justified in my pursuit for the upgrade to warlike service recognition, because I did believe I had served in a war zone. Public information sources reveal that in the conflict some 2000 people were killed, 6500 were wounded and over 1.5 million were displaced as refugees; Israel had flown over 10,000 bombing sorties and fired over one million cluster bombs from aircraft into southern Lebanon, and there were thousands of rockets, bombs and artillery shells fired across the border during the period. The UN, the Lebanese government and the world's media had all declared the events of July 2006 as 'warlike', which seemed to me to be overwhelming and definitive. The footage I had taken from PB Khiam was also influential in my submission for warlike service as it clearly showed the conditions we were operating in during the war. As a result, I was of the firm belief that the service of the four Australians serving in Lebanon (Brad, Amanda, Birchy and I) during the war should be recognised as such by the Australian government too.

However, Australia's legislation on service recognition—determining whether an operation is classified as 'peacetime', 'non-warlike' or 'warlike'—was written in 1920 and in my opinion is outdated. The traditional criteria to qualify for warlike service did not adequately reflect the operational environments into which we send our soldiers. The criteria stipulate that for an operation to be classified warlike, soldiers must be armed and there needs to be an identified enemy. Working as unarmed peacekeepers meant that we hadn't met these criteria, even though there was a war taking place around us. Ironically, we were at the receiving end of bombs dropped by jets where it made no difference if we were carrying rifles or not. And, since neither Israel nor Hezbollah were considered the 'enemy' to UN peacekeepers, my submission for warlike service recognition was rejected.

But our case did fall under the principle of 'incurring danger', which is what Greg Isolani used to challenge the ruling. This was supported by the vice chief of the Defence Force, Lieutenant General David Hurley, and the minister for Defence, John Faulkner, but it nonetheless met strong opposition from DVA and the prime minister and cabinet.

This was another battle I could well have done without. At my own personal expense, it would ultimately consume three years of my life.

23 The Bumpy Road Back

Rehabilitation is exhausting and frustrating. While I struggled to come to terms with the fate of my team-mates and gradually started to see small improvements, I continued treatment of my injuries sustained during the war. But it was not all smooth sailing. Although I felt better at times, I sometimes felt like I was even more out of control, now that I was catching glimpses of my old self again. I undertook a three-week live-in chronic pain management course in hospital, hoping to reduce my dependency on painkillers. Constant pain was morale destroying, leaving me wrung out every day and so I was desperate to find a solution.

The chronic pain course reminded me how much physical exercise, and running in particular, had meant to me before I was injured. Running was not just exercise—it was my daily escape, allowing me to clear my head and concentrate on my breathing, like an active form of meditation. The reward for zestful exercise had always been a natural endorphin high, which would do marvellous things for my self-esteem and confidence, something I now craved. I realised that I had for years taken my former physical abilities for granted.

With the knowledge that my injuries would probably prevent me from ever running again, I was trying to find a replacement for this physical activity. I was determined to get the most out of my body, within its new parameters. I worked hard with Kev Laws, my dedicated physiotherapist, and Tim Maguire, my brilliant chiropractor, as well as using acupuncture to free up the seized muscles and damaged nerves. I also attended spinal fitness classes run by a physio at Kev's practice, and followed a daily exercise regime in the gym. I set myself weekly physical goals, such as walking 200 metres—activities I would never have previously considered exercise at all, but which were now a huge physical challenge.

Although I could stand and walk, my range of movement was limited. I was advised by my treating doctors that I would continue to suffer chronic pain for the rest of my life and I would require weekly treatment to maintain movement. They also believed that my back injuries will gradually deteriorate over time. But I was lucky for so many reasons; most importantly I was surrounded by a great support network and my injuries could have been substantially worse. Many soldiers have endured far more debilitating injuries than me. But the problem with depression is that it robs you of optimism. At the time, I couldn't see the positives. Where I had previously been determined and strong, I now just didn't care anymore. I was consumed in my own world; my reactions to my situation were self-centred and introspective as I had lost perspective and awareness.

My family, friends and Clent continued to be steadfast constants throughout my darkness, uncertainty and anxiety. Like most of us, Clent has his fair share of faults. But he was my 'glass half full' man and an eternal optimist, whose positive attitude kept me going.

•

A year or more into my rehabilitation, one day, in the midst of what had become an all-too-common scene—me crying in self-pity on the shower floor—something changed deep inside me, it was a turning point. Instead of selfishly questioning why all of this had happened to me, I suddenly thought of Clent and all that he had endured over the past few years, as my life spiralled out of control. He had been so valiant, never showing so much as the slightest crack in his optimism. He would support and encourage me, even when I was at my most vile and demoralised. I said to myself, *Matti, since when did you become a victim? This is not who you are. Don't let them take everything from you.*

With a picture in my mind of Clent's smile breaking through the negative thoughts that had taken over my life, I came to the conclusion that he deserved better . . . far better, in fact! I slowly picked myself up from the floor of the shower and turned off the water. As I dried myself, I was even more resolute: *Clent deserves to have back the woman he fell in love with two years ago.* And I wanted to be that girl again for him.

I immediately made a plan to get my life back on track, starting with small steps. The next morning, when Clent's alarm went off, I too got out of bed; I ironed him a fresh business shirt. This normally insignificant act then became my whole reason to get up in the morning. It was a small thing, but to me at the time it was a vitally important task—something to spur me into action each day. It was the beginning of my slow but steady return to a more normal life.

After more than a year of hard work, I became stronger and a little more mobile. The return of my physical independence also formed the foundation for a return to happiness. Although activity still caused me pain, just getting out of the house, which I had made my sanctuary for far too long, was a positive thing.

Looking back at this time in my life, I think my experience of hitting complete rock bottom prompted my determination to divert off the dark path I was on and make the U-turn into a positive recovery. I started to gradually get in touch with the 'old' me again.

•

On 23 December 2007, my life really took a dramatically positive, upward turn. While on a trip back to Alstonville to see my family for Christmas, Clent cajoled me to go for a walk up to the headland overlooking my favourite beach in the world, Lennox Head. The beach and the entire region held so many wonderful memories for me, right back to playing in the surf as a child with my brother.

As I looked out, reminiscing and evoking better times, I noticed Clent getting down on bended knee. Dressed to the nines in his best holiday board shorts and singlet, he produced a stunning engagement ring and asked me to marry him.

I did not need to give the decision a moment's thought and immediately beamed: 'Yes!' He had made me the happiest girl in the world! Lennox Head would forever hold even more sentiment for me now. His proposal also dissolved the fear I had been privately carrying, that he would eventually leave me. In hindsight I now realise Clent was never going to leave me—and, knowing me so well, he had delayed his proposal of marriage until I had turned the corner. He knew I would have misinterpreted this as an act of charity or sympathy had he proposed earlier. He waited until I had regained that spark of fighting spirit and was on the up.

The timing of Clent's proposal was impeccable. My brother, Mark, had just flown back to Australia from London to spend Christmas at my parents' house. Clent's parents and his youngest brother, Kelv, were also in town for the festive season celebrations, so both families could share in our exciting news. The champagne flowed freely.

It was then that I learnt Clent had actually asked my parents for my hand in marriage back in 2006, when he had met them in Turkey, shortly before escorting them to visit me in Lebanon. He had also shared with them his plan to propose to me during our planned dive holiday at Sharm el-Sheikh in Egypt and had decided on an engagement ring at a jeweller's in Tyre. But during the war, as bombs rained down, it was definitely not safe to trek across town to check on the ring, and we left before hostilities ended. Who could have predicted that the Hezbollah ambush, sparking a war with Israel, would have got in the way of Clent's marriage proposal? When I spoke with my parents from the bunker of PB Khiam, during the first week of the war, my mother had been very upset. Little did I know then that this was partly through fear that I might die not knowing that Clent planned to marry me.

With my new Version 2 engagement ring, and a smile that could not be removed from my face for love nor money, the festive season that year at Byron Bay became my most memorable ever. But there was a lot to be done before a wedding could take place.

Since my back injury, I had gained over 15 kilos—almost a quarter of my total body weight. So, in addition to all the usual wedding arrangements that needed to be made, I also decided to use the upcoming wedding as motivation to lose those extra kilos. Not all that different from many other brides-to-be, I'm sure. I jokingly named the weight-loss regime 'Operation Supermodel', but I was determined to regain my old body in time for the big day. Discipline had always been one of my strengths, and I summoned up all of my determination so as to feel like I was my old self again in time for our wedding day.

Just shy of one year later and having succeeded in my quest to lose the weight, I felt incredible as we celebrated our wedding day in Byron Bay with 45 of our closest family and friends, from all over the world. It really was a celebration of life, love and commitment. Each and every one of our guests had played a significant role in our recovery from the events in Lebanon.

The day was awash with emotions. The wedding telegrams, in particular, brought most guests unstuck—one minute we would all be hysterical with laughter, the next wiping away the tears, particularly as we heard the beautiful sentiments penned by the wives of my team-mates killed on PB Khiam. These messages touched the hearts of everyone. In particular, the telegram from Wolf's wife, Cynthia:

Dear Matti and Clent,

I am thrilled to have this opportunity to express my feelings on your wedding day. I know Wolf, as Matti knew him, would want me to do so. Although Paeta (Wolf) and I were married for nine short years, our love, understanding and devotion to each other was as strong as love eternal. Do not live life with regret. Take every opportunity life gives you as a gift. If opportunity lacks, then steal the gift of time. Life can be short or long—it matters not. How you live life, laugh, love and are loved in return is all that matters in the end.

All our love, Cynthia and Paeta.

My gift to Clent was a song I had secretly written for him which I performed with my guitar. The song, I hoped, described the journey we had been on to that point in our lives. In the three years we had known each other, our lives had become entwined through adversity and triumph. We felt we made a pretty good team and, together, we could tackle just about anything that came our way.

•

After the high of our wedding, the continuing battle with the government for future health cover quickly brought me back to reality. I was still going by ambulance to the hospital emergency department in crippling pain almost every week or two with my abdominal condition, which remained undiagnosed. The attacks were sudden and incapacitating. I would experience great difficulty in breathing and such intense pain that it would induce vomiting.

DVA continued to refuse to cover the illness until there was a confirmed diagnosis and I could prove that my military service caused the condition. The fact that I had been fit and well prior to joining the army, and before deploying to tropical disease areas in the Solomon Islands, did not count as sufficient evidence of a service-related condition.

Meanwhile, the army continued its efforts to discharge me on medical grounds while I remained on sick leave. I fought to delay my discharge date twice, arguing that I should not be medically discharged until after a determination had been made about my health cover under DVA. It was a difficult situation. I knew I could no longer serve in the army as a result of the injuries I had sustained in Lebanon, but at least in the army my health was covered for the frequent hospital visits for the undiagnosed abdominal attacks. But I no longer felt like a soldier; instead, I felt like a burden on the system.

From the first time I had started to get these attacks, in the Solomon Islands, I knew that some questioned the legitimacy of the condition. Because a diagnosis could not be determined, there was an insinuation at work that I was feigning my illness. However, my blood tests proved there was something drastically wrong—inflammatory markers in my blood would become dramatically elevated during an attack, before settling to more normal levels several days later. I couldn't fake my own blood results. Something was wrong, but the doctors just could not determine what it was.

I was also told by colleagues of malicious rumours that were circulating in the military community that I had faked my injury in Lebanon to escape the war zone. Being accused of deserting is one of the most horrific accusations against an army officer and I could not believe my integrity was being questioned. I imagined these rumours were being generated by ill-informed staff, who weren't aware that there was video evidence of the accident or that the MRI taken in Cyprus and initially reported as inconclusive was later found by doctors in Australia to show several fractured and wedged vertebrae. If only the true extent of my injuries had been discovered originally, I might have been spared years of pain. Away from the workplace, I now had with no opportunity to defend my reputation. The rumours weighed on my mind heavily and compounded my poor mental state. In the end, I had to conclude that I only needed to concern myself with the views of those people I respected and admired—their opinion was what really mattered. But at times this was easier said than done.

During my military career we were always assured that, although we were at times performing high-risk activities, we would be looked after if injured. But, despite having served in the army for fifteen years, including participation in five operations, and having sustained injuries in the theatre of war, I suddenly found out it was not a straightforward process to get health cover.

The Defence Department and DVA are two separate government departments that, seemingly, have little communication with each other. In discussions with the minister for Veterans' Affairs, he summarised his department's position on my case by saying: 'Defence broke you, and Defence should fix you, before you are handed over to DVA.' As I have learnt, the soldier required to deal with both departments is often caught in the middle. Soldiers are left to battle on their own for health cover with DVA without the support of the military chain of command. Although there are good people within DVA working to improve these processes, from discussions with other veterans, I found that the difficulties I experienced are not uncommon. I felt that during the claim process I was dealing with uncompassionate staff who had little knowledge or experience of anything military, let alone what I, the injured soldier, might have suffered (and continue to suffer).

While the military promise to look after their injured, in fact it is DVA that is responsible for medically retired personnel and, sadly, DVA sometimes falls short. Our soldiers unquestioningly put Queen and country ahead of personal obligations, but in return they struggle to access their entitlements, because the process to do so is extremely convoluted. On average, according to my lawyer, DVA takes over three years to settle a claim (assessing the injury as permanent and stable); however, the military cannot be expected to keep soldiers on sick leave for three or more years while DVA is making these determinations. As a result, soldiers are often discharged without knowing what their health entitlements are, and they fall into the gap between the departments without health cover.

My case was aided greatly by the fact that I had an expert lawyer involved and I was a keynote speaker at a forum attended by the minister for Veterans' Affairs. As a result of my address the minister himself became personally involved in my case. However, most soldiers will not have these opportunities and the system should work without the need for these interventions. My case was particularly complicated, but I have met so many veterans who walked away from their claims as the process was just too difficult and they were not well enough to fight it.

In the battle to diagnose my abdominal condition, Clent and I left no stone unturned, desperately hoping to find a cure by consulting doctors and specialists across the country and around the world. But it was a doctor in Canberra, Colonel Stephen Rudzki, the Director of Army Health, who finally discovered the cause of all my abdominal agony, in early 2009. He diagnosed the cause of the attacks as a rupture in my diaphragm and prescribed a successful regime of treatment that has moderated the symptoms, frequency and intensity of my attacks.

He traced my condition back to when I first started experiencing symptoms in the Solomon Islands, and concluded that I had sustained a small tear in my diaphragm while on arduous patrol in the Solomons jungle, searching for Jimmy Rasta. During those patrols up and down mountains, I often slipped and occasionally fell; at the time I would usually be carrying some 25 kilograms in my daypack and webbing, which is carried on your upper body. The small tear became chronic when exacerbated in the vehicle accident in Lebanon. He said that when I was thrown into the APC's windscreen, in addition to my spinal injuries, the tear in my diaphragm had become much larger and this had created scar tissue, entrapping the vagus nerve, which controls breathing and diaphragm function. The scar would periodically aggravate the nerve causing the diaphram to go into spasm. This explained why the condition had become so much worse since the vehicle accident.

My relief at hearing that it was not a potentially life-threatening, terminal illness—which other specialists continued to test for—was beyond words. Although an inoperable condition, with Dr Rudzki's diagnosis now in hand and a successful treatment plan, DVA finally accepted liability for the condition and provided health cover, allowing me to be medically discharged from the army. After an exhausting three-year campaign, with the assistance of my lawyer, we had finally succeeded in gaining health cover for my injuries. I was discharged from the army on 4 May 2009.

•

By this time, except for the occasional severe diaphragm attack which, to this day, still leaves me requiring ambulance services and emergency admission to hospital, my health had stabilised enough for me to be fit to travel. I would now be able to visit the gravesites of my team-mates killed in Lebanon. I needed to pay my respects to my mates who had not returned, and to pass on my condolences to their families in person.

Clent and I knew this would be a tough trip, but it was one that we felt we had to make. I hoped it would relieve me of my recurrent nightmares, and help me achieve a sense of reality about the attack on PB Khiam and the passing of my team-mates. Their deaths had continued not to feel real. I also hoped for some form of closure on this chapter of my life, so Clent and I could move forward with our lives.

I had written to the families of my deceased team-mates and arranged to meet them. On 28 June 2009, our plane descended into Toronto airport, Canada. Clent took my hand in his; I was a bundle of nerves.

I had met Wolf's wife, Cynthia, in Lebanon in 2006 and we had got on very well. I felt like I knew her, because Wolf had loved talking about his soulmate, 'Cyn', and his beloved family, including their two children and two border collie dogs. But our lives were completely different now, and this was a most difficult situation. Cynthia had been a widow for almost three years and the anniversary of Wolf's death was just a few weeks away.

My stomach was all over the place and I didn't have the faintest idea of what to say or how to behave. What words would adequately express the sorrow and sympathy I felt for her loss? I suddenly questioned the decision to visit at all and wondered if our being here would cause Cynthia more distress than good. I so hoped it wouldn't.

Once we got inside the airport and amid the mass of people in the arrivals hall, I recognised Cynthia immediately. We embraced and I hugged her for a long time, as tears streamed down my face. All I could find to say over and over again was, 'I'm so sorry I couldn't bring Wolf home. I'm so sorry, Cyn. I'm so sorry. I'm so sorry.' She cried too. I had this irrational, self-imposed sense that I should have done something to save Wolf and the boys. In Cynthia's arms, I felt this burden of responsibility lifting slightly—it was so good to see her.

Cynthia drove us an hour south that afternoon, to Burlington, to visit Wolf's grave. All of a sudden I did not feel prepared for this moment and I hugged Cyn for what seemed like an eternity in front of Wolf's tombstone. More tears of sorrow. All the years of grief and anguish seemed to be pouring out of me now that I was here at his resting place. It was as though Wolf's passing was suddenly real and my survival became even more incredible.

I had sometimes wanted to trade places with Wolf since his death. He had a wife and family who loved him dearly. I had seen the grief and anguish on their faces at the funeral in Canada and that had deepened my sense of survivor guilt. Words by letter or email had seemed so inadequate. I had hoped that travelling halfway around the world three years later, to visit his grave at my first opportunity after being discharged from the military, would express the words that I had not been able to find to say.

I explained to Cynthia that I had a special request and an obligation to fulfil to Wolf. Back at PB Khiam, I had promised him and Big Mack that I would have cold beers waiting for them in Tyre when they rotated from the base a few days after me. As bizarre as it sounded, I wanted to bring some beers to Wolf's grave and make good on my promise to him. Cynthia loved the idea and said: 'You really did know Wolf well! He'd love the idea of Aussies flying around the world to bring him beers at his gravesite. Let's do it tomorrow.' I was relieved that she wasn't offended by my strange request.

The following morning we were back with a six-pack of Wolf's favourite ales at the beautiful tree-lined cemetery that overlooked the water. We made a toast and recited Wolf's paratrooper motto of 'Fair winds and soft landings' before I poured a bottle of the beer around his tombstone. Then Cynthia and Clent gave me some time on my own with Wolf. I felt awkward at first, sitting at the foot of his grave; but then, like the surge of a tidal wave, I couldn't stop as all of the grief and anger poured out of me. I cried and cried my heart out.

That evening Cynthia and I stayed up until the wee hours talking about the war. Cynthia told me that she had received a phone call at about 7 p.m. Lebanon time the night of the bombing. She could not hear, due to the static and broken connection, but she was sure it was Wolf calling her. She had told him that the line was too broken and he should hang up and try calling again, so he might get a better connection; the last thing she said was that she loved him. But the phone did not ring again. She had an unsettled feeling, so she took the dogs for a walk while hoping Wolf would call back on her mobile phone; but he never did.

Shortly after she returned from her walk, she was in the kitchen preparing dinner when a breaking news story interrupted the program on the television—a photograph of Wolf flashed on the screen and the accompanying audio said that he was suspected to have died at PB Khiam, after an Israeli air strike had destroyed the post. Cynthia was stunned and utterly shocked to hear the news via the media. She called Wolf's army unit, who could not confirm the information, as they too did not know about the incident. The harsh reality of today's journalists reporting from war zones around the world means that news is instant. Defence forces sometimes do not have enough time to confirm details and inform families through official notification processes prior to the news being aired. It was a horrific way for Cynthia to hear of the passing of her husband, and I cannot begin to imagine what she and the family went through as a result.

Wolf had previously worked at the Canadian Peace Training Centre in Kingston, Ontario, about four hours' drive from Toronto. When the Commanding Officer of the centre learnt of my upcoming visit, he asked if I would share my experiences with his staff. So the day after we had visited Wolf's grave, I fought back my emotions as I delivered a one-hour presentation on the lessons learnt from the 2006 Lebanon War, in the hope that this would save lives in the future. The presentation was all the more difficult to deliver given Wolf's wife, son and former colleagues were in the audience and having so recently visited his grave.

After my address I spoke with Colonel Bill Lewis, a retired officer who had also served with the UN in Lebanon in the 1990s during the First Gulf War period. Bill had so much to talk about from his time serving with the UN in Lebanon and I could have spent days exchanging stories with him. For the first time since the war, I recalled the many good times and happy memories from my year in the Middle East, rather than only details of the war. I found myself swapping stories about the joy of living submersed within the Middle Eastern culture and about the lifelong friendships I had forged with those serving from so many different nationalities. My time with Bill gave me a new perspective on my experience.

Bill had heard how I had been awarded two Lebanese war medals and that I had attempted unsuccessfully to have a second replica set made, which could be mounted alongside my other Australian medals. (The process of mounting medals in a group can cause damage to the medals so veterans often choose to use replicas rather than the original medals for mounting.) On the day of our departure from Canada, Bill went out of his way to hand-deliver a special present to me. His gift was a small box which held two Republic of Lebanon war medals.

Bill explained that, during his mission in Lebanon, he had bought the war medals for US$5 from a local man who was selling them off the bonnet of his Mercedes 300 in the fleamarket of the town of Ebel El Saki, not far from PB Khiam. Bill had been drawn to the medals because they seemed so exotic and meaningful, which would make them great souvenirs. He thought it was strange to be able to buy military war medals off the street, but then again, everything was for sale in Lebanon. By another amazing coincidence, he had bought exactly the same two war medals that I had been awarded. Bill clarified that he wanted me to have the medals to use as my replica set; he believed it was his fate to have purchased them all those years ago and to have kept them just so he could give them to me now. I was stunned and again tears welled in my eyes. It almost felt like I had cried throughout my entire week-long stay in Canada! I attempted to politely decline Bill's generous offer, but he would not have a bar of it. He insisted that I keep them and wear them with pride on Anzac Day, remembering my dear friends in Canada.

With my replica Lebanon medals safely stowed, we then flew from Canada to Finland, where we experienced the highs of reuniting with old UN friends. Elation gave way to grief as we went with Big Mack's family to visit his gravesite. With his family's blessing, we repeated the toast with a beer at his resting place—Big Mack's father, Pentti, said that his son would have absolutely loved that we flew all the way from Australia to have a beer with him. We got some strange looks from passers-by in the cemetery though, which Big Mack also would have found amusing.

Shortly after Big Mack's death, and still in a state of intense grief, Pentti had been diagnosed with cancer and, despite many procedures, he lost his battle with the illness a year later. Pentti had seen a photograph of Big Mack and me on the observation platform of PB Khiam during the war, and he explained that my arrival in Finland and the opportunity to meet and talk with me signified to him 'a blessing and a prayer answered'.

Big Mack's mother, Turttu, had thoughtfully prepared a massive sponge cake for Clent's birthday, which fell on the day of our visit and exactly four years since evacuating on the ship to Cyprus. In their humble farmhouse, over coffee and through broken English, Turttu surprised me by saying that she felt her son lived on through me. This was an unexpected notion for me; but I was happy to console them in their grief, if only a little, by sharing my account of the time I had spent with their wonderful son. They were a lovely and generous family, still terribly shocked by their loss.

The sadness of discussing Big Mack's death was balanced by a magical two weeks spent in Finland with my other Finnish team-mate, Jarno 'Smiley' Limnell. Though their personalities were very different, Big Mack and Jarno had gone through military training together and had worked closely afterwards. They were best mates. Now, Jarno was also finding it difficult to accept the loss of Big Mack and the circumstances surrounding his passing. In many ways, it was helpful for me to see that others too were still coming to terms with the events of the Lebanon War. It wasn't just me struggling on my own.

We spent a large part of our stay at Jarno's family's summer cottage, an hour or so from Helsinki by car, on the edge of the Baltic Sea. This picturesque property was nestled in a thick forest and had a small jetty providing access to the sea. It was an idyllic escape and the perfect location for my emotional discussions with Jarno about the war. These chats were often followed by the uplifting Finnish tradition of drinking vodka and cognac in the sauna and then cooling off in the freezing saltwater of the sea. I had shared the Finnish sauna experience several times with Big Mack and the other Finns while in Lebanon, so it only seemed fitting to be enjoying this tradition again as we toasted our dear friend.

Our time in Finland passed far too quickly; before we knew it we were on our way to visit more UN friends, this time in Norway.

During the war, my Norwegian team-mate Tore Rosseid had been due to replace me on PB Khiam, but had remained in Tyre to evacuate his family. In his place, Hans-Peter had volunteered to serve at PB Khiam as he was the team leader and he did not have any family in Lebanon to be evacuated. In a strange way, both Tore and I owe our lives to Hans-Peter. Tore explained that he had also struggled with the sense of guilt over this—it was a unique bond we shared. I appreciated immensely the time spent talking with Tore, sharing as we did our feelings as only people who served with us during the war would fully comprehend.

Tore told me that he had performed the grim task of trying to identify the bodies of our team-mates at PB Khiam. They believed Big Mack had been in the corner of the bunker that had taken the direct hit from the bomb, and this was why his remains were not recovered until ten days after the bombing. I know that his passing would have been swift and pain-free, although this did not make it any easier for his family.

Tore and I shared the photos and videos we had each taken during the war. Although this was confronting, difficult and at times simply unbearable, after a morning of discussions I actually started to feel a little better. I no longer felt isolated and the venting of my grief was quite therapeutic.

The remainder of our stay in Norway was truly blissful. We experienced the beauty of the Norwegian fjords, the diverse culture, amazing food and unique climate, not to mention the generous hospitality of the Rosseid family, who will always be lifelong friends. Our week in Norway was gone in the blink of an eye, but we took away with us amazing memories.

I would have loved to have then travelled to China, but unfortunately it had proven difficult to make contact and coordinate a visit with Du's wife. I hope one day to meet with Du's family and visit his grave too. Although I had been in contact with Hans-Peter's family, it was strange, but I did not feel ready to visit my Austrian team-mate's grave during this trip. Perhaps it was because

Hans–Peter had replaced me on PB Khiam, a decision that cost him his life; as a result, his sacrifice prompted a more acute sense of survivor guilt with me. I do intend to pay my respects to him and his family at some point in the future, when the timing is right.

Our trip had been an emotionally challenging journey, but one that was extremely cathartic. My life seemed to be slowly returning to normality and a sense of balance. By the time we landed back in Australia I felt like I had cried enough tears to flood the world; but in the process, I had purged my innermost anguish and grief. The emotions that had been bottled up for three years had been released, leaving me feeling relieved and even energised. Through the blessing and support of my team-mates' families and friends, I felt like the great weight of survivor guilt had been shifted. I now felt free to find my old self again, and I yearned to make a positive contribution with my life and to make my fallen team-mates proud.

My experiences during the war would never be erased; they would remain with me forever and play a big part in shaping my character. But it was up to me to determine whether that shaping would have a positive or negative effect—I now had a choice. I felt like I was back in control. For the first time since being injured, I was feeling confident and driven to succeed. With a whole new perspective on my past and a fresh approach to my future, I was spurred into action and nothing was going to hold me back.

I had been given a second chance at life and I was not going to waste it. I couldn't wait to start a new chapter and see where my journey would take me next.

Epilogue

The Bombing of PB Khiam

I desperately wanted answers to the many questions I had about the events leading up to the deaths of my team-mates in Lebanon. Why, for instance, did Israel target a UN base? And why did the UN leave the unarmed peacekeeping force in place after so many days of danger, near misses and direct hits to the bases?

During the two years after the 2006 Lebanon War, information gradually came to light about the fatal bombing of PB Khiam on 25 July. There were two official boards of inquiry, one conducted by the UN and the other by the Canadian military. However, during these investigations, Israel would not allow the operational commanders involved in the incident to be interviewed. The findings from both inquiries were limited because of this.

From the information obtained, it was revealed that there were about 15,000 people in the township of El Khiam prior to the war. These people were densely congregated in concrete housing, in what was a relatively small area at the peak of a hill and along the ridge line that overlooked the Marjayoun valley. On the fateful day that PB Khiam was destroyed, my team-mates reported 91 aerial bombs and 95 artillery shells landing in and around the community of El Khiam.

Given that a 1000-pound bomb delivered by a jet can destroy a five-storey building, it is bewildering to think that nearly 100 of these lethal missiles, as well as 95 artillery shells, exploded in such a small area. This is incredibly high-saturation bombing. For those residents who chose to remain in the area and seek shelter in their homes, the scenes on the streets in El Khiam that day must have been horrific and bloody.

On the afternoon of the fatal attack, my team-mates themselves survived fourteen dangerously close near misses from 1000-pound aerial bombs that landed less than 500 metres from the base. A further nineteen artillery shells landed less than 150 metres from them.

There were three distinct waves of attack from Israel. As night fell, at 6.29 p.m., my team-mates reported another eight near misses and four direct hits to the base from Israeli artillery fire. One of the rounds that exploded into the compound was a direct hit on the door of the bunker, blocking access through this entry point to the underground shelter, making it unsafe to remain at the post. A cold chill shoots through my body every time I imagine what it must have been like for my team-mates at PB Khiam that afternoon.

I sometimes wonder—usually at night, when the mind wanders before sleep—how my team-mates were feeling during those last six hours of continual danger. The direct hits and even the near misses must have been terrifying. Every minute would have felt like an hour, waiting in that bunker, wondering if each breath would be their last; yet at the same time they would have been trying to remain focused on the job, doing their best to ignore negative thoughts. Knowing them, I am quite sure they would not have voiced concern for their own safety—stoic and professional to the very end.

I was alarmed to learn that my team-mates had requested to be evacuated from PB Khiam after the third wave of attack, at about 6.30 p.m. Knowing my colleagues, they would have held out at the compound for as long as they could, bravely performing their duties. By requesting to evacuate, I expect they judged their chances of survival were diminishing and they really needed to leave the area, immediately.

But it took nearly an hour for the UN commanders from UNTSO, UNIFIL and OGL to agree to an evacuation and for this message to reach PB Khiam. And even then, the evacuation was scheduled to occur the following morning, some twelve hours later.

That hour of waiting for an answer, as Israel continued its barrage of fire, must have been difficult for my team-mates. And then to hear that approval was only granted for the following day, I imagine, would have perplexed them more. Tragically, the evacuation came too late. The last contact with the base was at 7.25 p.m. Then the radio fell silent. All communication with PB Khiam was lost.

We now know that, between 7.25 p.m. and 7.30 p.m., an Israeli fighter jet fired a 1000-pound aerial bomb with a precision laser-guided system onto the base. It was a direct hit on the bunker of PB Khiam, instantly killing all four of my team-mates. The guys didn't stand a chance.

With the loss of communication with the base, the UN brought forward the evacuation and a rescue team arrived at the compound just before 10 p.m., to find the disturbing remains of what was left of PB Khiam. The entire base was virtually destroyed.

The rescue effort was hampered by the continued barrages of artillery fire from Israel in and around Khiam throughout that night and into the next day. The Indian soldiers from the UNIFIL rescue team risked their own lives as they searched through the rubble to recover the bodies. Three bodies were retrieved on the night of the bombing; the fourth was not recovered until ten days later, on 4 August. The two patrol base dogs, Gwynn and Ghajar, were also killed in the blast and I was told they were found being protected by Wolf's body.

It would have been a horrendous scene and a grim task for the rescue team. Our Lebanese interpreter, Eddie, had remained at PB Khiam until the morning of the fatal bombing, when Wolf convinced him he should leave the base and return to his house in El Khiam. As a result, Eddie survived the bombing.

I later learnt that, of the 45 UN positions in southern Lebanon, 36 experienced near misses and sixteen sustained direct hits from Israeli fire. Of the four UNTSO patrol bases, two were compromised: PB Khiam was completely destroyed and PB Ras sustained three direct hits, damaging the main building substantially. The UN reported 145 near misses and sixteen direct hits to their positions during the 33-day war. Of these, over 50 near misses and four direct hits, plus two splashes from artillery shells, were sustained at PB Khiam alone.

UN headquarters staff in Jerusalem have acknowledged that these figures are underestimates, as it was proven that some reports of near misses from the UNTSO patrol bases in Lebanon were not received in the UN headquarters in Jerusalem. The reason for this is not known for sure, althought these reports might have been blocked by Israeli electronic jamming of communications. More bombs than are indicated in the official records narrowly missed UN positions during the 2006 war in Lebanon.

It was a costly battle for the UN. In addition to the extensive damage to property and the deaths of four peacekeepers on PB Khiam, a UN civilian and his wife were also killed after an Israeli fighter jet delivered its payload in Tyre. Another UNTSO team member, Captain Roberto Punzo, an Italian serving at PB Hin, was shot in the back by a Hezbollah soldier, almost killing him, and several UNIFIL soldiers, plus myself, were injured during the conflict.

Over time and in the light of these details about the events of the war, I continued to question why the UN had decided to leave the unarmed peacekeeping force in place after so many days of near misses and direct hits that endangered the lives of the UN personnel.

UNTSO is a force given the task of observing and monitoring a peace agreement; at the outset of the war, I can understand that we needed to remain in position, to report violations of the peace treaty. This was the job we were sent to do. Small skirmishes often abated after twelve or so hours; but several days into the war, it was clear that there was no longer a peace to keep. At that point, we had reported hundreds of violations of the peace agreement. In my opinion, the risk of injury or death to the UN observers far outweighed the benefit of keeping the unarmed force in place.

The decision not to withdraw the peacekeeping force after PB Ras had sustained three direct hits by Israel on day eight of the war—six days before PB Khiam was destroyed—played heavily on my mind. I also pondered the request from my team-mates to evacuate the base on the night of the bombing and the fatal decision by the UN to delay their evacuation by twelve hours. The decision to delay, I can only assume, would have been made because of the difficulties associated with attempting to evacuate at night and because of problems in coordination with the Israeli Defence Force and between the two UN missions, UNTSO and UNIFIL. Nevertheless, despite these difficulties, it turned out to be possible to send a UN rescue team later that night, when communications were lost with the base. Of course, by this time it was too late; they would only be evacuating the dead bodies.

There were a number of findings and recommendations for the UN in its operations in the Middle East. Of note was the recommendation that the UN needs to ensure that sufficient attention is given to the reports by peacekeepers of near misses to UN bases. Furthermore, these reports also need to be forwarded to the highest officials, as appropriate, within the UN to allow them to take decisive action.

Questions were also raised regarding the fortification of UN bases and the lack of overhead protection from shrapnel on the observation platforms. If peacekeepers are expected to continue operating in such environments, then the bases need to be equipped to protect observers. Many UN processes and procedures also need to be trained and rehearsed, including medical evacuation procedures and how food and water resupply is to be executed during periods of conflict.

One vital issue for the UN during the war was its communications. I was surprised that, unlike my service in the Australian Defence Force, the UN communications were ineffective and, more importantly, insecure. When reporting, we were sometimes required to use our own personal mobile phones, with local sim cards purchased off the street, and personal email accounts, using Gmail, Hotmail or Yahoo. These means of communication are unreliable and cannot be guaranteed to function during a conflict, when it is vital to have contact with command and for reports of near misses to be received at higher headquarters.

During my long road to rehabilitation and recovery, these unanswered questions surrounding the deaths of my team-mates troubled me and continue to do so. I understood the Middle East to be a very complicated region; there is no clear black and white, but all shades of grey—and the Lebanon War of 2006 was no different. The history of conflict between Israel and Hezbollah is long and problematic, making it difficult to assess one incident of conflict in isolation in a balanced and fair manner. As widely reported, however, the 2006 Lebanon War was provoked by Hezbollah's capture of two Israeli soldiers. This resulted in Israel responding, but with what many have suggested was a disproportionate level of force. This should have come as little surprise, however, as Israel openly declares its intentions to respond with maximum impact.

This Israeli policy has obvious consequences, including the loss of innocent civilian lives. The town of El Khiam was a Hezbollah stronghold. In an area harbouring these guerrilla fighters, I can understand the Israeli Defence Force wanting to use strong force to protect Israeli troops while launching assaults through this region. But, to my mind, that does not excuse Israel for ignoring six hours of repeated requests from the UN to shift their fire away from PB Khiam.

Although the Israeli government has accepted full responsibility for the fatal attack and the deaths of the four peacekeepers at PB Khiam, they claim that it was an accident—an operational error, rather than a deliberate targeting of a UN base. The investigation teams found this explanation difficult to understand in the light of the available facts. PB Khiam was a distinctive, clearly marked and highly identifiable position, and had been in existence for over 30 years; the base was well known to Israeli forces and commanders; Israel stated it was not observing where its bombs were falling, which would seem contrary to standard operating procedures; and investigators could not understand why Israel did not stop firing at PB Khiam, despite the numerous and repeated appeals over six hours from the UN for Israel to hold their fire. There is still a number of unanswered questions around the firing on the UN compound, making it difficult to get closure for many of the families and people involved. Until all questions are answered adequately, it is difficult to move on.

Despite the lingering uncertainty surrounding the bombing, and based on the evidence obtained, I feel that there are three entities—Israel, Hezbollah and the UN—which share in varying degrees responsibility for the deaths of my team-mates: Israel, for not taking more care when firing in close proximity to UN positions; Hezbollah, for their tactic of firing rockets from within civilian-populated areas and close to UN bases, which was inevitably going to draw retaliatory fire; and the UN, for not evacuating the unarmed peacekeepers sooner.

The more information I gathered about the night my team-mates died, the more I felt frustrated at the futile loss of life on PB Khiam—it could have been avoided. I can only hope that the lessons learnt during the 2006 Lebanon War are implemented by all parties concerned. At least then soldiers currently serving, and those of future generations, will not be left to suffer the same fate, and my team-mates—who made the ultimate sacrifice in the name of peace—will not have lost their lives in vain.

Author's Note

When I returned to Australia after visiting the graves of my team-mates and passing on my condolences to their families, I needed a positive project to pursue to get my life back on track. After I delivered a keynote address at a veterans' forum in Melbourne, I was approached by an audience member, Mr Denny Neave, who heads up Big Sky Publishing. Denny encouraged me to write my story, offering me a publishing contract the very next day. I discussed the opportunity with a number of people including my medical specialists, who all felt that telling my story would not only be therapeutic and help me gain some form of closure, but might also help other people dealing with similar issues.

Through a series of networks and coincidences the project came to life. Colonel Andy Condon put me in contact with Dr Bob Breen, a military historian working at the Australian National University who had first-hand experience of several Australian peacekeeping operations. Bob had previously assisted General Peter Cosgrove and General Jim Molan with their memoirs and was willing to assist me too. General Cosgrove and General Molan also offered me their support and introductions to their contacts in the publishing world. As the idea of writing a book gained momentum, I was surrounded by an amazing group of supporters who continued to encourage me. One positive step led to another.

In another small-world coincidence, I was introduced via my godmother, Susan Crawford, to communication and publicity guru Glen-Marie Frost, who has since become a trusted friend and mentor. Glen-Marie called on Helen Grasswill, a producer from *Australian Story*, who was keen to film a documentary on my life story.

In early 2010, my submission for recognition of warlike service for the four Australians based in Lebanon during the 2006 Lebanon War continued. Through the efforts of the vice chief of the Defence Force, Lieutenant General David Hurley, the Defence Force twice recommended the upgrade to warlike service. Although this recommendation was supported by the minister for Defence, John Faulkner, the upgrade was opposed by DVA and blocked by the Department of Prime Minister and Cabinet. I was informally advised this decision was based on financial reasons and the desire not to set a precedent for other veterans' submissions. The Nature of Service department, which reviews the submissions, was headed up by Brigadier David Webster, who continued to advocate my case despite being short-staffed. An email from Brigadier Webster stated that I was just one case in 83 submissions waiting for determinations, some of which dated back to World War II. As a result of the efforts of General Hurley, Minister Faulkner, Brigadier Webster and my lawyer, Greg Isolani, the upgrade to warlike service was reviewed and approved by Prime Minister Rudd in May 2010.

That same month, after the *Australian Story* documentary aired on ABC television, the book project became a reality, with interest from several international publishing houses. I settled with Allen & Unwin, who offered me the wise guidance and tutelage of Richard Walsh as I wrote my first book.

I have written this book with a motto in mind: 'To educate, commemorate and inspire'. There are several organisations that can learn lessons from my experience and I hope that, in the sharing of my story, processes will be changed so that other members of the Defence Force do not have to endure similar circumstances. Several individuals and organisations let me down and, whether this was unintentional or not, it certainly exacerbated an already tough situation, and delayed my journey back to wellness. I write in disappointment, not in anger, as I believe it is important to focus on improving the processes for the future rather than on the individuals responsible.

While the UN has its fair share of faults, it also conducts incredible work in vulnerable communities around the world. Without a better alternative, I believe the UN needs more support and better resourcing to ensure its service personnel are adequately equipped so that the risks are reduced. The saying 'the more we sweat in peace the less we bleed in war' epitomises the emphasis that should be placed on our peacekeeping efforts.

As we continue to send our troops into harm's way, we should support our men and women in uniform. Our military personnel conduct themselves honourably in extraordinary circumstances. They have incredible stories of their own. Mine is but one of many and I feel privileged to have the opportunity to share my experiences.

I sustained injuries within a military environment; however, injury, depression and post-traumatic stress disorder are not limited to war veterans—they can happen to anyone. Police officers, emergency department personnel, firefighters, SES volunteers, paramedics and others often witness death and destruction and experience horrific flashbacks and post-traumatic stress. I hope that my story may be of assistance to those suffering any of these symptoms who find themselves in need of optimism.

Rehabilitation after injury or depression takes considerable strength and determination. Despite the encouragement from professionals and loved ones, I believe the turnaround needs to be self-initiated. No matter how much love my supporters surrounded me with, it wasn't until I found my own inner drive that I was able to get my life back on track and take advantage of the help that was on offer. I am sure that if I can do it, then others can too. Persevere—it's worth the hard work. My advice to those suffering depression is to seek help early from medical practitioners or from organisations such as beyondblue (www.beyondblue.org.au).

I have found that sharing my story has been extremely cathartic and I now enjoy helping others through keynote addresses and presentations on my experiences. The feedback at the end of my presentations, and the inundation of letters and emails after the *Australian Story* documentary, indicate that there are a lot of people facing similar events in their own lives.

For anyone who has suffered setbacks in their life—you are not alone. I hope that my story may give you heart that you too can find something tangible to hold on to during the dark days, ensuring that your best years are ahead of you and not behind.

Acknowledgements

This book would not have been possible without the remarkable efforts of an entire team of people—I owe you all an infinite debt of gratitude. My deep appreciation goes to my literary agent and dear friend Glen-Marie Frost for her steadfast support, inspiration and believing in me and this book. My mentor, Andy Condon, who played a crucial role in getting my story off the ground and for so much more. Bob Breen, who was instrumental in the early stages of this book and for providing me wise counsel and advice on the military aspects of my story.

I also owe endless thanks to Richard Walsh for his invaluable tutelage, editorial guidance and encouragement, particularly on those days when I felt writing a book was beyond me. Sue Hines, Vanessa Pellatt and the entire team at Allen & Unwin for their hard work and patience. My heartfelt thanks to Tracey Allen for her proofreading, enthusiasm and late night messages of friendship and support.

I am fortunate to have had the opportunity to work with some great people to ensure the problems I experienced are fixed. I would like to highlight the wonderful work of Ron Tattersal, an ex-serviceman who has worked tirelessly in a voluntary capacity for many years assisting countless veterans gain entitlements and support from DVA. Ron has also played a critical role in improving the army's battlefield casualty management program, which will save lives.

Chief of the Army, Major General Ken Gillespie, and his staff are acknowledged for their work in recognising the gap in support for injured and medically retired soldiers and for creating the 'Wounded Digger Program', which is a step closer to getting much-needed assistance to our soldiers and veterans. I wish to note the efforts of Jennifer Collins, the deputy commissioner of DVA in New South Wales, who is making the transition for injured personnel from the Defence Force to DVA more effective and less convoluted.

I'd also like to acknowledge all the physios, chiropractors and medical staff who patch up people like me and who have been so crucial in getting me physically strong enough to survive the long hours required to write a book. To Rohan Dempster for helping me find my sense of humour during the days that I wanted to give up.

I am most grateful to all my friends in Australia and around the world—too numerous to mention individually—for their love and messages of encouragement. A special thanks to Brad, Amanda and Birchy for their mateship, valued support and recovering my personal belongings from my apartment in Tyre in the middle of the war. My possessions from Lebanon are not just souvenirs, but items that hold so many treasured memories.

Warm wishes to Susan Crawford for her generosity, devoted friendship and providing me with a bed and a hot meal in Sydney. I am also deeply indebted to my family, who are always supportive— even when they doubt the wisdom of my decisions—for being there when I needed them the most.

My heartfelt appreciation and love to my husband, Clent, without whom this book would not have been possible. I am truly blessed to have him in my life.

Finally, I would like to acknowledge and honour those who have given their lives or sustained injuries in the service of peace.

Afterword

In 2010 Matina Jewell was the subject of a two-part documentary about her experiences as a UN peacekeeper during the 2006 Lebanon War, screened on ABC television's *Australian Story*. At the same time, in an interesting coincidence, her submission to have her service in Lebanon upgraded to 'warlike service' came before Prime Minister Kevin Rudd again, and this time the upgrade was approved.

As a result of her case, the criteria for war service recognition, particularly for peacekeeping operations, is now under review. It is hoped the current legislation being used to determine war service recognition, which was written in 1920, will be modified to adequately reflect current operational environments.

Matina continues to actively pursue better health outcomes for military personnel, both serving and retired. She is especially focused on adequate health cover for younger veterans and ex-servicewomen under DVA, because she believes this organisation's health cover remains fundamentally structured to support older, male veterans. She has worked with DVA to improve a number of areas where the system fails Australia's injured Defence personnel, and she is also seeking to ensure that service personnel injured on operations are not medically discharged from the Defence Force without knowing what their health entitlements are under DVA.

She advocates that the Defence Force should intervene when military personnel serving on representation duties—such as with the UN—are injured, because the UN may not have the ability to conduct medical evacuation of our soldiers to Australian standards. Matina hopes that by telling her story other soldiers and veterans will be spared what she has endured and she aims to use her story as a catalyst for positive change.

She is a member of the Federal Commission for the ANZAC Centenary, where she works alongside two former prime ministers, Bob Hawke and Malcolm Fraser, providing advice to government on how best to commemorate 100 years of military service to the Australian community during the upcoming commemorative period of 2014 to 2018.

Matina is the ambassador of the Australian Peacekeeper and Peacemaker Veterans' Association and also the ambassador of the Australian Peacekeeping Memorial Project. To help signify and mark the contribution our Australian troops have made now and into the future, she is working with a team of dedicated people, including the governor-general, Quentin Bryce, to raise funds to build a peacekeeping monument in front of the Australian War Memorial on ANZAC Parade. Donations to this cause are greatly appreciated and can be made via the website www.peacekeepingmemorial.org.au